LEADERSHIP
A Communication Perspective

Michael Z. Hackman
University of Colorado—Colorado Springs

Craig E. Johnson
George Fox College

WAVELAND
PRESS, INC.
Prospect Heights, Illinois

Consulting Editors

Joseph A. DeVito
Robert E. Denton, Jr.

For information about this book, write or call:

Waveland Press, Inc.
P.O. Box 400
Prospect Heights, Illinois 60070
(708) 634-0081

Table of Contents

Preface

Leadership has been investigated by scores of researchers in disciplines ranging from psychology and sociology to political science and philosophy. These researchers have poked, probed, and dissected the process of leadership in an attempt to gain a clearer understanding of the unique characteristics of leading and following. Those of us in communication have, in the words of communication theorist Lee Thayer, "been strangely silent" on the topic of leadership.[1] Fortunately, communication experts are beginning to pay more attention to leadership as a growing number of researchers recognize that leading is a symbolic process. Many colleges and universities now offer courses in organizational communication and leadership as part of their communication curricula.

This book offers an introduction to the topic of leadership from a communication perspective. We believe that leadership is best understood as a product of human communication. Because leading is communicating, leaders are made, not born. Leadership competence increases with communication competence. For this reason, *Leadership: A Communication Perspective* emphasizes both theory and practice. Each chapter blends a discussion of research and theory with practical suggestions for improving leadership effectiveness. Case studies, summaries of significant research, and exercises which offer the opportunity for active participation appear in each chapter.

Part I introduces the fundamentals of leadership. Chapter 1 examines the relationship between leadership and communication. Chapters 2 and 3 survey the research on leader communication style and summarize the development of leadership theory. Chapters 4 and 5 focus on two elements—power and influence—that are essential to the practice of leadership. Part II is an overview of leadership in specific contexts. Chapters 6, 7, and 8 discuss leadership in group, organizational and public settings. Chapter 9 summarizes the ways that leaders can continue to develop creatively and ethically.

Students and colleagues provided us with many of their own leadership stories along with encouragement, advice and support. In particular, we want to thank Frank E.X. Dance and Alvin Goldberg of the University of Denver and Pamela Shockley-Zalabak of the University of Colorado-Colorado Springs. Special thanks goes to our research assistants Carrie Brown, Melissa Lampe, Kevin O'Neil, Melissa Rowberg, Rich Seiber and Penny Whitney and to our editor at Waveland, Carol Rowe, who was a constant source of encouragement and inspiration. Our gratitude is also extended to Gail Myers for his thorough review of our original manuscript. Our greatest appreciation goes to our families. Without their sacrifices, this project would never have been completed. It is to them that this book is dedicated.

> **To Tammy, Nikolas, Jane and my parents — your love, faith and support warmed my heart. To my dog Sunny, who patiently sat beneath my desk every day while I wrote — you warmed my feet.**
>
> **To Mary — now we can spend more time together.**
>
> **To Aaron and Derek — now you can spend more time on the computer.**

Michael Z. Hackman
University of Colorado-Colorado Springs

Craig E. Johnson
George Fox College

[1] Thayer, L. (1988). Leadership/communication: A critical review and a modest proposal. In G. M. Goldhaber & G. A. Barnett (Eds.), *Handbook of organizational communication* (pp. 231-263). Norwood, NJ: Ablex Publishing.

Part I

Fundamentals of Leadership

1

Leadership and Communication

3

The Leadership Paradox

James MacGregor Burns, a political activist, historian and professor of government, described the paradox that frustrates those who study leadership. "Leadership," Burns wrote, "is one of the most observed and least understood phenomena on earth."[1]

Leadership attracts universal attention. Historians, philosophers and social scientists have attempted to understand and to explain leadership for centuries. From Confucius to Plato to Machiavelli, many of the world's most famous scholars have theorized about how humans lead one another.[2] One reason for the fascination with this subject lies in the very nature of the human experience. Leadership is all around us. We get up in the morning, open the newspaper or turn on the radio or television and discover what actions leaders all over the word have taken. We attend classes, work, and interact in social groups—all with their own distinct patterns of leadership. Our daily experiences with leadership are not that different from the experiences of individuals in other cultures. Leadership is an integral part of human life in rural tribal cultures as well as in modern industrialized nations.

Despite all the attention, leadership truly remains an enigma—one of the "least understood phenomena on earth." Theoretical explanations of leadership have shifted dramatically from one model to another. Researchers once searched diligently to discover the character traits of leaders. They abandoned this search and began, instead, to look for those factors in the environment that make a leader effective or ineffective. The newest shift is toward an examination of how a leader creates a symbolic focus or vision for a group.

We all have a personal stake in the success or failure of leadership. Even if we never personally seek to be leaders, our lives will be affected by those acting in leadership roles. Followers prosper under effective leaders and suffer under ineffective leaders whatever the context: government, corporation, church or synagogue, school, athletic team or class project group. The study of leadership, then, is more than academic. Understanding leadership has practical importance for all of us. See Figure 1.1 for a dramatic example of how important leadership can be.

We hope this book will help bridge the gap between observing leadership and understanding leadership. Understanding involves both intellectual comprehension and practical application. We encourage you to learn about the nature of leadership in order to develop your personal leadership skills. For this reason, each chapter features important

Figure 1.1   Case Study

Death on the Mountain

The Oregon Episcopal School's annual climb to the top of Mt. Hood on Monday, May 12, 1986 should have been routine. It was not. The hiking group included fifteen high school students, two faculty members and a guide. Father Tom Goman, an experienced climber, was the leader. Although a number of other groups cancelled their climbs because weather forecasts predicted the onset of freezing rain and snow, the Episcopal School forged ahead. Five students turned back because of altitude sickness shortly after the hike started. The others continued up the mountain. A fierce snowstorm hit before they reached the summit. The climbers took refuge from the whiteout conditions in a tiny snow cave. They tried to preserve body heat by lying on top of one another.

The guide and one student climbed down the mountain on Tuesday to seek help. Winds of sixty miles-per-hour hindered rescue efforts. On Wednesday, the bodies of three students were found in the snow; the cave was not found until Thursday. Only two of the eight climbers who remained in the snow cave survived the ordeal.

Questions about the decisions of trip leader, Father Tom Goman, still remain. Why did he decide to go through with the climb when others cancelled due to the weather? Why didn't Goman, considered a cautious man, turn back when the weather worsened? Why didn't the hikers (who carried a gas stove, one sleeping bag and food and water for a day) take extra food and ice axes that many experienced climbers find essential for every climb? Since Father Goman was among the victims, the answers to these questions can only be suppositions. However, this tragedy demonstrates the importance of leadership. In high risk situations, leaders literally make the difference between life and death.

Discussion Questions

1. Have you ever followed a leader in a life or death situation? How did you determine that this person was worthy of your trust?
2. Have you ever been the leader in a high risk activity? How did you approach this task?
3. Leaders in dangerous situations like combat, whitewater rafting or mountain climbing often expect absolute obedience. Is there ever a time when followers should challenge the authority of these leaders?

Source: Trippett, F. (1986, May 26). Oregon killer. *Time*, p. 24; and press reports in *The Oregonian* and *The Columbian* newspapers.

research related to leadership and a set of application exercises. Our focus includes, but is not limited to, organizational leadership. Although we will use many examples from the corporate world, we will also look at leadership in a number of other settings including small groups, politics, social movements, education and the military.

While we examine leadership in a wide variety of situations, our perspective remains the same. We believe that leadership is best understood from a communication standpoint. In this chapter we define leadership and identify key leadership skills. In addition, we describe how you can begin to develop the skills necessary to become an effective leader. Let's begin by considering the special nature of human communication and the unique qualities of leadership.

Defining Leadership

The Nature of Human Communication

As we have noted, leadership is a fundamental element of the human condition. Wherever society exists, leadership exists. Any definition of leadership must account for its universal nature. Leadership seems to be linked to what it means to be human. As communication specialists, we believe that what makes us unique as humans is our ability to create and manipulate *symbols*. Communication theorist Frank Dance defines symbols as abstract, arbitrary representations of reality agreed upon by human users.[3] For instance, there is nothing in the physical nature of this book that mandates labeling it a "book." We have agreed to use this label, or symbol, to represent a bound collection of pages in text; this agreement is purely arbitrary. The meaning of a symbol, according to Leslie White, does not come from the intrinsic properties of the idea, concept or object being represented. The value is "bestowed upon it by those who use it."[4] Words are not the only symbols we use; we attach arbitrary meanings to many nonverbal behaviors as well. Looking someone in the eye symbolizes honesty to Americans. However, making direct eye contact in some other cultures is considered an invasion of privacy. Meaning is generated as the product of human creation.

Communication is based on the transfer of symbols. This transfer allows for the creation of meaning within individuals. As you read this text, the words we have written are transferred to you. The meanings of these words are subject to your interpretation. It is our goal to write in a way that allows for clear understanding, but factors such as your cultural background, your previous experience, your level of interest as well as our writing skills influence your reception of our message. The goal of communication is to create a shared reality between message sources and receivers.

The human ability to manipulate symbols allows for the creation of reality. Simply labeling someone as "motivated" or "lazy," for example, can lead to changes in behavior. Followers generally work hard to meet the high expectations implied in the "motivated" label; they may lower their performance to meet the low expectations reflected in the "lazy" label. This phenomenon, discussed in detail in Chapter 7, is known as the Pygmalion Effect.

A single symbolic act can alter our view of reality. Although an increase in personal freedom within communist bloc countries was noted in the first few years after Mikhail Gorbachev came to power in the Soviet Union, many remained unconvinced that any real change in Soviet policy had occurred. In 1989 when the Berlin Wall was finally dismantled, the world view of the Soviet reform movement changed dramatically. The destruction of the best known symbol of communism signaled a new era in international relations. The Soviet Union transformed from "evil empire" to "revolutionary empire" as the result of one powerful symbolic act.

Symbols not only create reality, they enable us to communicate about the past, present and future. We can evaluate our past performances, analyze current conditions, and set agendas for the future. In addition, symbolic communication is purposive and goal driven. We consciously use words, gestures and other symbolic behaviors in order to achieve our goals. The purposeful nature of human communication differentiates it from animal communication.[5] The communication patterns of animals are predetermined. For example, wolves normally travel in small groups known as packs. Dominance within the pack is predetermined based on such characteristics as size, physical strength, and aggressiveness. Humans, on the other hand, consciously select from an array of possibilities for achieving their goals. Human leadership is not predetermined as in the animal world, but rather varies from situation to situation and from individual to individual.

Leadership shares all of the features of human communication described above. First, *leaders use symbols to create reality*. Leaders use language, stories and rituals to create distinctive group cultures. Second, *leaders communicate about the past, present and future*. They engage in evaluation, analysis and goal setting. Effective leaders create a desirable vision for followers outlining what the group should be like in the future. Third, *leaders make conscious use of symbols to reach their goals.* We will have more to say about how leaders adapt their behaviors to reach their goals later in the chapter. In the meantime, let's take a closer look at the characteristics of human communication.

The Human Communication Process

Noted communication scholar Dean Barnlund identified five principles that reflect the basic components of human communication.[6]

Communication is not a thing, it is a process. Communication is not constant, it is dynamic and ever-changing. Unlike a biologist looking at a cell through a microscope, communication scholars focus on a continuous, on-going process without a clearly defined beginning or end. Take a typical conversation, for example. Does a conversation begin when two people enter a room? When they first see each other? When they begin talking? Barnlund, and others, would suggest that a conversation actually "begins" with the experiences, skills, feelings and other characteristics that individuals bring to an interaction.

Communication is not linear, it is circular. Models depicting the process of communication have evolved from a linear explanation, first developed by ancient Greek rhetoricians over two thousand years ago, to a circular explanation, offered by Barnlund. In the earliest description of the communication process, a source transmitted a message to a receiver in much the same way that an archer shoots an arrow into a target. Only the source had an active role in this model. The receiver merely accepted messages. This view, known as an action model, is diagrammed below.

An Action Model of Communication

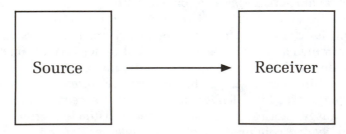

The action model provided an incomplete depiction of the communication process because the response of the receiver was ignored. Reactions to messages, known as feedback, were included in the next explanation of communication—the interaction model. The interaction model described communication as a process of sending messages back and forth from sources to receivers and receivers to sources. From this perspective, diagrammed below, communication resembles a game of tennis.

An Interaction Model of Communication

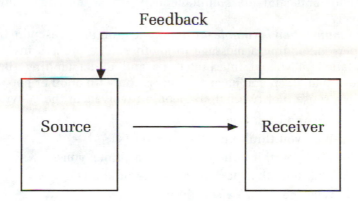

The evolution of the circular explanation of communication was completed with the development of Barnlund's transactional model. The transactional approach assumes that messages are sent and received simultaneously by source/ receivers. The on-going, continuous nature of the process of communication is implicit in this model.

A Transactional Model of Communication

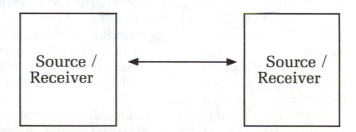

In the transactional model, communicators simultaneously transmit and receive messages. Effective communicators pay close attention to the messages being sent to them as they talk with others. The typical classroom lecture demonstrates how we act as senders and receivers at the same time. Even though only one person (the instructor) delivers the lecture, students provide important information about how the lecture is being received. If the lecture is interesting, listeners respond with smiles, head nods and questions. If the lecture is boring, class members may fidget, fall asleep or glance frequently at their watches. These responses are transmitted throughout the lecture. Thus, both the instructor and students simultaneously act as message source and receiver.

Communication is complex. Communication involves more than just one person sending a message to another. The process involves the negotiation of shared interpretations and understanding. Barnlund explains that when you have a conversation with another person there are, in a sense, not two but six people involved in the conversation.

1. Who you think you are
2. Who you think the other person is
3. Who you think the other person thinks you are
4. Who the other person thinks he or she is
5. Who the other person thinks you are
6. Who the other person thinks you think he or she is

Communication is irreversible. Like a permanent ink stain, communication is indelible. If you have ever tried to "take back" something you have said to another person you know that while you can apologize for saying something inappropriate, you cannot erase your message. Many times in the heat of an argument we say something that hurts someone we care for. After the argument has cooled down we generally say we are sorry for our insensitive remarks. Even though the apology is accepted and the remark is retracted, the words will never be completely forgotten. The other person may still wonder, "Did he/she really mean it?" We can never completely un-communicate.

Communication involves the total personality. A person's communication cannot be viewed separately from the person. Communication is more than a set of behaviors. It is the primary defining characteristic of a human being. Our view of self and others is shaped, defined and maintained through communication.

Now that you have a better understanding of the process of human communication, we will examine the special nature of leadership communication.

Leadership: A Special Form of Human Communication

One way to isolate the unique characteristics of leadership is to look at how others have defined the term. Unfortunately, there seem to be as many definitions of leadership as there are people interested in the topic. A common theme of many proposed definitions of leadership is that leaders exert influence over others in order to reach group goals. One way to identify leaders is to determine who is influencing whom. For example, Paul Hersey defines leadership as "any attempt to influence the behavior of another individual or group."[7] Bernard Bass argues that "an effort to influence others is attempted leadership." When others actually change, then leadership is successful.[8]

Leader influence attempts are not random or self-centered. Instead, leaders channel their influence and encourage change in order to reach group goals. Note the group orientation in the following definitions:

> "the process (act) of influencing the activities of an organized group toward goal setting and goal achievement."[9]

> "by virtue of [the leader's] special position in the group he [she] serves as a primary agent for the determination of group structure, group atmosphere, group goals, group ideology, and group activities."[10]

Placing leadership in the context of group achievement helps to clarify the difference between leadership and persuasion. Persuasion involves changing attitudes and behavior through rational and emotional arguments. Since persuasive tactics can be used solely for personal gain, persuasion is not always a leadership activity. Persuasion is only one of many influence tools available to a leader.

Combining our discussion of human communication with the definitional elements above, we offer the following communication-based definition of leadership:

> ***Leadership is human (symbolic) communication which modifies the attitudes and behaviors of others in order to meet group goals and needs.***

Leaders vs. Managers

Before we finish the task of defining leadership, we need to distinguish between leadership and management. Management is often equated with leadership. For example, many management consulting firms use the term "leadership" in the titles of their training seminars. However, leading differs significantly from managing. Managers may act as leaders, but very often they do not. Similarly, employees can take a leadership role even though they do not have a managerial position. Leadership experts James Kouzes and Barry Posner of Santa Clara University suggest the following exercise to highlight the differences between leaders and managers. Take a sheet of paper and make two columns. In the first column, identify the activities (events or actions) of leaders. In the second column, list the activities of managers. Now compare the two lists. Kouzes and Posner predict that you will associate leaders with change, crisis, and innovation and that you will associate managers with organizational stability. According to these authors: "When we think of leaders, we recall times of turbulence, conflict, innovation, and change. When we think of managers, we recall times of stability, harmony, maintenance, and constancy."[11]

Perhaps the key difference between a leader and a manager lies in the focus of each. While the manager is more absorbed in the status quo, the leader is more concerned about the ultimate direction of the group. Warren Bennis and Burt Nanus surveyed ninety successful corporate and public leaders in an attempt to understand leadership better. They found that *managers are people who do things right and leaders are people who do the right thing*.[12] As Bennis and Nanus further explain, managers are problem solvers who focus on physical resources. Leaders, on the other hand, are problem finders, focusing on spiritual and emotional resources.

Confusing efficiency with effectiveness provides another contrast between management and leadership. Management is frequently concerned with efficiency. Nonetheless, an organization can be efficiently run yet fail if it does not respond to changing conditions or meet the needs of members. Bennis notes: "Leading does not mean managing; the difference between the two is crucial. There are many institutions that are very well *managed* and very poorly *led*. They may excel in the ability to handle all the routine inputs every day, yet they may never ask whether the routine should be preserved at all."[13]

An employee may assume a leadership role even though she or he is not a manager. Consider the example of a Procter and Gamble employee at a Jif peanut butter plant. While shopping in his neighborhood supermarket, the employee noticed that the labels on several jars of Jif peanut butter were crooked. He bought all of the stock with the poorly mounted labels assuming that Procter and Gamble would not want its image tarnished by sloppy workmanship. His leadership efforts have since become part of the folklore of Procter and Gamble.[14]

Both management and leadership are important. However, Americans have given much more emphasis to management training than to leadership training. Colleges and universities are more likely to offer management degrees than leadership degrees. Since leadership is critical for the ultimate success of groups and organizations, we think that a great deal more attention should be given to training leaders.

Leadership Communication Skills

Viewing leadership from a communication perspective recognizes that leadership effectiveness depends on developing effective communication skills. Frank Dance and Carl Larson identify three functions of human communication.[15] First, *symbolic communication links humans to other humans and to the physical environment.* Conversations, parties, weather reports, meetings and so on tie us to one another and to the world. Second, *higher mental processes develop as a result of symbol usage.* Language makes reasoning and conceptualizing possible. Third, *human communication allows for the regulation of our own behavior as well as the behavior of others.* We can suggest, plead, command or convince—to name a few of the possible means to regulate behavior.

Each of the functions of human communication identified by Dance and Larson plays a critical role in effective leadership. Successful leaders are experts in processing cues from the environment. They attend to current events, to the activities of other groups and organizations, to their own group norms and cultures, as well as to the physical environment. Most importantly, they solicit feedback from others. Listening which accurately interprets verbal and nonverbal messages is a primary linking skill. Effective leadership also involves the establishment and maintenance of satisfying group relationships. Creating a trusting, cooperative work atmosphere and building an effective team are key linking abilities.

Thinking and reasoning skills are essential to leaders since leaders direct groups toward goals. The term "envisioning" best describes the type of conceptual activity needed for leadership. Leaders must be able to take the inputs they receive from linking with others and the environment and convert them into an agenda or vision for the future. In many cases, these visions are creative in nature; that is, they combine previously existing needs, wants and demands into new images or realities.

We noted earlier that influence is an important element in the definition of leadership. Skills that involve regulating the behavior of others are part of the leader's repertoire. To influence others successfully, leaders must be able to:

1. Develop perceptions of credibility
2. Develop and use power bases effectively
3. Make effective use of verbal and nonverbal influence cues
4. Develop positive expectations for others
5. Manage change
6. Gain compliance
7. Negotiate productive solutions

We discuss these skills in greater detail in later chapters. Figure 1.2 illustrates the importance of communication skills for leadership. In a survey of 428 personnel managers, oral and written communication skills were the most significant factors for employment success. The tools necessary for job success are equally essential for successful leadership.

Figure 1.2   Research Highlight

How Important Are Communication Skills?

Table 1 lists the skills that members of the American Society of Personnel Administrators chose as most important in helping college graduates get their first jobs.

Table 1

Factors/Skills Important for Successful Job Search

Rank/Order	Factors/Skills
1	Oral (speaking) communication
2	Listening ability
3	Enthusiasm
4	Written communication skills
5	Technical competence
6	Appearance
7	Poise
8	Work experience
9	Resume
10	Specific degree held
11	Grade point average
12	Part-time or summer employment
13	Accreditation of program

14	Leadership in campus/community activities
15	Participation in campus/community activities
16	Recommendations
17	School attended

The top four factors/skills needed to get a job are communication related (**note**: there is no way to express enthusiasm except through communication). Factors like work experience, type of degree, accreditation of program, recommendations and school attended are less important. The same pattern emerged when the researchers asked the personnel managers to indicate what factors are needed in order to be a success on the job.

Table 2

Factors/Skills Important for Successful Job Performance

Rank/Order	Factors/Skills
1	Interpersonal/human relations skills
2	Oral (speaking) communication skills
3	Written communication skills
4	Persistence/determination
5	Enthusiasm
6	Technical competence
7	Personality
8	Work experience
9	Dress/grooming
10	Poise
11	Interviewing skills
12	Specific degree held
13	Physical attractiveness
14	Grade point average
15	Resume
16	School attended
17	Letters of recommendation

Communication skills are just as important for doing a job successfully as they are for getting a job. Once again, oral and written communication abilities appear at the top of the list. In Table 2 as in Table 1, grade point average, resume, school attended, and letters of recommendation rank below communication abilities.

The researchers went on to ask for the "ideal management profile" and found (not surprisingly by now) that communication skills received high ratings. Ideal managers are able to 1) work one on one, 2) gather information to make decisions, 3) work in small groups, 4) listen, and 5) give effective feedback. Knowledge of finance, marketing, and accounting rated near the bottom of the list.

Source: Curtis, D. B., Winsor, J. L., & Stephens, R. D. (1989). National preferences in business and communication education. *Communication Education, 38*, 6-14. Tables used by permission.

For further reading:
DiSalvo, V., Larson, D., & Seiler, W. (1976). Communication skills needed by persons in business organizations. *Communication Education, 25,* 269-275.
DiSalvo, V. (1980). A summary of current research identifying communication skills in various organizational contexts. *Communication Education, 29,* 283-290.
Hanna, M. (1978). Speech communication training needs in the business community. *Central States Speech Journal, 29,* 163-172.
Sypher, B. D., & Zorn, T. (1986). Communication-related abilities and upward mobility: A longitudinal investigation. *Human Communication Research, 12,* 420-431.

Playing to a Packed House:
Leaders as Impression Managers

From a communication standpoint, leaders are made, not born. We increase our leadership competence as we increase our communication skills. We can compare the leadership role to a part played on stage to illustrate how effective communication skills translate into effective leadership.

Sociologist Erving Goffman adapts Shakespeare's adage that life is a stage and we are all actors on it to argue that most communication interactions can be viewed as performances complete with actors, stages, dialogues, and dressing rooms.[16] Let's look at a typical date, for example. The date is a performance which may take place on any number of stages: the dance floor, the living room, the movie theater, the football game. The actors (the couple) prepare in their dressing rooms at home before the performance and may return to the same locations for a critique session after the date ends. Particularly on the first date, the interactants may work very hard to create desired impressions—they engage in "impression management." Each dating partner tries to manage the perceptions of the other person by using appropriate behaviors, which might include dressing in the latest fashions, acting in a courteous manner, engaging in polite conversation, and paying for meals and other activities.

Leaders also engage in impression management. When leaders perform, they play to packed houses. People in organizations, for example, carefully watch the behavior of the CEO for information about the executive officer's character and for clues as to organizational priorities, values, and future direction. They seek answers to such questions as: "Can I trust him/her?" "What kind of behavior gets rewarded around here?" "Is he or she really interested in my welfare?" "Is dishonesty tolerated?" "Are we going to survive the next five years?"

Successful leaders use communication as a tool to reach their ends; they match their behaviors with their goals. If they want to emphasize customer service, they spend more time with customers and reward good service providers. If they want to foster cooperation, they downplay power and status cues and emphasize listening. These leaders promote communication on a first-name basis and refuse such luxuries as executive washrooms and reserved parking places. Effective leaders know what they want to accomplish, what communication skills are needed to reach their goals, and how to put those behaviors into action.[17]

To see how impression management works, change one aspect of your usual communication and watch how others respond. If friends have told you that you seem unfriendly because you are quiet when meeting new people, try being more assertive the next time you meet strangers at a party. If you make a conscious effort to greet others, introduce yourself and learn more about them, you may shake your cool, unfriendly image.

Many people are uncomfortable with the idea of impression management. They equate playing a role with being insincere since true feelings and beliefs might be hidden. While this is a very real danger, followers continually watch for inconsistencies and often "see through" performances of insincere leaders. Frequently, we have no choice but to play many roles. We are forced into performances as job applicants, students, dating partners and leaders each day. The real problem is that we often mismanage the impressions we make. Our behaviors may make us appear dull or untrustworthy when we really are interesting and honest.

Some fear that leaders can manipulate impressions to mislead the group. This is a legitimate concern (we'll discuss the ethical dimension of leadership in greater detail in Chapter 9). Because impression management can be used to further group goals or to subvert them, it should be judged by its end product. Ethical impression management meets group wants and needs and, in the ideal, spurs the group to reach higher goals. Unethical impression management subverts group needs and lowers purpose and aspiration.[18]

Summary

Leadership is an integral part of the human experience. There are leaders in every type of human society. In this chapter, we suggested that leadership is best understood as a form of human (symbolic) communication. Human communication is: 1) a process, 2) circular in nature, 3) complex, 4) irreversible, and 5) the characteristic that defines the total personality. Leaders use symbols to modify the attitudes and behavior of others in order to reach group goals. While managers value efficiency and focus on maintaining the status quo, leaders value effectiveness and focus on the future of the group or organization.

Three clusters of communication skills are essential for leaders: 1) linking, 2) envisioning, and 3) regulating. Linking skills include monitoring the environment, creating a trusting climate and team building. Envisioning involves creating new agendas or visions out of previously existing elements. Regulating means influencing others by developing credibility and power, using effective verbal and nonverbal communication, creating positive expectations, managing change, gaining compliance, and negotiation. Successful leaders match their communication behaviors to their goals through a process called impression management. They monitor their actions to create desired impressions in the minds of others. Ethical leaders use impression management to reach group goals rather than to satisfy selfish, personal goals.

Application Exercises

1. Make a list of the characteristics of leaders and managers as described on page 12. Are your characteristics the same as those described by Kouzes and Posner? To clarify the differences between leaders and managers, describe someone who is an effective leader and then someone who is an effective manager. How do these two people differ? Share your descriptions with others in class.

2. Develop your own definition of leadership. How does it compare to the one given in the chapter?

3. Brainstorm a list of the ways that leaders employ symbols to lead.

4. Communication Encounter Analysis

   Evaluate your effectiveness as an impression manager by analyzing a recent communication encounter (a date, a class presentation, a job interview, etc.)

   a. Identify your behaviors and the behaviors of the other person(s) in the encounter.

   b. What were your goals in this situation? Theirs?

   c. Determine the success or failure of your impression management. Did you make the impression you wanted? Why or why not? What could you do next time?

   d. What insights can you draw from this performance that you could apply to a leadership situation?

   e. Write up your findings.

Endnotes

[1] Burns, J. M. (1978). *Leadership*. New York: Harper & Row, p. 2.

[2] For more information on the history of leadership study, see: Bass, B. M. (Ed.) (1981). *Stodgill's handbook of leadership*. New York: Free Press, Ch. 1.

[3] Dance, F. E.X. (1982). A speech theory of human communication. In F. E.X. Dance (Ed.), *Human communication theory* (pp. 120-146). New York: Harper & Row, p. 126.

[4] White, L. A. (1949). *The science of culture*. New York: Farrar, Strauss and Cudahy, p. 25.

[5] Information concerning differences among human and animal communication systems is extensive. The following sources serve as a good starting point for reading in this area:

Adler, M. J. (1967). *The difference of man and the difference it makes*. New York: Holt, Rinehart and Winston.

Sebeok, T. A., & Rosenthal, R. (Eds.). (1981). *The Clever Hans phenomenon: Communication with horses, whales, apes, and people.* (Annals of the New York Academy of Sciences, Vol. 364). New York: New York Academy of Sciences.

Sebeok, T. A., & Umiker-Sebeok, J. (1979). *Speaking of Apes: A critical anthology of two-way communication with man*. New York: Plenum.

Terrace, H. S., Pettito, L. A., Sanders, R. J., & Bever, T. G. (1979). Can an ape create a sentence? *Science, 206*, 891-902.

Walker, S. (1983). *Animal thought*. London: Routledge & Kegan Paul.

[6] Barnlund, D. C. (1962). Toward a meaning-centered philosophy of communication. *Journal of Communication, 12*, 197-211.

[7] Hersey, P. (1984). *The situational leader*. Escondido, CA: Center for Leadership Studies, p. 14.

[8] Bass, B. M. (1960). *Leadership, psychology, and organizational behavior*. New York: Harper & Row, p. 90.

[9] Stogdill, R. M. (1950). Leadership, membership and organization. *Psychological Bulletin, 47*, p. 4.

[10] Krech, D., & Crutchfield, R. S. (1948). *Theory and problems of social psychology*. New York: McGraw-Hill, p. 417.

[11] Kouzes, J. M., & Posner, B. Z. (1987). *The leadership challenge: How to get extraordinary things done in organizations*. San Francisco: Jossey-Bass, pp. 31-32.

[12] Bennis, W., & Nanus, B. (1985). *Leaders: The strategies for taking charge*: New York: Harper & Row, p. 21.

[13] Bennis, W. (1976). *The unconscious conspiracy: Why leaders can't lead*. New York: AMACOM, p. 154.

[14] Peters, T., & Austin, N. (1985). *A passion for excellence: The leadership difference*. New York: Warner Books, p. 328.

[15] Dance, F. E.X., & Larson, C. (1976). *The functions of human communication: A theoretical approach*. New York: Holt, Rinehart and Winston.

[16] Goffman, E. (1959). *The presentation of self in everyday life*. Garden City, NY: Doubleday.

[17] For more information on the prerequisites for effective goal directed (instrumental) communication see:

Hart, R. P., & Burks, D. M. (1972). Rhetorical sensitivity and social interaction. *Speech Monographs*, 39, 75-91.

Hart, R. P., Carlson, R. E., & Eadie, W. F. (1980). Attitudes toward communication and the assessment of rhetorical sensitivity. *Communication Monographs*, 47, 3-22.

[18] The term "transformational" was coined by James MacGregor Burns to describe the type of leadership that creates high moral purpose. We'll have more to say about transformational leadership in Chapter 3.

2

Leadership Communication Styles

Overview

The Dimensions of Leadership Communication Style

Authoritarian, Democratic, and Laissez-Faire Leadership

Task and Interpersonal Leadership

Summary

Application Exercises

The Dimensions of Leadership Communication Style

Think of the leaders you have worked with in the past. Chances are you enjoyed interacting with some of these people more than others. The leaders you enjoyed working with were most likely those who created a productive and satisfying work climate. Under their guidance, you probably accomplished a great deal and had a pleasant and memorable experience.

One factor that contributes to variations in leader effectiveness is communication style. Leadership communication style is a relatively enduring set of communicative behaviors that a leader engages in when interacting with followers. A leader's communication style may reflect a philosophical belief about human nature or may simply be a strategy designed to maximize outcomes in a given situation. Regardless, the communication style a leader selects contributes to the success or failure of any attempt to exert influence.

Researchers have identified a number of leadership communication styles in the past half-century. These varying styles can be pared down to two primary models of communication: one model compares *authoritarian*, *democratic*, and *laissez-faire* styles of leadership communication; a second model contrasts *task* and *interpersonal* leadership communication. Let's look more closely at these two models of communication.

Authoritarian, Democratic, and Laissez-Faire Leadership

One of the earliest investigations of leadership communication style was undertaken by Kurt Lewin, Ronald Lippitt, and Ralph White.[1] Lewin and his colleagues studied the impact of *authoritarian*, *democratic* and *laissez-faire* leadership communication styles on group outcomes.

Leaders adopting these three styles of communication interact with followers very differently. The authoritarian leader maintains strict control over followers by directly regulating policy, procedures and behavior. Authoritarian leaders create distance between themselves and their followers as a means of emphasizing role distinctions. Many authoritarian leaders believe that followers would not function effectively without direct supervision. The authoritarian leader generally feels that people left to complete work on their own will be unproductive. Examples of authoritarian communicative behavior include a police officer directing traffic, a teacher ordering a student to do his or her assignment, and a supervisor instructing a subordinate to clean a work station.

Democratic leaders engage in supportive communication that facilitates interaction between leaders and followers. The leader adopting the democratic communication style encourages follower involvement and participation in the determination of goals and procedures. Democratic leaders assume that followers are capable of making informed decisions. The democratic leader does not feel intimidated by the suggestions provided by followers but believes that the contributions of others improve the overall quality of decision-making. The adage that "two heads are better than one" is the motto of the democratic leader. A group leader soliciting ideas from group members, a teacher asking students to suggest the due date for an assignment, and a district manager asking a salesperson for recommendations regarding the display of a new product are examples of democratic communicative behavior.

Laissez-faire, a French word roughly translated as "leave them alone," refers to communication affording followers a high degree of autonomy and self-rule. The laissez-faire leader does not directly participate in decision-making unless he or she is requested to do so by followers. Examples of laissez-faire communicative behavior include a group leader quietly observing group deliberations (providing information and ideas only when asked), a teacher allowing students to create their own assignments, and a research and development manager allowing his or her subordinates to work on product designs without intervention.

How can you tell if a leader is using an authoritarian, democratic, or laissez-faire style? One easy way to determine a leader's style is to pay close attention to the leader's communication. The following communication patterns are indicative of these three styles of leadership:

Authoritarian	Democratic	Laissez-Faire
Set goals individually	Involve followers in goal setting	Allow followers free rein to set their own goals
Control discussion with followers	Facilitate discussion with followers	Avoid discussion with followers
Set policy and procedures unilaterally	Solicit input regarding the determination of policy and procedures	Allow followers to set policy and procedures
Dominate interaction	Focus interaction	Avoid interaction
Personally direct the completion of tasks	Provide suggestions and alternatives for the completion of tasks.	Provide suggestions and alternatives for the completion of tasks only when asked to do so by followers

Authoritarian	Democratic	Laissez-Faire
Provide infrequent positive feedback	Provide frequent positive feedback	Provide infrequent feedback of any kind
Exhibit poor listening skills	Exhibit effective listening skills	May exhibit either poor or effective listening skills
Use conflict for personal gain	Mediate conflict for group gain	Avoid conflict

Lewin and his colleagues taught these communication styles to adult leaders who supervised groups of ten-year-old children working on hobby projects at a YMCA. The authoritarian leader was instructed to establish and to maintain policy and procedures unilaterally, to supervise the completion of task assignments directly, and to dictate follower behavior in all situations. The democratic leader was told to encourage the participation of followers in the determination of policy and procedures related to task completion and follower behavior. The laissez-faire leader was instructed to avoid direct involvement in the establishment of policy and procedures by supplying ideas and information only when asked to do so by followers.

The responses of the children in these experiments led to the formation of six generalizations regarding the impact of leadership communication style on group effectiveness.[2]

1. *Laissez-faire and democratic leadership communication styles are not the same.* Groups with laissez-faire leaders are not as productive and satisfying as groups with democratic leaders. The amount and quality of work done by children in laissez-faire groups was less than that of democratic groups. Additionally, the majority of children in laissez-faire groups expressed dissatisfaction despite the fact that more than two-and-a-half times as much play occurred in these groups.

2. *Although groups headed by authoritarian leaders are often most efficient, democratic leaders also achieve high efficiency.* The greatest number of tasks were completed under authoritarian leadership. This productivity was dependent on the leader's direct supervision. When the authoritarian leader left the room, productivity dropped by nearly 40% in some groups. Democratic groups were only slightly less productive. Further, productivity in these groups remained steady with or without direct adult supervision.

3. *Groups with authoritarian leadership experience more hostility and aggression than groups with democratic or laissez-faire leaders.*

Hostile and aggressive behavior in the form of arguing, property damage, and blaming occurred much more frequently in authoritarian groups than in other groups.

4. *Authoritarian led groups may experience discontent that is not evident on the surface.* Even in authoritarian led groups with high levels of productivity and little evidence of hostility and aggression, absenteeism and turnover were greater than in democratic and laissez-faire groups. Further, children shifted from authoritarian groups to more permissive groups exhibited tension release behavior in the form of energetic and aggressive play.

5. *Followers exhibit more dependence and less individuality under authoritarian leaders.* Children in authoritarian groups were more submissive than those in other groups. These children were less likely to initiate action without the approval of the leader and less likely to express their opinions and ideas than children in the democratic and laissez-faire groups.

6. *Followers exhibit more commitment and cohesiveness under democratic leaders.* Children in democratic groups demonstrated a higher degree of commitment to group outcomes. The climate in democratic groups was generally supportive and friendly.

A number of follow-up studies to the work of Lewin, Lippitt, and White have provided additional information about the effects of authoritarian, democratic, and laissez-faire leader communication. Figure 2.1 summarizes these findings.

The findings related to leadership communication style suggest the leader adopting authoritarian communication can expect: high productivity (particularly when he or she directly supervises followers); increased hostility, aggression, and discontent; and decreased commitment, independence, and creativity among followers. This style of communication would seem best suited for tasks requiring specific compliance procedures and minimal commitment or initiative. Routinized, highly structured, or simple tasks are often effectively accomplished under authoritarian leadership. Authoritarian leadership is also recommended when a leader is much more knowledgeable than his or her followers, when groups of followers are extremely large, or when there is insufficient time to engage in democratic decision-making. Certainly a military combat leader would not stop to discuss the possibilities of advancing or retreating while under enemy fire.

Democratic leadership communication contributes to relatively high productivity (whether or not the leader directly supervises followers)

Figure 2.1   Research Highlight

The Effect of Authoritarian, Democratic and Laissez-Faire Leadership Communication Styles

A number of researchers have studied the effects of the Authoritarian, Democratic and Laissez-Faire leadership communication styles. Some of the most important findings are summarized below.

Authoritarian Leadership	Democratic Leadership	Laissez-Faire Leadership
Increases productivity (Shaw, 1955; Hise, 1968)	Lowers turnover and absenteeism rates (Argyle, et al., 1958)	Decreases innovation (Farris, 1972)
Produces more accurate solutions when leader is knowledgeable (Cammalleri, et al., 1973)	Increases follower satisfaction (Mohr, 1971; Bass, et al., 1979)	Decreases follower motivation and satisfaction (Aspegren, 1963)
More positively accepted in larger groups (Vroom and Mann, 1960)	Increases follower participation (Hespe and Wall, 1976)	Increases productivity and satisfaction for highly motivated experts (Weschler, et al., 1952; Meltzer, 1956)
Enhances performance on simple tasks, decreases performance on complex tasks (Rudin, 1964)	Increases follower commitment to decisions (Ziller, 1954)	Decreases quality and quantity of output (Muringham and Leung, 1976)
Increases aggression level among followers (Day and Hamblin, 1964)	Increases innovation (Farris, 1972)	
Increases turnover rates (Ley, 1966)		

Sources:

Argyle, M., Gardner, G., & Ciofi, F. (1958). Supervisory methods related to productivity, absenteeism, and labor turnover. *Human Relations, 11*, 23-40.

Aspegren, R. E. (1963). A study of leadership behavior and its effects on morale and attitudes in selected elementary schools. *Dissertation Abstracts, 23*, 3708.

Bass, B. M., Burger, P. C., Doktor, R., & Barrett, G. V. (1979). *Assessment of managers: An international comparison*. New York: Free Press.

Cammalleri, J. A., Hendrick, H. W., Pittmen, W. C., Jr., Blout, H. D., & Prather, D. C. (1973). Effects of different leadership styles on group accuracy. *Journal of Applied Psychology, 57*, 32-37.

Day, R. C., & Hamblin, R. L. (1964). Some effects of close and punitive styles of supervision. *American Journal of Sociology, 69*, 499-510.

Farris, G. F. (1972). The effect of individual roles on performance in innovative groups. *R & D Management, 3*, 23-28.

Hespe, G., & Wall, T. (1976). The demand for participation among employees. *Human Relations, 29*, 411-428.

Hise, R. T. (1968, Fall). The effect of close supervision on productivity of stimulated managerial decision-making groups. *Business Studies, North Texas University*, pp. 96-104.

Ley, R. (1966). Labor turnover as a function of worker differences, work environment, and authoritarianism of foremen. *Journal of Applied Psychology, 50*, 497-500.

Meltzer, L. (1956). Scientific productivity in organizational settings. *Journal of Social Issues, 12*, 32-40.

Mohr, L. B. (1971). Organizational technology and organizational structure. *Administrative Science Quarterly, 16*, 444-459.

Muringham, J. K., & Leung, T. K. (1976). The effects of leadership involvement and the importance of the task on subordinates' performance. *Organizational Behavior and Human Performance, 17*, 299-310.

Rudin, S. A. (1964). Leadership as psychophysiological activation of group members: A case experimental study. *Psychological Reports, 15*, 577-578.

Shaw, M. E. (1955). A comparison of two types of leadership in various communication nets. *Journal of Abnormal and Social Psychology, 50*, 127-134.

Vroom, V. H., & Mann, F. C. (1960). Leader authorization and employee attitudes. *Personnel Psychology, 13*, 125-140.

Weschler, I. R., Kahane, M., & Tannenbaum, R. (1952). Job satisfaction, productivity, and morale: A case study. *Occupational Psychology, 26*, 1-14.

Ziller, R. C. (1954). Four techniques of group decision making under uncertainty. *American Psychologist, 9*, 498.

and to increased satisfaction, commitment, and cohesiveness. This style of communication is best suited for tasks that require participation and involvement, creativity, and commitment to decisions. The only significant drawbacks to democratic leadership are that democratic techniques are time consuming and can be cumbersome with larger groups.

The leader adopting the laissez-faire communication style may be accused of leadership avoidance. This communication style results in decreased productivity and less satisfaction for most followers. Further, laissez-faire groups may be less innovative than those with leaders employing authoritarian or democratic communication styles. However, laissez-faire leadership can be highly effective with groups containing motivated and knowledgeable experts. These groups often do not require direct guidance and produce better results when left alone. A group of medical researchers, for example, might function very effectively when provided with the necessary information and materials without any direct guidance or intervention by a leader. Take a look at the case study in Figure 2.2 to see what happens when highly motivated and knowledgeable followers are supervised too closely.

Production
Board has
given new
CEO -
2 years
to do this)

Organization
now "leader" appointed from outside
to change the organizational somewhat do functional
structure + increase creativity + outside

Figure 2.2

Case Study

The Importance of Leadership Communication Style:
SuperNova Microcomputer

Jay Brooks is the project director of a product development team at SuperNova Microcomputer. His team of thirty employees has been assigned to develop a new "highly user friendly" computer system for the home market. This group of thirty consists of the best technicians within the organization.

Unfortunately, Jay's team has been experiencing numerous difficulties and delays in the development of the new computer system. A number of team members have complained to the president of SuperNova, Sam Lowell, that Brooks is stifling creativity within the team and that Laura Martin, the project assistant, would be a much more effective leader for the team. "We could get this project moving if Laura was in charge," claims one team member.

Brooks, who was hired from a major competitor six months ago, is a very directive leader. He holds a meeting every morning from 8 a.m. to 10 a.m. in which every unit within the overall team presents their latest innovations. All new ideas must be cleared through Brooks before further research and work are undertaken. Many team members have complained about these meetings, claiming that "Brooks might as well build this system by himself if he is going to approve every chip." In addition, all team members must complete a worksheet isolating the specific tasks they have undertaken each day. This worksheet, wryly called "form 1984" by members of the team, is a major source of dissatisfaction among team members.

Laura Martin has been with SuperNova Microcomputer since its inception a decade ago. Laura was passed over for the job as project director because Sam Lowell felt that she was not as technically competent as she needed to be. Laura was disappointed but she accepted the decision because, overall, she has been very happy at SuperNova. Indeed, Laura has been instrumental in promoting the open, democratic, employee-oriented management style that is characteristic of SuperNova. As project assistant she interacts frequently with all members of the team. She has discovered that many of the members of the team feel unappreciated. One team member complains, for example, "We are expected to create one of the most advanced home computer systems in existence, but we are treated like a bunch of rebellious third graders."

Sam Lowell is disturbed because the project is falling way behind schedule. After only six months, major delays have pushed back the target date for the project by a full year. The team members themselves don't seem to be aware that they are falling behind any projected schedule; they only seem to realize that the project is bogging down.

Things have gotten so bad in the last couple of weeks that a number of team members are threatening to quit. If these people leave, the entire project will be jeopardized. Further, rumors are spreading through the team that upper management is disappointed with productivity and may replace several key team members. All in all, members of the team seem very frustrated.

large group
each member or team within
group has clearly defined
responsibilities
have limited time to

"We just want to build the best product that we can," says one team member, adding, "I only wish they would let us."

Discussion Questions

1. What recommendations would you make concerning the leadership of the product development team at SuperNova Microcomputer?
2. Which leadership communication style(s) would be most effective in working with the product development team? Why?
3. How would you suggest a leader might get the product development team back on schedule?
4. What recommendations would you make concerning the overall operation at SuperNova Microcomputer?

produce a planning document

In summary, researchers have concluded that the democratic style of leadership communication is often most effective. In general, the benefits derived from democratic communication far outweigh any potential costs. Democratic leadership is associated with increased follower productivity, satisfaction and involvement/commitment. The negative element of democratic leadership is that it can become mired in lengthy debate over policy, procedures, and strategies. In most cases, the increase in follower involvement and commitment more than make up for any such delays. Authoritarian leadership is effective in terms of output (particularly when the leader directly supervises behavior) but generally ineffective in enhancing follower satisfaction and commitment. Laissez-faire leadership damages productivity, satisfaction, and commitment in most groups. The one exception is a group of highly knowledgeable and motivated experts. In many situations, the costs associated with the authoritarian and laissez-faire styles of leadership can seriously hamper a leader's effectiveness.

Task and Interpersonal Leadership

Closely related to the authoritarian, democratic, and laissez-faire model of leadership style is the task and interpersonal model. Task and interpersonal styles have been variously labeled by researchers. Task oriented communication has been referred to as:

* Production oriented
* Initiating structure
* Theory X management
* Concern for production.

Interpersonal oriented communication has been called:

* Employee oriented
* Consideration
* Theory Y management
* Concern for people.

Despite the differing labels, conceptualizations of task and interpersonal leadership communication have been quite similar.

The leader employing the task style is primarily concerned with the successful completion of task assignments. The task oriented leader demonstrates a much greater concern for getting work done than for the people doing the work. The task leader is often highly authoritarian. In contrast, the interpersonal leader is concerned with relationships. This style, similar to the democratic style, emphasizes teamwork, cooperation, and supportive communication.

Ernest Stech describes the typical communication patterns of task and interpersonal oriented leaders in his book, *Leadership Communication*.[3] He lists the following distinctions between these two styles of leadership.

Task Orientation	Interpersonal Orientation
Disseminate information	Solicit opinions
Ignore the positions, ideas and feelings of others	Recognize the positions, ideas and feelings of others
Engage in rigid, stylized communication	Engage in flexible, open communication
Interrupt others	Listen carefully to others
Make demands	Make requests
Focus on facts, data, and information as they relate to tasks	Focus on feelings, emotions and attitudes as they relate to personal needs.
Emphasize productivity through the acquisition of technical skills.	Emphasize productivity through the acquisition of personal skills
Most often communicate in writing	Most often communicate orally
Maintain a "closed door" policy	Maintain an "open door" policy

From the late 1940s until the early 1960s several groups of researchers worked to identify and to label the dimensions of leadership communication. These researchers used different methodologies and measurement techniques but came to similar conclusions. Each of the research teams suggested that leadership consists of two primary communication dimensions: task and interpersonal. Although each group of researchers applied their own unique label to the communication styles they discovered, they were essentially talking about the same set of communicative behaviors.

The similarity in findings among these researchers is not surprising. Leadership boils down to two primary ingredients: work that needs to be done and the people who do the work. Without these ingredients there is no need for leadership! Let's focus now on four of the most significant attempts to identify the communication patterns of leaders: (1) the Michigan leadership studies, (2) the Ohio State leadership studies, (3) McGregor's Theory X and Theory Y, and (4) Blake and Mouton's Managerial Grid.

The Michigan Leadership Studies

Shortly after World War II, a team of researchers at the University of Michigan set out to discover which leadership practices contributed to effective group performance. To determine the characteristics of effective leaders, the Michigan researchers looked at both high and low performing teams within two organizations. Twenty-four groups of clerical workers in a life insurance company and seventy-two groups of railroad workers were studied in an attempt to identify the factors contributing to satisfactory and unsatisfactory group leadership.[4]

From their observations of these work groups, the Michigan researchers noted a distinction between what they called "production oriented" and "employee oriented" styles of leadership communication. Production oriented leaders focus on accomplishing tasks by emphasizing technical procedures, planning, and organization. The production oriented leader is primarily concerned with getting work done. Employee oriented leaders focus on relationships between people and are particularly interested in motivating and training followers. Employee oriented leaders demonstrate a genuine interest in the well-being of followers both on and off the job.

The Michigan researchers believed that the production oriented and employee oriented styles were opposing sets of communicative behaviors. They suggested these leadership communication styles could be described along a continuum as illustrated in Figure 2.3. A leader could choose either a production oriented style, an employee oriented style, or a neutral style of communication. According to the Michigan research, leaders who exhibited employee oriented styles had more productive and satisfied work groups.

Figure 2.3

Employee Oriented Versus Production Oriented
Leadership Communication Styles

Neutral

[---]

Employee Oriented   Production Oriented

This one dimensional view of leadership communication style was short lived.[5] Follow-up studies performed by the University of Michigan researchers suggested that it was possible for leaders to adopt both production oriented *and* employee oriented styles. Further, leaders who demonstrated high concern for both production and people were found to be more effective than leaders who exhibited only employee oriented or production oriented communication.[6] Production oriented and employee oriented leadership styles were not polar opposites but rather two distinct dimensions of leadership communication style.

The Ohio State Leadership Studies

At the same time that the Michigan researchers were involved in their observations of work groups, an interdisciplinary team of researchers at Ohio State University attempted to identify the factors associated with leadership communication.[7] The Ohio State researchers developed a questionnaire they called the Leader Behavior Description Questionnaire (LBDQ). The LBDQ was administered to groups of military personnel who were asked to rate their commanders.

Statistical analysis of the LBDQ indicated two primary dimensions of leadership. These dimensions were labeled *consideration* and *initiating structure*. Consideration consisted of: interpersonal oriented communication designed to express affection and liking for followers; the consideration of followers' feelings, opinions, and ideas; and the maintenance of an amiable working environment. Inconsiderate leaders criticized followers in front of others, made threats, and refused to accept followers' suggestions or explanations. Initiating structure referred to task related behaviors involved in the initiation of action, the organization and assignment of tasks, and the determination of clear-cut standards of performance.

Consideration and initiating structure were believed to be two separate dimensions of leadership. As a result, a leader could rate high or low on either dimension. This representation of leader communication style allowed for the development of a two dimensional view of leadership. As depicted in Figure 2.4, the Ohio State researchers believed that it was possible for a leader to demonstrate varying amounts of task (initiating structure) or interpersonal (consideration) communication.

Figure 2.4

**A Two Dimensional View of Leadership
Communication Style**

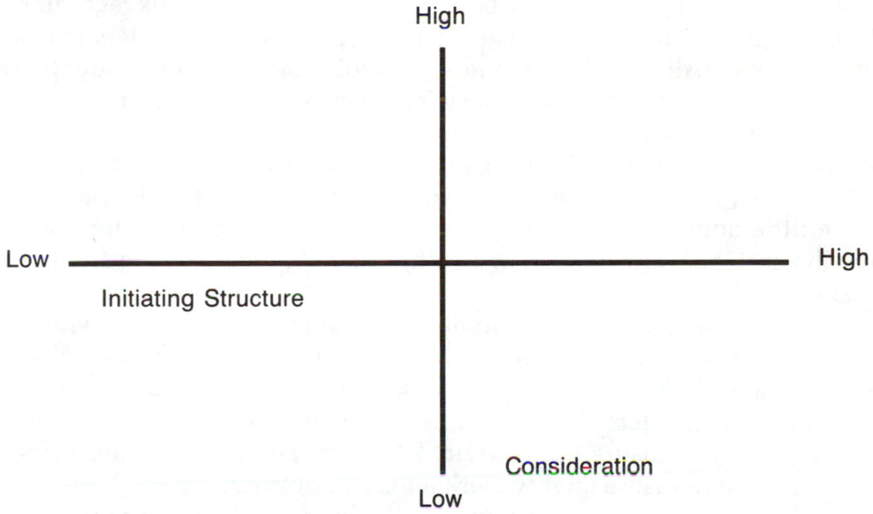

High

Low ———————————————————————— High

Initiating Structure

Consideration

Low

Conclusions drawn from the Ohio State research focusing on the use of task and interpersonal styles of leadership communication are complicated by variations in methodology and instrumentation. Over the years, several different versions of the LBDQ have been used to measure task (initiating structure) and interpersonal (consideration) related messages. As a result, the findings of the Ohio State team are inconsistent. In general, both consideration and initiating structure are important to effective leadership. Considerate leadership communication seems to increase follower satisfaction while decreasing hostility and strife. Initiating structure appears important in guiding and organizing the completion of tasks.[8]

McGregor's Theory X and Theory Y

In the late 1950s, Douglas McGregor, a professor of management at the Massachusetts Institute of Technology, attempted to isolate the ways in which attitudes and behaviors influence organizational management. The result of this investigation was McGregor's classic work *The Human Side of Enterprise*.[9] In his book, McGregor identifies two basic approaches to supervision—Theory X management and Theory Y management.

Theory X and Theory Y represent basic approaches for dealing with followers. Both approaches are based on a set of assumptions regarding human nature. Theory X managers believe that the average person has an inherent dislike for work and will avoid engaging in productive activities whenever possible. Managers must coerce, control, direct and threaten workers in order to insure performance. Indeed, Theory X management assumes that most people actually desire strict supervision as a means of insuring security. If workers are told what to do they can have little doubt that they are performing as expected. This approach emphasizes task supervision with little or no concern for individual needs.

Theory Y managers work to integrate organizational and individual goals. Theory Y assumes that work is as natural as play or rest. Work is not viewed as inherently unpleasant but rather as a source of satisfaction. Therefore, threats, punishment and direct supervision are not necessary to insure productivity. Personal commitment and pride are sufficient to insure quality workmanship. Further, Theory Y argues that the average person seeks responsibility as an outlet for imagination and creativity. This approach emphasizes individual commitment by recognizing individual needs as well as organizational needs.

The leader employing a Theory X orientation adopts a task oriented approach. This leader focuses on methods for getting work done. Little consideration is given to those doing the work. The Theory Y leader, on the other hand, focuses on the unique characteristics of the individuals performing tasks. The tasks themselves are not ignored but are viewed in terms of the people involved.

The Theory X—Theory Y dichotomy has been criticized for being an overly simplistic attempt to identify polarized extremes of human nature. McGregor responded to his critics by explaining that Theory X and

Theory Y are not polar opposites but, rather, independent dimensions isolating options from which a leader might select depending on the situation and the people involved.

Blake and Mouton's Managerial Grid ®

One of the most commonly cited examples of the task and interpersonal approach to leadership communication style is Robert Blake and Jane Mouton's Managerial Grid.[10] Blake and Mouton identify communication styles based on the degree of concern for production (task orientation) and concern for people (interpersonal orientation) exhibited by a leader. These communication styles are plotted on a graph with axes ranging from one to nine.(See Figure 2.5.)

The five plotted leader communication styles are:

1,1 Impoverished Management. The impoverished leader demonstrates a low concern for tasks and a low concern for relationships. The leader with a 1,1 orientation does not actively attempt to influence others but rather assigns responsibilities and leaves followers to complete tasks on their own.

9,1 Authority-Obedience. This leader is highly concerned with the completion of task assignments but demonstrates little concern for personal relationships. The primary function of the 9,1 oriented leader is to plan, direct, and control behavior. Followers are viewed as human resources who facilitate the completion of tasks. Input from followers is not encouraged as the 9,1 oriented leader attempts to dominate decision-making.

5,5 Organization Man Management. This middle-of-the-road leader is adequately concerned with production and people. In an attempt to involve followers, the 5,5 leader engages in compromise. Organization man leaders do not rock the boat—they push enough to achieve adequate productivity but yield if they believe increasing the workload will strain interpersonal relationships. As a result, the 5,5 leader often achieves mediocre results.

1,9 Country Club Management. The country club leader is more concerned with interpersonal relationships than with the completion of tasks. The 1,9 leader seeks to establish a supportive, friendly environment. Although country club leaders may want tasks to be completed effectively, they will emphasize factors that contribute to the personal satisfaction and happiness of followers. The 1,9 leader sees his or her primary responsibility to provide a positive working environment.

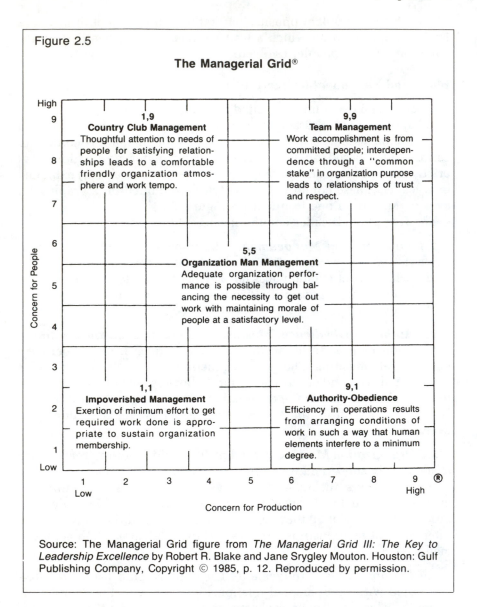

Figure 2.5

The Managerial Grid®

Source: The Managerial Grid figure from *The Managerial Grid III: The Key to Leadership Excellence* by Robert R. Blake and Jane Srygley Mouton. Houston: Gulf Publishing Company, Copyright © 1985, p. 12. Reproduced by permission.

9,9 Team Management. Team leadership involves a high concern for both production and people. The 9,9 leadership style is the ideal in which successful execution of task assignments as well as individual support and caring are emphasized. The 9,9 leader nurtures followers so that they are able to achieve excellence in both personal and team goals. Under team leadership, both leader and followers work together to achieve the highest level of productivity and personal accomplishment.

Leaders generally adopt one leadership communication style which they use in most situations. This is called a *dominant style*. A second Grid orientation in the model may be used as a backup style. For example, a leader might generally adopt a 5,5 leadership communication style but might shift to a 9,1 style when pressured to get orders out to an important customer.

The most effective leadership communication style, according to Blake and Mouton, is team management (9,9). Implementation of the 9,9 style in organizational contexts is associated with increased productivity and profitability, increased frequency of communication, and improved leader-follower relations.[11]

Summary

In this chapter, we examined the typical communicative behaviors of leaders adopting the authoritarian, democratic, laissez-faire, task, and interpersonal styles of leadership communication.

Authoritarian leaders maintain strict control over followers by directly regulating policy, procedures, and behavior. Democratic leaders engage in supportive communication that facilitates interaction between leaders and followers. Laissez-faire leaders allow followers a high degree of autonomy and self-rule and will not directly participate in decision-making unless requested to do so by followers.

The leader employing the task style is primarily concerned with the successful completion of task assignments. The task oriented leader demonstrates a much greater concern for getting work done than for the people doing the work. The interpersonal leader is concerned with relationships. This style emphasizes teamwork, cooperation, and supportive communication.

The research focusing on leadership communication style suggests the leader adopting authoritarian communication can expect high productivity (particularly when he or she directly supervises followers); increased hostility, aggression and discontent; and decreased commitment, independence, and creativity among followers. Democratic leadership communication contributes to relatively high productivity (whether or not the leader directly supervises followers), and increased satisfaction, commitment, and cohesiveness. Followers under laissez-faire leadership tend to be less productive and less satisfied. The only situation in which laissez-faire leadership may be effective is with groups containing highly motivated and knowledgeable experts.

Task and interpersonal oriented styles have been observed by (1) the Michigan leadership studies, (2) the Ohio State leadership studies, (3) McGregor, and (4) Blake and Mouton. Although the results are inconsistent at times, generally the use of *both* task and interpersonal oriented communication styles is associated with effective leadership.

Application Exercises

1. Make a list of the qualities that you believe to be important to effective leadership. Compare your list with the communicative behaviors listed on pages 23 and 24. Do effective leaders seem to adopt one leadership communication style more than others?

2. Identify the leadership communication styles you respond to most favorably. Why?

3. In what types of situations do you believe each of the leadership communication styles identified in this chapter would be most effective? Least effective?

4. Try to think of historical examples of leaders who adopted one of the five grid positions identified by Blake and Mouton. Which of these leaders was most effective? Why?

5. Identify as many alternatives to the styles of leadership communication outlined in this chapter as you can. Discuss with others in class the various styles you identify.

6. Read the case study below. Answer the questions at the end of the case. Discuss your opinions with others in class.

The Laid Back Leader

Roland Ortmayer is a most unusual leader. Ort—as he is known to his friends—has been head football coach at the University of La Verne for over forty years. In a profession in which winning is the measure of success, Ort has lost more games than he has won. That does not trouble Ort, as he prefers to have the better team win, even if that team is the opposition. If Ort's view on competition seems unusual, consider the following:

* *Ort does not require his players to attend practices*. "I think there is something wrong with a player if he practices every day," Ort claims.
* *Ort does not recruit players*. He believes that players should attend La Verne because of its academic programs, not because of the football team.
* *Ort does not believe that football players should lift weights*. There is too much physical work that needs to be done to waste time lifting useless weight, the coach explains.
* *Ort does not have a playbook*. According to Ort, if all the plays are scripted in advance there is no incentive to be creative.
* *Ort never holds team meetings*. Practice lasts from 3:45 to 5:30 p.m. Beyond that a player's time is his own.
* *Ort has no team rules and he has never kicked a player off his team*. "If a player does something that would warrant punishment of some kind, then he is the one who needs to be here the most," Ort explains.
* *Ort lines the field before each game and washes the team's uniforms each Sunday*. According to Ort, these activities make him "feel closer to the guys."

Ort's laid back style of leadership might not be as effective at a larger institution where there is pressure to recruit top notch athletes and win big games. But at tiny La Verne, Ort is respected by administrators, faculty and students alike. He coaches with compassion and understanding and helps his young men learn the value of competing and trying to be the best they can be.

Discussion Questions

1. Under what conditions is the laissez-faire style of leadership most effective?
2. What strategies does Ort employ to increase commitment among his players?
3. How should a leader's success be measured? Do you agree with the definition of leadership presented in Chapter 1 which claims that leaders help followers achieve their goals and meet their needs.
4. How would you rate Ort as a leader? Would you like to play on his team?

Source: Looney, D.S. (1989, September 4). A most unusual man. *Sports Illustrated*, pp. 118-124.

Endnotes

[1] Lewin, K., Lippitt, R., & White, R. K. (1939). Patterns of aggressive behavior in experimentally created "social climates." *Journal of Social Psychology, 10,* 271-299.

[2] White, R., & Lippitt, R. (1968). Leader behavior and member reaction in three "social climates." In D. Cartwright and A. Zander (Eds.), *Group dynamics* (pp. 318-335). New York: Harper & Row.

[3] Stech, E. L. (1983). *Leadership communication.* Chicago: Nelson-Hall, Ch. 4.

[4] See: Katz, D., Maccoby, N., Gurin, G., & Floor, L. (1951). *Productivity, supervision, and morale among railroad workers.* Ann Arbor: University of Michigan, Institute for Social Research.

Katz, D., Maccoby, N., & Morse, N. (1950). *Productivity, supervision, and morale in an office situation.* Ann Arbor: University of Michigan, Institute for Social Research.

[5] Although the one dimensional view of leadership communication has been criticized as being overly simplistic, some one dimensional models are still routinely discussed in leadership courses. For an example of a commonly cited one dimensional model see:

Tannenbaum, R., & Schmidt, W. H. (1958). How to choose a leadership pattern. *Harvard Business Review, 36,* 95-101.

[6] Kahn, R. L. (1956). The prediction of productivity. *Journal of Social Issues, 12,* 41-49.

[7] Stogdill, R. M., & Coons, A. E. (1957). *Leader behavior: Its description and measurement.* Columbus: Ohio State University, Bureau of Business Research.

[8] Stogdill, R. M. (1965). *Managers, employees, organizations.* Columbus: Ohio State University, Bureau of Business Research.

[9] McGregor, D. (1960). *The human side of enterprise.* New York: McGraw-Hill.

[10] Blake, R. R., & Mouton, J. S. (1985). *The managerial grid III: The key to leadership excellence.* Houston: Gulf Publishing.

[11] See:

Blake, R. R., & Mouton, J. S. (1978). *The new managerial grid.* Houston: Gulf Publishing, pp. 178-179.

Blake, R. R., Mouton, J. S., Barnes, L. B., & Greiner, L. E. (1964). Breakthrough in organization development. *Harvard Business Review, 42,* 133-155.

3

Theoretical Approaches to Leadership

Understanding and Explaining Leadership

Much of what was written about leadership prior to the twentieth century was based on non-experimental observation. The increasing use of "scientific" procedures and techniques to measure human behavior, which blossomed in the early twentieth century, changed the way in which scholars looked at leadership. Over the past ninety years, four primary approaches for understanding and explaining leadership have evolved: the *Traits Approach*, the *Situational Approach*, the *Functional Approach*, and the *Transformational Approach*.

Early social scientists believed that leadership qualities were innate. Either individuals were born with the traits needed to be a leader or they would always lack the physiological and psychological characteristics necessary for successful leadership. This perspective, known as the Traits Approach, maintained that nature played a key role in determining leadership potential. The search for inherent leadership traits served as the impetus for hundreds of research studies between the turn of the century and the end of World War II. Since the late 1940s, the popularity of the Traits Approach has steadily declined. For the most part, present-day researchers no longer accept the notion of the born leader.

The Traits Approach gave way to a situational explanation of leadership. The Situational Approach argues that the traits, skills, and behaviors necessary for effective leadership vary from situation to situation. Think of a successful leader you know. He or she may lead a student club, social group, or religious congregation. Now imagine this leader as a union boss, lab supervisor, or military commander. Is it difficult to picture this person playing different leadership roles effectively? A leader is not always successful in every situation. A leader's effectiveness depends on his or her personality, the behavior of followers, the nature of the task, and many other situational factors. The eighteenth President of the United States, Ulysses S. Grant, is an excellent example of how a leader's effectiveness varies between situations. Grant was a highly effective military leader but was considered inept as President.

While many researchers have attempted to identify factors influencing leadership effectiveness in various situations, others have studied the functions of leadership. The Functional Approach looks at the way leaders behave. The underlying assumption of the Functional Approach is that leaders perform certain functions that allow a group or organization to operate effectively. An individual is considered a leader if he or she performs these functions by engaging in identified leader behaviors. The Functional Approach has been applied primarily to group leadership. The perspective is important to communication scholars as it attempts to identify specific communicative behaviors associated with leadership.

The final approach to leadership, known as the Transformational Approach, has emerged in the past decade. The driving force behind the Transformational Approach is a series of research projects focusing on the characteristics of extraordinary leaders. These inspiring leaders transform both themselves and their followers by envisioning bold new possibilities for the utilization of human and material resources. The Transformational Approach focuses on the techniques involved in elevating leaders and followers to higher levels of motivation and morality. One of the primary methods of transformational leadership is the creation of vision. Vision refers to a leader's sense of future direction and purpose. The leader with vision creates an image of the future which serves to inspire followers to reach previously unimagined heights.

The Traits, Situational, Functional, and Transformational approaches all represent perspectives for understanding and explaining leadership. These approaches provide frameworks that guide leadership theory and research. You may discover that the four approaches at times overlap and at other times contradict one another. Currently, no single approach provides a universal explanation of leadership behavior. Indeed, each approach provides important information that helps us to understand and to explain the complicated process of leadership. Let's look at these four approaches to leadership in greater detail.

The Traits Approach to Leadership

In the early part of the twentieth century, it was widely believed that leaders possessed unique physical and psychological characteristics that predisposed them to positions of influence. Researchers were not completely sure which characteristics were most important, but they assumed that an individual's physical and psychological features were the best indicators of leadership potential. Scores of leadership studies focused on factors such as height, weight, appearance, intelligence, and disposition. Other studies looked at status, social skill, mobility, popularity and other social traits in order to determine which of these characteristics were most strongly correlated with leadership. Researchers wanted to know, for example, were leaders: Tall or short? Bright or dull? Outgoing or shy?

In 1948, Ralph Stogdill published a review of 124 studies and surveys appearing in print between 1904 and 1947 which examined traits and personal factors related to leadership.[1] Stogdill's review uncovered a number of inconsistent findings. Leaders were found to be both young and old, tall and short, heavy and thin, extroverted and introverted, and physically attractive as well as physically unattractive. Further, the strength of the relationship between a given trait and leadership prowess varied significantly from study to study. Stogdill concluded, "A person does not become a leader by virtue of the possession of some combination of traits, but the pattern of personal characteristics of the leader must bear some relevant relationship to the characteristics, activities, and goals of the followers."[2]

Based on his review, Stogdill identified six general factors he believed to be associated with leadership. These factors included both personal traits as well as components of the leadership situation.

1. *Capacity*. Personal traits related to leadership such as intelligence, verbal fluency, originality, and judgement affect a leader's capacity. Generally, those perceived as leaders are more intelligent and more able to express their ideas in clear and cogent terms. We now realize that many of these "traits" can be acquired through appropriate training and practice. Many organizations realize the value of life-long learning as a means for enhancing personal capabilities. Hewlett Packard CEO John Young, for example, suggests that life-long training and development are necessary for employees to achieve their full potential.[3]

2. *Achievement*. Skills and abilities acquired through education and training constitute personal achievements. Achievements may be measured by academic credentials, specific knowledge, or task skills. Finishing your college degree, learning how to give an effective oral presentation, or mastering the technique for programming a computerized order system are achievements that might enhance your ability to lead others.

3. *Responsibility*. Leaders are responsible. A leader is dependable, persistent, and demonstrates a desire to excel. Acting responsibly encourages others to look to you for leadership. Next time you are in a group, try to communicate to others that you are responsible: arrive on time for all group meetings, contribute ideas frequently, and volunteer to complete necessary tasks. You may soon notice others in the group looking to you for leadership.

4. *Participation*. Leaders are willing to get involved. To be a leader one should participate in group activities, be sociable, cooperative, adaptable, and use humor appropriately. Leaders are active and useful contributors. Leaders are not always the most talkative members of a group or organization, but they are rarely among the least frequent contributors.

5. **Status**. Socioeconomic status, position, and popularity are related to leadership. On average, leaders tend to come from a higher socioeconomic background and to be more popular than their followers. This is not to say that individuals are precluded from leadership by their social status. Only in the rare instance in which a certain social status is required to gain a particular leadership position (such as the citizenship requirement to be President of the United States) does social status prevent an individual from achieving a formal leadership position. Differences in status between leaders and nonleaders may be somewhat artificial, however. Leaders are often perceived as having higher status or as being more popular simply because they are playing the role of leader.

6. **Situation**. Leadership varies from situation to situation. Being a leader in one situation does not guarantee a leadership role in another situation. Few, if any, of us are leaders all of the time. No particular set of innate traits, in and of themselves, guarantee leadership. The unique combination of traits, skills, and abilities each individual possesses contributes to potential leadership in varying situations. An expert on wilderness survival might not be viewed as a leader in a corporate boardroom. Conversely, most corporate executives would probably not be nominated to lead an expedition to Antarctica.

In 1974, Stogdill again published an exhaustive review of traits research. This time he analyzed 163 traits studies published between 1949 and 1970.[4] Fewer inconsistencies were uncovered in the traits research of the 1950s and '60s, but Stogdill remained convinced that personality traits *alone* did not adequately explain leadership. Once again, Stogdill concluded that *both* personal traits and situational factors influenced leadership.

In many instances, Stogdill's work has been cited as evidence that personal traits have no bearing on leadership. Stogdill himself did not hold this view. In 1974, he wrote:

> [I] have been cited frequently as evidence in support of the view that leadership is entirely situational in origin and that no personal characteristics are predictive of leadership. This view seems to overemphasize the situational and underemphasize the personal nature of leadership. Strong evidence indicates that different leadership skills and traits are required in different situations. The behaviors and traits enabling a mobster to gain and maintain control over a criminal gang are not the same as those enabling a religious leader to gain and maintain a large following. Yet certain general qualities — such as courage, fortitude, and conviction — appear to characterize both.[5]

Recently, researchers have reanalyzed previous reviews of trait research using advanced statistical techniques.[6] The updated analyses suggest that personal characteristics do have an influence on perceptions of leadership. Certain traits such as intelligence, dominance, and gender may be important in explaining who is *perceived* as a leader. These findings do not directly imply that traits are predictive of leadership effectiveness. Rather, they suggest that certain traits may enhance the perception that someone has the ability to lead others. These perceptions seem particularly important in gauging political leadership. Research indicates that characteristics such as intelligence, honesty, altruism, and foresight are commonly perceived as qualities of effective political leaders.[7]

The notion that certain personal traits guarantee leadership effectiveness has never been satisfactorily supported. Certain traits can be advantageous in certain situations, but personal traits alone do not predispose individuals to success as a leader. Every tall person will not become a great basketball player, and every outgoing and intelligent person will not become a great leader. While many people possessing desirable personal traits have risen to positions of influence, just as many who lack the personal characteristics deemed necessary for leadership have been successful leaders. The assumption that leaders are *born* is not accurate. A more reasonable assumption is that leaders are *made* through training and experience.

The Situational Approach to Leadership

As the Traits Approach became less plausible as an explanation of leadership behavior, many researchers began to pursue situational explanations for leadership. These situational approaches, often called contingency approaches, assume that leadership behavior is contingent upon variations in the situation.[8] For example, the strategy for effectively leading a high tech research and development team is much different from the strategy for most effectively leading a military combat unit. The differences in leadership style might be attributed to task and relational structure, superior-subordinate interactions, the motivation of followers, or any one of a number of other situational factors. Three of the most commonly studied situational approaches are Fiedler's Contingency Model of Leadership, Path-Goal Theory, and Hersey and Blanchard's Situational Leadership Theory.

Fiedler's Contingency Model of Leadership

One of the earliest, and most often cited, situational models is Fred Fiedler's Contingency Model of Leadership.[9] In the early 1950s, Fiedler became interested in interpersonal communication in therapeutic relationships. He discovered that competent therapists viewed themselves as more similar to their patients than less competent therapists did. Fiedler wondered how these findings related to group performance and leadership. He decided to assess how workers perceived fellow workers. He developed a measure of Assumed Similarity between Opposites (ASo) to score differences in ratings of most and least-preferred coworkers.

Ratings of least-preferred coworkers (LPC) became the primary element in Fiedler's Contingency Model of Leadership. Fiedler claims that our ratings of others with whom we do not like to work provide us with valuable information about our leadership behavior. This information can help us identify the situations in which we might most effectively lead others. Before continuing with this Chapter, take a moment to complete the LPC scale provided in Figure 3.1.

Highly negative evaluations of a least preferred coworker result in low LPC scores; favorable evaluations result in higher LPC scores. According to Fiedler, low-LPC leaders are more concerned with tasks, and high-LPC leaders demonstrate greater concern for relationships. The effectiveness of a leader in a given situation is influenced by three primary factors that control the amount of influence a leader has over followers. These are (1) the leader's position power, (2) task structure, and (3) the interpersonal relationship between leader and members.

Position Power. A leader gains power by virtue of his or her position within a group or organization. Positions that afford a leader the ability to reward and punish provide substantial position power. The leader of a classroom problem-solving group has little power to reward or punish group members as compared to an employer who can offer a raise or a bonus, a more appealing work schedule, or long term job security.

Task Structure. Some tasks are highly structured. These tasks have very specific procedures, agreed upon outcomes, and are generally easy for leaders to evaluate. The production of a circuit board on an assembly line is an example of a structured task. Other tasks are highly unstructured. These tasks may be accomplished in a number of different ways. In these situations, it is very difficult for a leader to determine the best method of task completion, and evaluations of performance are extremely difficult to make. The writing of a television or movie script would be an example of an unstructured task.

Figure 3.1

Fiedler's Least-preferred Coworker (LPC) scale

Think of the person with whom you work least well. He or she may be someone you work with now or someone you worked with in the past. This person does not have to be the person you liked the least but should be the person with whom you had the most difficulty in getting a job done. Describe this person as he or she appears to you.

Please give your immediate, first reaction to the items listed below. Simply look at the words on both ends of the line and place an "X" at the spot that most closely describes your perception of the person with whom you work least well. Remember that there are *no right or wrong answers*. Work rapidly; your first answer is likely to be the best. Please do not omit any items, and mark each item only once.

pleasant	8	7	6	5	4	3	2	1	unpleasant
friendly	8	7	6	5	4	3	2	1	unfriendly
rejecting	1	2	3	4	5	6	7	8	accepting
helpful	8	7	6	5	4	3	2	1	frustrating
unenthusiastic	1	2	3	4	5	6	7	8	enthusiastic
tense	1	2	3	4	5	6	7	8	relaxed
distant	1	2	3	4	5	6	7	8	close
cold	1	2	3	4	5	6	7	8	warm
cooperative	8	7	6	5	4	3	2	1	uncooperative
supportive	8	7	6	5	4	3	2	1	hostile
boring	1	2	3	4	5	6	7	8	interesting
quarrelsome	1	2	3	4	5	6	7	8	harmonious
self-assured	8	7	6	5	4	3	2	1	hesitant
efficient	8	7	6	5	4	3	2	1	inefficient

| gloomy | 1 | 2 | 3 | 4 | 5 | 6 | 7 | 8 | cheerful |
| open | 8 | 7 | 6 | 5 | 4 | 3 | 2 | 1 | guarded |

Scoring of the LPC

The LPC score is obtained by summing the item ratings above. An average can be computed by dividing the total score by twenty. In samples collected by Fiedler, low LPC scores ran from an average of 1.2 to 2.2. High LPC scores ranged from approximately 3.2 to 4.1.

Source: Fiedler, F. E. (1967). *A theory of leadership effectiveness*. New York: McGraw-Hill. Used by permission.

Leader-Members Relations. A leader builds a relationship with his or her followers through interaction. A good relationship is characterized by loyalty, affection, trust, and respect. Poor relationships result in lower motivation and commitment.

Fiedler plotted each of the three situational variables for leaders on a continuum from favorable to unfavorable to create his Contingency Model (see Figure 3.2). The most favorable conditions for leaders exist when the relationship between the leader and followers is good, the task is highly structured, and the leader's position power is strong. The least favorable conditions exist when the relationship between the leader and followers is poor, the task is highly unstructured, and the leader's position power is weak. The effectiveness of a leader in a given situation, according to Fiedler, is influenced by LPC scores. Leaders with low LPC scores (task orientation) are most effective when conditions are either highly favorable or unfavorable for the leader. Notice that in Figure 3.2 the tails on each end of the graph represent the correlation between group performance and low leader LPC scores. The hump in the center of the graph indicates a relationship between high LPC scores (relational orientation) and group performance. High-LPC leaders are most effective when situational variables are neither extremely favorable or unfavorable.

Criticism of Fiedler's Contingency Model has been fierce.[10] Most of the criticism of Fiedler's theory has focused on the development of the LPC measure and the methods used to distinguish the effect of position power, task structure, and leader-member relations on leader effectiveness. Additional concerns have been expressed regarding the utility of the Contingency Model. Since LPC scores are relatively

Figure 3.2

Correlations Between Leaders' LPC Scores and Group Effectiveness Under Conditions Ranging from Favorable to Unfavorable for Leaders

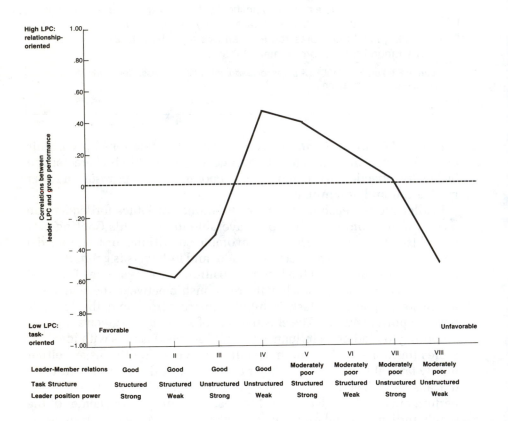

Source: Fiedler, F. E. (1967) *A theory of leadership effectiveness*. New York: McGraw-Hill. Used by permission.

consistent personality measures, situations must be adapted to fit leaders, as opposed to leaders modifying behavior to fit situations.

Fiedler's most recent research does not focus on LPC scores but looks instead at the impact of intellect and knowledge on leader effectiveness.

Fiedler's new theory of leadership, called Cognitive Resource Theory, assumes that the more intelligent and knowledgeable a leader is, the better his or her plans and decisions will be. Cognitive Resource Theory suggests that situational factors such as leader directiveness, situational stress, group supportiveness, and the nature of the task influence group performance.[11] At the present, the relationship between the Contingency Model and Cognitive Resource Theory is not fully developed.

Path-Goal Theory

Path-Goal Theory is based on a theory of organizational motivation called Expectancy Theory. Expectancy Theory claims that followers are more motivated to be productive when they believe that successful task completion will provide a path to a valuable goal. According to Robert House and his associates, leaders play an important role in influencing follower perceptions of task paths and goal desirability.[12] It is a leader's responsibility to communicate clearly what is expected of followers and what rewards can be anticipated when tasks are successfully completed. Take, for example, a group of students assigned to give a classroom presentation. How might the leader of such a group apply Expectancy Theory? By providing specific expectations for individual task assignments and reinforcing the group goal (a quality product that will receive a good grade), the group leader can increase the motivation and satisfaction level of followers.

According to House and Mitchell, the ability to motivate followers is influenced by a leader's communication style as well as by certain situational factors. Four communication styles are identified.

1. *Directive Leadership*: procedure related communication behavior that includes planning and organizing, task coordination, policy setting, and other forms of specific guidance.

2. *Supportive Leadership*: interpersonal communication focusing on concerns for the needs and well-being of followers, and the facilitation of a desirable climate for interaction.

3. *Participative Leadership*: communication designed to solicit opinions and ideas from followers for the purpose of involving followers in decision making.

4. *Achievement-Oriented Leadership*: communication focusing on goal attainment and accomplishment, emphasizing the achievement of excellence by demonstrating confidence in the ability of followers to achieve their goals.

In Path-Goal Theory, two situational variables are most influential in the selection of appropriate leadership communication style: the nature of followers and the nature of the task. Follower characteristics thought to be important include follower needs, abilities, values, and personality. Important task factors include task structure and clarity. These factors influence motivation and satisfaction levels among followers and determine the most effective leader communication style (see Figure 3.3).

Directive leader communication is most effective when followers are inexperienced or unsure, or when the task is unstructured. In these situations, followers might have a low expectation of their ability to perform satisfactorily. This expectation can lead to decreased motivation and satisfaction. In general, when expected behavior and task assignments are ambiguous, such as in a new position or job function, followers need directive leadership. On the other hand, if behavioral expectations are clearly understood and followers are competent in performing tasks, directive leadership lowers motivation and satisfaction. Nobody likes to have someone looking over her/his shoulder when the task is clear and performance is not problematic.

When followers confront structured tasks that are stressful, tedious, frustrating, difficult, or dissatisfying, such as working on an assembly line, a leader can make the situation more tolerable by engaging in supportive leader communication. In situations such as these, followers might have the necessary skills to complete tasks effectively but may lack confidence or commitment. This lack of confidence or commitment can produce a low self-expectation, resulting in poor performance. Supportive communication bolsters confidence and commitment and offers social rewards that can enhance motivation and satisfaction. Simply recognizing the difficulty of a task and expressing your appreciation for a follower's efforts can increase motivation and satisfaction levels. Supportive communication will contribute less to motivation and satisfaction when tasks are already stimulating and enjoyable.

Situations in which tasks are unstructured and behavior expectations are ambiguous are good opportunities for participative leader communication. Participating in decision making allows followers to think critically about expected behavior and task performance. Becoming more intimately involved with an unclear task can serve to increase understanding and motivation. A follower struggling to develop a program to simplify a new computerized accounting system might benefit from participative communication. Participative communication stimulates understanding and clarity and can increase satisfaction, particularly when uncertainty is uncomfortable for followers. In situations where the task is highly structured and followers are aware

Figure 3.3

The Relationship Between Leader Behavior and Follower
Motivation and Satisfaction: Path-Goal Theory

Leader Communication Style	Directive	Supportive	Participative	Achievement-Oriented
To enhance motivation and satisfaction use when:	Followers are inexperienced or unsure.	Followers are skilled, but lack confidence or commitment.	Followers are unsure. (particularly if uncertainty prompts apprehension).	Followers possess necessary skills.
	Task is unstructured.	Task is structured. (particularly if task is stressful, tedious, frustrating, difficult, or dissatisfying).	Task is unstructured.	Task is unstructured.

of behavior expectations, participative leadership will have a minimal effect on motivation and satisfaction according to Path-Goal Theory.

Achievement-oriented leader communication serves to increase a follower's confidence in his or her ability to realize challenging goals. By emphasizing excellence and demonstrating confidence in a follower's abilities, a leader can create a positive performance expectation. We are more likely to produce excellent results when we know others have expressed confidence in our ability to excel. The expectations of his coach and teammates might offer a partial explanation for the incredible success of Michael Jordan, the star of professional basketball's Chicago Bulls. When asked what his game plan was, his coach once claimed, "We give the ball to Michael, and get out of his way." Achievement-oriented communication is most effective in unstructured situations. Followers performing highly structured tasks will not be as effectively motivated by achievement-oriented messages.

Path-Goal Theory attempts to explain follower motivation and satisfaction in terms of leader behavior and task structure. Although the theory neglects many situational variables that might potentially be important, such as power, organizational climate, and group cohesiveness, Path-Goal Theory provides a viable explanation of the relationship among leaders, followers, and tasks.

Hersey and Blanchard's Situational Leadership Theory

Paul Hersey and Kenneth Blanchard suggest that the maturity level of followers plays an important role in selecting appropriate leadership behavior.[13] As in the Fiedler model and Path-Goal Theory, Hersey and Blanchard divide leader behavior into task and relationship dimensions. The appropriate degree of task and relationship behavior exhibited by a leader is dependent on the maturity level of followers.

According to Hersey and Blanchard, follower maturity consists of two major components that can be plotted along a continuum: job maturity and psychological maturity. Job maturity refers to demonstrated task-related abilities, skills, and knowledge. An intern making rounds for the first time has low job maturity. A budget officer preparing a yearly financial statement for the twentieth consecutive year has high job maturity. Psychological maturity relates to feelings of confidence, willingness, and motivation. A factory worker bored and unchallenged by a repetitive task has low psychological maturity while a teacher committed to excellence in the classroom has high psychological maturity. Maturity levels can fluctuate as a follower moves from task to task or from one situation to another.

Four combinations of job maturity and psychological maturity indicate follower readiness:

Readiness Level 1: Low job maturity and low psychological maturity (follower lacks skills and willingness).

Readiness Level 2: Low job maturity and high psychological maturity (follower lacks skills, but is willing).

Readiness Level 3: High job maturity and low psychological maturity (follower is skilled, but lacks willingness).

Readiness Level 4: High job maturity and high psychological maturity (follower is skilled and willing).

According to Situational Leadership Theory, the maturity level of followers dictates effective leader behavior (see Figure 3.4). By adapting the Blake and Mouton Managerial Grid discussed in Chapter 2, Hersey and Blanchard suggest appropriate task and relational orientations for each of the four levels of follower maturity. Immature, Level One followers require specific guidance or "telling." The most effective leader behavior with Level One followers is high task directed communication and low relationship directed communication. Task related messages serve to direct and guide follower behavior. The use

Figure 3.4

Hersey and Blanchard's Situational Leadership Theory

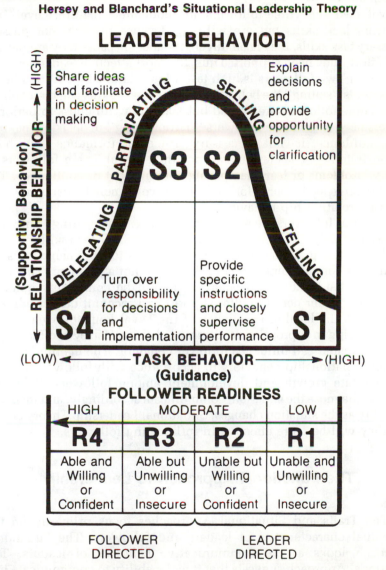

LEADER BEHAVIOR

(Supportive Behavior)
RELATIONSHIP BEHAVIOR → (HIGH)

PARTICIPATING — S3 — Share ideas and facilitate in decision making

SELLING — S2 — Explain decisions and provide opportunity for clarification

DELEGATING — S4 — Turn over responsibility for decisions and implementation

TELLING — S1 — Provide specific instructions and closely supervise performance

(LOW) ← TASK BEHAVIOR → (HIGH)
(Guidance)

FOLLOWER READINESS

	HIGH	MODERATE		LOW
	R4	R3	R2	R1
	Able and Willing or Confident	Able but Unwilling or Insecure	Unable but Willing or Confident	Unable and Unwilling or Insecure

FOLLOWER DIRECTED   LEADER DIRECTED

Source: Paul Hersey and Ken Blanchard, *Management of Organizational Behavior Utilizing Human Resources, 5/E*, © 1988, p. 171. Reproduced by permission of Prentice-Hall, Inc., Englewood Cliffs, New Jersey.

of supportive, relationship directed communication should be avoided at this level as such messages might be interpreted as a reward for poor performance.

Level Two and Three followers are moderately mature. Level Two followers lack skills but are willing. Because they do not possess necessary task skills, they need direct guidance. Because they are putting forth effort, they need support. Thus, the most effective leader behavior with Level Two followers is high task/high relationship. At this level, the leader is "selling" the belief that the necessary skills can be acquired. Level Three followers are skilled but lack the willingness to perform. Leaders need to get these followers "participating" in decision making. Task guidance is not necessary since performance has been demonstrated, but leaders must encourage Level Three followers to discuss problems or fears hampering commitment or confidence. The most effective leader behavior facilitates involvement by using low task and high relationship behavior.

Level Four followers are skilled and willing. "Delegating" authority to these mature performers is the best strategy. Since task skills are well developed, task guidance is not necessary. Relationship behavior is not required as commitment and confidence are not a problem. This does not mean that relationship behavior should be completely ignored. Certainly a leader needs to offer support and recognition periodically to maintain the level of excellence of the Level Four follower.

By engaging in appropriate leadership behavior, Hersey and Blanchard suggest a leader can influence follower behavior. The manipulation of task and relationship behaviors in accordance with follower maturity can facilitate growth and development among followers. If leaders carefully diagnose the situation, communicate accordingly, and maintain flexibility as the situation changes, Situational Leadership Theory claims that they will be more effective in influencing followers.

The Functional Approach to Leadership

The Traits and Situational Approaches focus primarily on the individual characteristics of leaders and followers. The Functional Approach looks at the communicative *behavior* of leaders. The Functional Approach suggests that it is the ability to communicate like a leader that determines leadership. Imagine that while driving you witness an accident. Several motorists, including you, stop to offer assistance. Who will become the leader in this emergency situation? Will the leader be the person with the most knowledge regarding first aid? Perhaps. Will the leader be the person with the right combination of motivation and maturity for the situation? Maybe. Most likely the leader will be the person who starts behaving like a leader. Leadership functions in this situation might include assigning tasks ("You call 911"), initiating action ("I'll put my jacket on him so he'll be warm"), giving support ("The ambulance will be here in just a few minutes"), and mediating conflict ("Let's not worry about whose fault it was until everyone is feeling better"). By performing the functions of leadership, an individual will be viewed as a leader by others.

One of the earliest contributions to the Functional Approach was Chester Barnard's 1938 classic, *The Functions of the Executive*.[14] Barnard's seminal work isolated communication as the central function of organizational leadership. Since then, a number of researchers have attempted to identify the various behaviors associated with leadership in organizations and groups. Kenneth Benne and Paul Sheats were pioneers in the classification of functional roles in groups.[15] Benne and Sheats analyzed group communication patterns to identify the various roles played by group members. They identify three types of group roles: *task-related roles*, *group building and maintenance roles*, and *individual roles*.

Task-related roles contribute to the organization and completion of group tasks. Task-related roles include:

> *The initiator*: defines the problem, establishes agenda and procedure, proposes innovative strategies and solutions in times of difficulty. The initiator makes statements such as: "I see our problem as maintaining our market share," or "Let's begin by just throwing out some possible ways to approach this problem."

> *The information/opinion seeker*: solicits ideas, asks questions about information provided by others, asks for evaluations of information and procedure. The information/opinion seeker makes statements such as: "Why do you think our production costs will increase in the next quarter?", or "Do you think we are spending enough time discussing possible solutions?"

> *The information/opinion giver*: presents and evaluates facts and information, evaluates procedure. The information/ opinion giver makes statements such as: "I think we will serve our students better by offering more night courses next

semester,'' or ''I learned in my Group Communication course that we shouldn't offer solutions until we have thoroughly analyzed the problem.''

The elaborator: provides examples and background as a means for clarifying ideas, speculates how proposed solutions might work. The elaborator makes statements such as: ''A bake sale may be an effective way to raise money. Last year, the Ski Club made $500 from their bake sale.''

The orienter/coordinator: summarizes interaction, looks for relationships among ideas and suggestions, focuses group members on specific issues and tasks. The orienter/coordinator makes statements such as: ''That suggestion seems to fit with Glenn's idea about training,'' or ''Maybe if we all come to the next meeting with a few pages of notes we could put together an outline for our presentation.''

The energizer: stimulates or arouses the group to achieve excellence, promotes activity and excitement. The energizer makes statements such as: ''If we can get this product out on schedule I think it will revolutionize the industry.''

Group building and maintenance roles contribute to the development and maintenance of open, supportive, and healthy interpersonal relationships among group members. Group building and maintenance roles include:

The encourager: supports and praises the contributions of others, communicates a sense of belonging and solidarity among group members, accepts and appreciates divergent viewpoints. The encourager makes statements such as: ''I agree with Susan,'' or ''I am confident that our group will do a great job next week,'' or ''I can appreciate your concern about reaching a decision too quickly. We must be careful not to jump to premature conclusions.''

The harmonizer/compromiser: mediates conflict, reduces tension through joking, attempts to bring group members with opposing points of view closer together. The harmonizer/compromiser makes statements such as: ''What's the worst thing that could happen if we don't get this project done on time? Okay, what's the second worst thing that could happen?'', or ''Is there any way you and Brett can both get what you want from this decision?''

The gatekeeper: encourages the involvement of shy or uninvolved group members, proposes regulations of the flow of communication through means such as time and topic limitation. The gatekeeper makes statements such as: "I'd be interested to hear what Meg has to say about this," or "Why don't we limit our discussion of the budget to twenty minutes."

The standard-setter: expresses group values and standards, applies standards to the evaluation of the group process. The standard-setter makes statements such as: "Our goal has always been to develop user-friendly products," or "Let's try to be critical of ideas, not people. That has always been our policy in the past."

Individual roles not supportive of the task or group relationships can minimize group effectiveness. Although a certain degree of individuality is healthy, individual-centered behaviors do not contribute to task completion or relationship development and maintenance. Individual roles include:

The aggressor: attacks the ideas, opinions, and values of others, uses aggressive humor, makes personal judgments. The aggressor makes statements such as: "It is better to keep your mouth shut and appear stupid than to open it and remove all doubt," or "Pete's concern for equal work loads is the reason this group is so unproductive."

The blocker: resists the ideas and opinions of others, brings up "dead" issues after they have been rejected by the group. The blocker makes statements such as: "I don't care if we already voted on it; I still think the Traits Approach offers the best explanation of leadership."

The recognition-seeker: relates personal accomplishments to the group, claims to be more expert and knowledgeable than other group members on virtually every topic. The recognition-seeker makes statements such as: "I know I am not a nurse, but I might as well be considering how much time I spent with my husband when he was ill."

The player: maintains a non-caring or cynical attitude, makes jokes at inappropriate times. The player makes statements such as: "We can't get much accomplished in one hour. Let's knock off early and get a beer."

> *The dominator*: lacks respect for the views of others, disconfirms the ideas and opinions of others, frequently interrupts. The dominator makes statements such as: "Steve's idea doesn't seem worthwhile to me. The way to get this program to run is to do what I have suggested."

Roles associated with the successful completion of the task and the development and maintenance of group interaction help to facilitate goal achievement and the satisfaction of group needs. These roles serve a leadership function. Roles associated with the satisfaction of individual needs do not contribute to the goals of the group as a whole and are usually not associated with leadership. By engaging in task-related and group building/maintenance role behaviors (and avoiding individual role behavior), a group member can perform leadership functions and increase the likelihood that he or she will achieve leadership status within the group.

In addition to the Benne and Sheats categories, several other communicative behaviors associated with leadership have been identified. Figure 3.5 provides a listing of three sets of proposed leadership functions.

The Functional Approach provides guidelines for the behavior of leaders by suggesting the necessary functions that a leader should perform. In its present form, the Functional Approach does not provide a clear, well developed prescription for leader behavior. Many of the identified leader behaviors are vague and some are contradictory. How, for example, does a leader specifically act as an ideologist, increase interdependence among group members, or facilitate work? However, from a communication perspective, the Functional Approach does provide a useful framework for identifying communication behaviors that can contribute to the exercise of leadership.

The Transformational Approach to Leadership

In the past decade, the Transformational Approach has emerged as a new perspective for understanding and explaining leadership. The Transformational Approach was first outlined by James MacGregor Burns. Burns compared traditional leadership, which he labeled as "transactional," with a more "complex" and "potent" type of leadership he called "transforming."[16] The motivational appeals of the transactional leader are designed to satisfy basic human needs. The motivational appeals of the transformational leader go beyond basic needs in an attempt to satisfy a follower's higher level needs. According

Figure 3.5

The Functions of Leadership

Krech and Crutchfield (1948)

* executive
* planner
* policy-maker
* expert
* external group representative
* facilitator of internal relationships
* supplier of rewards and punishments
* arbitrator
* role model
* group symbol
* surrogate for individual responsibility
* ideologist
* parental figure
* scapegoat

Bowers and Seashore (1966)

* supporter of others
* interaction facilitator
* goal emphasizer
* work facilitator

Cartwright and Zander (1968)

* goal achievement (including: initiating action, focusing on goals, clarifying issues, developing procedural plans, and evaluating outcomes)
* maintenance behavior (including: keeping interpersonal relationships pleasant, mediating disputes, providing encouragement, involving reticent followers, and increasing interdependence among members)

Sources:
Krech, D., & Crutchfield, R. (1948). *Theory and problems of social psychology*. New York: McGraw-Hill.

Bowers, D. G., & Seashore, S. E. (1966). Predicting organizational effectiveness with a four-factor theory of leadership. *Administrative Science Quarterly, 2*, 238-263.

Cartwright, D., & Zander, A. (1968). Leadership and performance of group functions: Introduction. In D. Cartwright & A. Zander (Eds). *Group dynamics* (pp. 301-317). New York: Harper & Row.

to Abraham Maslow, five human needs exist in hierarchical order: physiological needs, safety needs, social needs, esteem needs, and self-actualization needs.[17]

The most basic human needs are *physiological*. Before we can concern ourselves with any other needs, we must satisfy basic necessities such as oxygen, food, water, and sleep. As you may have discovered, if you study for several days without sleeping, the need for sleep will take precedence over other less urgent needs.

When physiological needs are satisfied, we can turn our attention to the second level of the hierarchy, *safety* needs. Humans seek predictability and protection. We are generally most comfortable in environments that are familiar and free from danger. If you become lost in the desert in the heat of the day, your first priority will be finding a safer, cooler environment.

Once environmental factors have been satisfied, we can turn our attention to our *social* needs. Humans desire affiliation with others. We seek social connections with others through our group memberships and relationships with others.

Esteem needs become important when physiological, safety, and social needs are reasonably well satisfied. Esteem needs relate to our desire to feel good about ourselves. Esteem consists of internal feelings of competence, respect, and self-worth as well as external feedback and recognition which support positive esteem. The feeling of satisfaction you get when you finish a difficult assignment, and the ''A'' grade your instructor gives you for your hard work, both help to satisfy your esteem needs.

When all other needs are satisfied, we can focus on *self-actualization* needs. Self-actualization is the process of applying your own unique set of interests and abilities to become the best person you can possibly become. If you are self-actualized, Maslow claims you will feel a sense of fulfillment and purpose. He also suggests that those who achieve self-actualization have a strong urge to help others satisfy their self-actualization needs.

The transactional leader is most concerned with the satisfaction of physiological, safety, and social needs. To meet these needs, a transactional leader exchanges rewards or privileges for desirable outcomes—much the way a Marine drill sergeant would trade a weekend pass for a clean barracks. Transformational leaders also attempt to satisfy the basic needs of followers, but these leaders go beyond mere exchange by engaging the total person in an attempt to satisfy higher level needs of esteem and self-actualization. Transformational leadership is empowering and inspirational; it elevates leaders and followers to higher levels of motivation and morality. According to Burns, "The result of transforming leadership is a relationship of mutual stimulation and elevation that converts followers into leaders and may convert leaders into moral agents."[18]

In a series of research studies involving groups of military leaders, university students, corporate managers and educators, leadership expert Bernard Bass looked at the behavior of transactional and transformational leaders.[19] Bass identified two dimensions of transactional leadership and three dimensions of transformational leadership. Transactional leaders engaged primarily in passive behavior. The behaviors most often associated with transactional leadership involved establishing the criteria for rewarding followers and maintaining the status quo. Transformational leaders demonstrated active behaviors which included providing inspiration, emotional support, and intellectual stimulation. As Bass explains:

> Unlike the transactional leader who indicates how current needs of followers can be fulfilled, the transformational leader sharply arouses or alters the strength of needs which may have lain dormant. . . .It is leadership that is transformational that can bring about the big differences and big changes in groups, organizations, and societies.[20]

Several other researchers have recently attempted to describe the characteristics of transformational leaders. Tom Peters and Robert Waterman prompted a renewed interest in organizational leadership with the publication of their 1982 best seller, In Search of Excellence.[21] Peters and Waterman studied sixty-two successful American companies. They discovered that excellent companies were most often blessed with extraordinary leadership. Peters and another colleague, Nancy Austin, focused on this phenomenon of extraordinary leadership in their 1985 book, A Passion for Excellence.[22] Warren Bennis and Burt Nanus studied ninety successful leaders from business, government, education, and sport in an attempt to identify the strategies used by transformational leaders.[23] James Kouzes and Barry Posner surveyed over thirteen hundred managers in order to discover practices common to successful transformational leaders.[24]

The characteristics of transformational leaders identified by these researchers are strikingly similar. Five primary characteristics appear, in one form or another, in all of the classification systems dealing with extraordinary leaders. Transformational leaders are creative, interactive, visionary, empowering, and passionate.

Creative. Transformational leaders are innovative and foresighted. They constantly challenge the status quo by seeking out new ideas, products, and ways of performing tasks. Transformational leaders are not afraid of failure; they realize that failure is an important part of success. Without experimentation and failure, no worthwhile innovation can be developed. (See Figure 3.6 for a discussion of how the transformational leader approaches failure.)

Interactive. Transformational leaders are masterful communicators able to articulate and to define ideas and concepts that escape others. As stated in Chapter 1, the process of leadership depends on the existence of symbols which facilitate coordinated action. Transformational

---

Figure 3.6   Research Highlight

The Wallenda Factor

Warren Bennis and Burt Nanus interviewed ninety successful public and private leaders. Although the leaders Bennis and Nanus studied were different in many respects, they were similar in the way they responded to failure. They simply didn't concern themselves with failing. Indeed, many of these extraordinary leaders created euphemisms such as "glitch," "bollix," and "setback" to refer to their mistakes. As far as these leaders were concerned, their mistakes served as a learning tool. Bennis and Nanus called this positive approach to failure the "Wallenda Factor."

The Wallenda Factor originates from the famed tightrope aerialist, Karl Wallenda. Wallenda fell to his death in 1978 traversing a 75-foot high wire in downtown San Juan, Puerto Rico. The walk was among the most dangerous Wallenda had ever attempted. For months prior to the walk he worried about falling. He was so concerned about his safety that he personally supervised the installation of the tightrope for the first time in his career. Wallenda focused all of his energies on not falling, rather than on walking.

Focusing on what can go wrong virtually guarantees failure. Successful leaders put their energies into the task and don't concern themselves with potential failures. That is not to say that leaders ignore possible failure but rather that they don't fear failure. As one leader quoted by Bennis and Nanus explained: "There isn't a senior manager in this company who hasn't been associated with a product that flopped. That includes me. It's like learning to ski. If you're not falling down, you're not learning."

Source: Bennis, W. G., & Nanus, B. (1985). *Leaders: The strategies for taking charge*. New York: Harper & Row.

leaders transmit their ideas through images, metaphors, and models that organize meanings for followers. Extraordinary leadership is a product of extraordinary communication. To communicate successfully, a transformational leader must be aware of the needs and motivations of his or her followers. Only when a leader is involved with followers can he or she find ways to do things better. Peters and Austin suggest that Managing by Wandering Around (known as MBWA) is one way to become involved with followers. MBWA means walking the floor and interacting with followers on a regular basis. The transformational leader engaging in MBWA does not play the role of a cop on patrol but, rather, acts as a coach whose primary activities are listening, teaching, and helping followers with problems.

Visionary. More than anything else, transformational leaders communicate a vision to their followers. The vision is a concise statement of the direction in which the group or organization and its people are headed. An effective vision serves to rally followers in the attainment of a compelling and achievable goal. Uninspiring or unachievable visions are ineffective and may serve to demoralize followers. Extraordinary leaders at every level communicate compelling visions. Whether the vision is to have the best customer service in the industry or the fewest defects among three assembly lines, a sense of direction and purpose is essential to inspired leadership. The behavior exhibited by a transformational leader is the basis for reinforcing a vision. When the plant manager jumps into a delivery truck to rush an order to an important customer, people notice. This kind of dramatic behavior serves to reinforce priorities and values. (Read the case in Figure 3.7 for an example of a leader who failed to communicate his vision effectively.)

Empowering. Transformational leaders empower others. Even an extraordinary leader cannot accomplish a great deal without capable followers. Transformational leaders encourage participation and involvement. The exchange of ideas between leader and follower does not pose a threat to the transformational leader. These extraordinary leaders realize that individual achievement and success is the basis for team achievement and success.

Passionate. Transformational leaders are passionately committed to their work. They love the tasks they perform and the people they work with. This passion serves to motivate others. Transformational leaders are able to encourage others because they, first and foremost, encourage themselves.

The Transformational Approach to leadership is still in its infancy. Most of the observations of transformational leaders have been made in organizational settings. Many questions remain about the viability of

Figure 3.7   Case Study

When Vision Fails: Counter College

Counter College* is a small, private liberal arts school with a regional reputation for excellence. The school grew rapidly during the long tenure of its now retired president who added new buildings and graduate programs. Although the school prospered under the former president's laissez-faire leadership style, serious problems existed. The college had a low enrollment and needed to centralize operations. In addition, the trustees and faculty wanted to see Counter become nationally known for academic quality.

After a long national search, the board of trustees thought they had found the ideal president in Tom Stanley. Stanley was young and energetic, a graduate of Harvard and Yale who had served with the Ford Foundation in South America. He came to Counter College with the desire to turn it into the "Dartmouth of the West." He summarized his optimism and that of the college when he ended his inaugural address with the charge: "Let's get on with it!"

Although Stanley came to Counter with both a vision for the college's future and a mandate to lead, his attempts to redirect the organization soon floundered. Major reforms had not even started when he offended faculty by criticizing his predecessor. In addition, he vetoed the unanimous decision of a committee that had voted to tenure a sociology professor. Stanley argued that denying tenure would save the college a million dollars in salary over the thirty-year period of the faculty member's contract. Another review committee later supported his action. However, a small group of disgruntled faculty vowed to get even.

President Stanley's problems multiplied when he moved to restructure the college's undergraduate and graduate programs. He tried to make changes himself without consulting the faculty who had previously had a major voice in setting college policy. Soon the college polarized into pro-Stanley and anti-Stanley factions. Stanley attempted to centralize more and more power in the administration while faculty resisted. During the fourth year of Stanley's presidency, the faculty voted overwhelmingly to request his resignation. After three more years of division and controversy, the board of trustees voted not to renew his contract.

Outside consultants and accreditation committees acknowledge that Counter made academic and financial progress during Stanley's tenure. Yet, even his supporters admitted that he contributed to his downfall because he did not understand the academic culture and rejected the advice of those who did. His experience demonstrates that having an inspiring vision is not enough. To be effective, leaders must know how to communicate their visions effectively and how to enlist the cooperation of others.

Discussion Questions

1 Even if Stanley was right, was rejecting the tenure committee's decision worth the cost? Why or why not?

2. What leadership style should Stanley have used in this situation?

3. Can strong leaders emerge in an academic setting where decision making is shared?

4. What are the ways in which leaders can listen effectively?

5. Evaluate the actions of the board of trustees. What leadership role should nonprofit boards play in situations like this?

6. If Stanley could have another chance at Counter, what would you suggest he do differently?

* Although this case describes actual events, the names of both the college and the president have been changed.

Source: Carlin, P., & Heltzel, E. M. (1989, April 9). Chaos on campus. *Northwest Magazine*, pp. 8-12.

transforming leadership in less permanent contexts, such as a group that meets only once. The Transformational Approach represents a bold and exciting perspective for understanding and explaining leadership. The assumption that effective communication is a key to extraordinary leadership will undoubtedly be tested by researchers in the years to come.

Summary

Four primary approaches for understanding and explaining leadership have emerged over the past ninety years. In this chapter, we examined each of these approaches.

The Traits Approach suggests that leaders are born with specific characteristics that predispose them to positions of influence. Traits research, conducted primarily in the early part of this century, has failed to find a clear connection between personal and physical traits and leadership.

The Situational Approach claims that situational conditions influence leadership effectiveness. Three of the most commonly cited situational approaches are Fiedler's Contingency Model of Leadership, Path-Goal Theory, and Hersey and Blanchard's Situational Leadership Theory.

Fiedler claims that ratings of least favored coworkers interact with the position power of a leader, the structure of the task, and the leader-follower relationship to influence the effectiveness of a leader's style in a given situation. Path-Goal Theory focuses on a leader's communication style related to the nature of the task and to followers. Hersey and Blanchard suggest that the maturity level of followers determines the selection of appropriate task and relational orientations for leaders.

The Functional Approach offers suggestions for behaving like a leader. Leaders play task-related and/or group building and maintenance roles. They avoid selfish, individual roles which do not support the task or group relationship.

The Transformational Approach focuses on the actions of inspiring leaders as they attempt to meet the higher level needs of followers. Transformational leaders have been found to be creative, interactive, visionary, empowering, and passionate.

Application Exercises

1. Make a list of traits that might be perceived as characteristic of leadership. Determine the accuracy of your list by comparing it with the actual traits of some of the effective leaders you have seen.

2. Review the LPC scale. See if your LPC score is indicative of a task or relational orientation. Do you agree with Fiedler's assertions?

3. Either alone, or in a group, make a list of leadership functions. Try to engage in these behaviors the next time you participate in a group. See if others look to you for leadership.

4. Select a particular leader discussed in one of the books focusing on transformational leadership (*In Search of Excellence, Passion for Excellence, Leaders, or The Leadership Challenge*, for example). Analyze how effectively this leader applies transformational techniques. Does he/she meet the higher level needs of followers? Is he/she an effective communicator? Does he/she have a clearly stated vision?

5. Conduct interviews with several effective leaders. Try to identify which approach to leadership provides the best explanation for their success. Share your results with your classmates.

Endnotes

[1] Stogdill, R. M. (1948). Personal factors associated with leadership: A survey of the literature. *Journal of Psychology, 25*, 35-71.

[2] Stogdill, R. M. (1948), p. 64

[3] Young, J. (1984, March). Innovation and the education process. *T.H.E. Journal*, pp. 72-74.

[4] Stogdill, R. M. (1974). *Handbook of leadership*. New York: The Free Press.

[5] Stogdill, R. M. (1974), p. 72.

[6] See:

The reanalysis of: Barnlund, D. C. (1962). Consistency of emergent leadership in groups with changing tasks and members. *Speech Monographs*, 29, 45-52 by Kenny, D. A., & Zaccaro, S. J. (1983). An estimate of variance due to traits in leadership. *Journal of Applied Psychology, 68*, 678-685.

The reanalysis of: Mann, R. D. (1959). A review of the relationships between personality and performance in small groups. *Psychological Bulletin, 56*, 241-270 by Lord, R. G., De Vader, C. L., & Alliger, G. M. (1986). A meta-analysis of the relation between personality traits and leadership perceptions: An application of validity generalization procedures. *Journal of Applied Psychology, 71*, 402-410.

[7] Foti, R. J., Fraser, S. L., & Lord, R. G. (1982). Effects of leadership labels and prototypes on perceptions of political leaders. *Journal of Applied Psychology, 67*, 326-333.

[8] See, for example:

Burns, T., & Stalker, G. M. (1961). *The management of innovation*. Chicago: Quadrangle Books.

Lawrence, P. R., & Lorsch, J. W. (1967). *Organization and environment*. Cambridge: Harvard University Press.

Woodward, J. (1965). *Industrial organization: Theory and practice*. Oxford: Oxford University Press.

[9] See, for example:

Fiedler, F. E. (1967). *A Theory of leadership effectiveness*. New York: McGraw-Hill.

Fiedler, F. E. (1972). Personality, motivational systems, and the behavior of high and low LPC persons. *Human Relations, 25*, 391-412.

Fiedler, F. E. (1978). The contingency model and the dynamics of the leadership process. In L. Berkowitz (Ed.), *Advances in experimental social psychology* (pp. 60-112). New York: Academic Press.

[10] See, for example:

Ashour, A. S. (1973). The contingency model of leadership effectiveness: An evaluation. *Organizational Behavior and Human Performance, 9*, 339-355.

Kerr, S., & Harlan, A. (1973). Predicting the effects of leadership training and experience from the contingency model: Some remaining problems. *Journal of Applied Psychology, 57*, 114-117.

Schriesheim, C. A., & Kerr, S. (1977). Theories and measures of leadership: A critical appraisal. In J. G. Hunt and L. L. Larson (Eds.), *Leadership: The cutting edge* (pp. 9-45). Carbondale: Southern Illinois University Press.

[11] See, for example:

Fiedler, F. E. (1986). The contribution of cognitive resources and leader behavior to organizational performance. *Journal of Applied Social Psychology, 16,* 532-548.
Fiedler, F. E., & Garcia, J. E. (1987). *New approaches to effective leadership: Cognitive resources and organizational performance.* New York: Wiley.

[12] See, for example:

House, R. J. (1971). A path-goal theory of leader effectiveness. *Administrative Science Quarterly, 16,* 321-338.

House, R. J., & Mitchell, T. R. (1974). Path-goal theory of leadership. *Journal of Contemporary Business, 3,* 81-97.

[13] Hersey, P., & Blanchard, K. H. (1988). *Management of organizational behavior: Utilizing human resources* (5th ed.). Englewood Cliffs, NJ: Prentice-Hall.

[14] Barnard, C. I. (1938). *The functions of the executive.* Cambridge, MA: Harvard University Press.

[15] Benne, K. D., & Sheats, P. (1948). Functional roles of group members. *Journal of Social Issues, 4,* 41-49.

[16] Burns, J. M. (1978). *Leadership.* New York: Harper & Row.

[17] Maslow, A. H. (1970). *Motivation and personality.* New York: Harper & Row.

[18] Burns, J. M. (1978), p. 4.

[19] Bass, B. M. (1985). *Leadership and performance beyond expectations.* New York: The Free Press.

[20] Bass, B. M. (1985), p. 17.

[21] Peters, T. J., & Waterman, R. H.,Jr. (1982). *In search of excellence.* New York: Harper & Row.

[22] Peters, T .J., & Austin, N. K. (1985). *A passion for excellence: The leadership difference.* New York: Warner Books.

[23] Bennis, W. G., & Nanus, B. (1985). *Leaders: The strategies for taking charge.* New York: Harper & Row.

[24] Kouzes, J. M., & Posner, B. Z. (1987). *The leadership challenge: How to get extraordinary things done in organizations.* San Francisco: Jossey-Bass.

4

Leadership and Power

Power Orientations

Americans have contradictory feelings about power. On the one hand, we are fascinated by the power and wealth we see on television shows. We admire those with "clout" who move quickly and decisively to get things done. On the other hand, we loathe the corruption and greed that often comes with power. Financier Gordon Gekko in the movie *Wall Street* is a vivid example of what can happen when power goes unchecked. Driven by greed, Gekko (a fictional character based on some real-life Wall Street investors) violates securities laws, corrupts his associates and throws hundreds of people out of work. Our mixed feelings toward power are best reflected in our view of the presidency. The President of the United States is considered the most powerful leader in the world. Yet, a candidate for the presidency must present a humble image as "one of the people." News footage of candidates trudging through small villages in New Hampshire and commercials featuring presidential hopefuls standing in cornfields are staples of presidential campaigns.

To help clarify your view of power, complete the Power Orientation Scale in Figure 4.1. Alvin Goldberg, Mary Cavanaugh and Carl Larson developed this scale after surveying the attitudes of people with firsthand experience with power: law enforcement personnel, government managers and corporate executives.[1] Once you've completed the Power Orientation Scale, check your ratings with the explanations below.

1. ***Power Is Good***. You see power as something that is exciting and desirable to have. You may actively seek to obtain and to hold power.

2. ***Power as Resource Dependency***. You recognize the importance of having and controlling resources, particularly information.

3. ***Power as Instinctive Drive***. You perceive power as a natural instinct; seeking power is a normal, acceptable activity for everyone.

4. ***Power as Political***. If you know how important it is to "play politics" at work or in the community, you probably scored high on this orientation.

5. ***Power as Charisma***. This power orientation reflects 1) the thought that power is something that can be held in reserve and used when needed, and 2) the idea that powerful people can take strong actions and generate strong emotional responses from others. If you see power as charisma, you probably also believe that people with high

Figure 4.1

Power Orientation Scale
Instructions

The following are all statements about power. You may find that you agree strongly with some of these and disagree strongly with others. You may also find there are some statements you are uncertain about. Whether you agree or disagree with any of the statements, you can be sure that many other people feel the same as you do.

Mark each statement in the left margin according to how much you agree or disagree with it. Please mark every one.

Write + 1, + 2, + 3 or − 1, -2, -3, depending on how you feel in each case.

+ 1: I agree a little	-1: I disagree a little
+ 2: I agree on the whole	-2: I disagree on the whole
+ 3: I agree very much	-3: I disagree very much

____ 1. An advantage of having power is being able to get people to follow your orders.

____ 2. People in powerful positions are often rewarded for doing very little.

____ 3. Having power gives you independence.

____ 4. An advantage of being in a position of power is that people seem to treat you as somebody special.

____ 5. In the long run, it is better to avoid having power.

____ 6. Knowing things others don't know gives you power over them.

____ 7. You know you have power when other people must come to you for things they need.

____ 8. An advantage to being considered powerful is that other people want to be like you.

____ 9. A person can be powerful within one group and not within another.

____ 10. There is no such thing as power without purpose.

____ 11. The drive for power exists in all of us.

____ 12. An advantage of being in a position of power is being able to control the rewards and punishments of others.

____ 13. Powerful people are cautious about whom they confide in.

____ 14. Success and power go hand in hand.

____ 15. If you have power, you have a sense of security.

____ 16. The responsibility and challenge of power is exciting.

____ 17. People seek power for its own sake.

____ 18. Power is something to be avoided.

____ 19. Having information that others want and need gives a person a great deal of power.

____ 20. People know they are powerful when others are dependent on them.

____ 21. People usually deserve the power they get.

____ 22. How much power a person has varies considerably from one situation to another.

___ 23. People naturally try to avoid feeling powerless.

___ 24. Powerful people are easy to recognize, even in situations where they do nothing to demonstrate their power.

___ 25. Sometimes powerful people cannot avoid hurting others.

___ 26. The meek shall inherit the earth.

___ 27. Power means the ability to beat the competition.

___ 28. It takes political skill to become powerful.

___ 29. Sometimes it's necessary for a powerful person to tell people what they should think.

___ 30. An advantage to having power is the freedom it gives you.

___ 31. You can usually tell a powerful person as soon as he or she enters a room.

___ 32. I would like to be a powerful person.

___ 33. Power comes from being an expert in something.

___ 34. People instinctively seek power.

___ 35. Whether power is good or bad depends on the type of person who has it.

___ 36. Power should be used to do the greatest good for the greatest number of people.

___ 37. In general, powerful people do more harm than good.

___ 38. Having power means that people may not like you.

___ 39. Powerful people are likely to feel anxious.

___ 40. Remaining in power requires political skill.

Power Orientation Scale
Scoring Sheet

To determine your individual orientation to power, tabulate your score on each of the six dimensions of power identified below. To calculate your score, add a constant of +4 to each item response, reversing responses where indicated. For example, your score on **Power as Good** would be computed by taking the inverse of your response to item 5 of the Power Orientation Scale—"In the long run, it is better to avoid having power"—and adding +4. If you marked that statement +3, you would change it to –3 and add +4 for a final total of +1. You would then use the same procedure for items 16, 18, 32, and 37. Remember, do not reverse the number you marked on the Power Orientation Scale unless you are asked to do so.

To interpret your total scores look at the range of scores listed below each orientation. This identifies the minimum and maximum scores possible. The higher your score, the more you agree with that orientation to power. A high score on Power as Good, for example, indicates that you *personally* view power as exciting and desirable.

Power as Good	Power as Resource Dependency
Item: 5 _____ (R)everse	Item: 6 _____
16 _____	7 _____
18 _____ (R)everse	19 _____
32 _____	20 _____
37 _____ (R)everse	
Your Total: _____	Your Total: _____
Range: 5-35	Range: 4-28
Power as Instinctive Drive	**Power as Political**
Item: 11 _____	Item: 28 _____
23 _____	40 _____
34 _____	
Your Total: _____	Your Total: _____
Range: 3-21	Range: 2-14
Power as Charisma	**Power as Control and Autonomy**
Item: 24 _____	Item: 1 _____
31 _____	3 _____
	12 _____
	30 _____
Your Total: _____	Your Total: _____
Range: 2-14	Range 4-28

power are treated differently than people with low power. (For more information on charisma, see Chapter 8.)

6. ***Power as Control and Autonomy***. If you have this attitude toward power, then you see power both as the ability to exert control over other people as well as the ability to resist control from others (to remain autonomous).

Goldberg, Cavanaugh and Larson conducted follow-up studies to explore the relationship between power orientation and decision making and managerial performance. They found that district court judges who viewed power as resource dependency were more likely to make sentencing decisions based on the information contained in established guidelines. The highest producing real estate branch managers believed their power depended on controlling resources rather than people. Although the research linking power orientations and behavior is limited, the findings do suggest that our view of power will shape our leadership behavior.

Power and Leadership

Interdependent but Not Interchangeable

Sorting out the relationship between power and leadership can be confusing. Is using power the same as exerting leadership? Does having power automatically make you a leader? Power and leadership are obviously interdependent; however, they are not interchangeable. While power can exist without leadership, leadership cannot exist without power.

Imagine sitting in a lecture. A terrorist armed with a semiautomatic weapon bursts into the room, ordering the class to lie on the floor. The group obeys. The terrorist certainly exerted power—a very negative manifestation of power—since the class gave in to his demands. We would not label the terrorist a "leader," however. We define power as *the ability to influence others.* Leadership is impossible without power since a leader must modify attitudes and behaviors. Yet, influencing others does not automatically qualify as leadership; power must be exercised in pursuit of group goals to merit leadership classification. In the case of the terrorist, his power was exercised on behalf of his own interests and not those of the class. In other instances, powerful individuals do not use their power and thus fail to take a leadership role. The small group member who knows the most about a topic would be a natural candidate for group leadership. This person may refuse, however, to participate in the group's discussion.

Leadership experts Warren Bennis and Burt Nanus summarize the relationship between power and leadership this way: "Power is . . . the *capacity to translate intention into reality and sustain it.* Leadership is the wise use of this power . . . . Vision is the commodity of leaders, and power is their currency."[2]

Sources of Power

If power is the "currency of leadership," then understanding the sources and use of power is essential to effective leadership. The ability to influence others can be based on a wide variety of factors. John French and Bertram Raven have isolated five primary sources of power:[3]

1. *Coercive Power* is based on the ability to administer punishment or to give negative reinforcements. Examples of coercion range from reducing status, salary, and benefits to requiring someone to do

something they don't like. In the most extreme form, coercive power translates into brute physical force. Whistleblowers (employees who have pointed out unethical practices like cost overruns and safety hazards) often experience coercion. They may be fired, assigned to distasteful jobs or socially ostracized.[4]

Coercion is most effective when those subject to this form of power are aware of expectations and are warned in advance about the penalties for failure to comply. Leaders using coercive power must consistently carry out threatened punishments. A parent who punishes without first establishing expectations and the consequences for failure will be less effective than a parent who clearly sets the ground rules. The effective parent says: "I expect you home by 10:00. If you're not home by then, you will be grounded for the rest of the weekend." The user of coercive power must then follow through with the announced consequence. Threatening over and over again to ground a teenager for being late without ever carrying out the punishment significantly diminishes coercive power. The same is true in organizational settings. A supervisor who threatens to take action against a subordinate must carry out the threat if the coercive attempt is to be successful.

Failure to execute threats can produce a cycle of negative behavior. Warnings to punish represent attention. Although humans certainly prefer positive reinforcement, they will select negative reinforcement over no reinforcement at all (apathy). Humans would rather be punished than ignored. If a child is unable to attract positive attention, he or she may begin to misbehave in an attempt to attract negative attention. Employees in organizations are no different. "Problem" employees who receive warning after warning may simply need attention. Following the guidelines regarding the use of coercive power and offering positive reinforcement minimizes the negative behavior.

2. **Reward Power** rests on the ability to deliver something of value to others. Although the reward is often tangible (money, health benefits or grades, for example), it might be something intangible like warmth and supportiveness. Effective organizations use both tangible and intangible rewards to recognize superior performance.

Rewards must be desirable and attractive to serve as sufficient motivators. One of our students worked in a large organization which decided to change computing systems. The changeover took six months and required employees to work many hours of overtime. When the new system was finally in place, the corporation hosted a Friday afternoon party and rewarded those who had worked such long hours with t-shirts that said, ''I Survived the Changeover.'' The student and her coworkers were insulted. More suitable rewards — like giving workers the day off after so many weeks of overtime — might have been more appreciated and more attractive to employees.

3. ***Legitimate Power*** resides in the position rather than in the person. Persons with legitimate power have the right to prescribe our behavior within specified parameters: judges, police officers, teachers, and parents, for example. Although we may disagree with our supervisor at work, we go along with a decision because that person is ''the boss.'' The amount of legitimate power someone has depends on the importance of the position she or he occupies and our willingness to grant authority to the person in that position. We grant legitimate power based on particular circumstances. We will pull our cars to the side of the road when a police officer flashes his or her lights. This is a legitimate request. We would not, however, allow the officer to take apart our engine on the roadway so we could no longer speed. This is not a legitimate request.

4. ***Expert Power*** is based on the person not the position, in contrast to legitimate power. Experts are influential because they supply needed information and skills. In our culture, in particular, it is important to be perceived as expert. Those with credentials are more powerful than those without appropriate certification. When visiting a new physician, do you immediately check his/her diploma? Our culture mandates that certain credentials must be obtained before an individual can be considered a professional. Demonstrating practical knowledge and skills can also build expert power. For this reason, members of an organization often have little legitimate power but a great deal of expert power. Receptionists can be extremely influential because of what they learn through talking to employees, managers, customers and others. School janitors are often powerful because they know how to fix bulletin boards, open locked doors and so on.

5. ***Referent Power*** is role model power — the ability to influence others that arises when one person admires another. Professional athletes are among those who have this power. For example, those who push for mandatory drug testing in baseball, basketball and other sports argue that sports figures are role models for children. Role models are not confined to celebrities. We all have personal contact with people we admire. Referent power depends on feelings of affection, esteem and respect for another individual. This loyalty generally

develops over an extended period of time. Since referent power takes so long to nurture it should be used carefully. A supervisor who asks a subordinate to work overtime as "a personal favor" will succeed if the employee likes and respects the supervisor. Referent power will probably be effective the first weekend and possibly the second, but after several weeks the employee will tire of doing "favors" for his/her supervisor. Once depleted, referent power must be replenished by engaging in behavior that will produce new feelings of affection, esteem and support.

Deciding Which Types of Power to Use:
Cost/Benefit Ratios

A useful way of determining the relative advantages and disadvantages of each source of power is to view leadership as a transaction between leaders and followers. The relationship between leaders and followers is reciprocal. While leaders exert more influence than other group members, they are also influenced by followers. According to Social Exchange Theory, leaders must maintain profitable relationships with followers.[5] They do this by providing rewards like approval, information, or salary in return for such commodities as labor, compliance and commitment. When the relationship becomes unprofitable to either party (the costs outweigh the benefits), then the relationship is redefined or ended. Seeing leadership from a transactional viewpoint means that there are potential costs and benefits associated with using each power type. For example, coercion can be used by followers as well as by leaders. Students may punish instructors who rely heavily on threats and other coercive tactics by giving them low course evaluations. Politicians who legislate unpopular tax measures are often removed from office.

A list of the benefits and costs of each type of power is given below. The list (which incorporates the thoughts of the authors and a number of researchers) is not exhaustive.[6] In fact, we hope that you will add your own costs, benefits and conclusions to our list (see Application Exercise 2).

Coercive Power

Benefits	Costs
* Effective for gaining obedience	* Drains physical and emotional energy from user
* Appropriate for disciplinary actions	* Lowers task satisfaction of followers

* Achieves quick results	* Destroys trust and commitment
	* Becomes less effective over time (must be repeated with greater and greater force)
	* Followers may respond in kind

Reward Power

Benefits	Costs
* Culturally sanctioned	* Lower task satisfaction than with expert and referent power
* An effective attention-getter for group priorities	* Not consistently linked with high task performance
* Can enhance cooperation and a sense of self-worth	* Escalating financial and material costs to provide higher and higher tangible rewards to offer
* Can serve as an effective motivator	* Some groups, like nonprofit agencies, have limited tangible rewards to give
	* Ineffective if rewards are not desirable or attractive or if the wrong individuals are rewarded

Legitimate Power

Benefits	Costs
* Culturally sanctioned	* Lowers follower task performance
* Incorporates the weight of the whole organization	* Lowers follower task satisfaction
* Effective in gaining obedience	* May become less effective over time

Expert Power

Benefits	Costs
* High follower task satisfaction	* Takes a long time to develop
* High follower task performance	* Must possess the necessary knowledge and skills
* Drains little, if any, emotional energy from the user	* Not as effective in gaining obedience as coercion, reward or legitimate power, particularly in the case of misbehavior
	* May not be effective if followers do not share the leader's goals

Referent Power

Benefits	Costs
* High follower task satisfaction	* Takes a long time to develop
* High follower task performance	* Can diminish if overused
	* Must possess the necessary knowledge and interpersonal skills
	* Not as effective in gaining obedience as coercion, reward or legitimate power, particularly in the case of misbehavior

The cost/benefit ratios listed above suggest that leaders should rely heavily on expert and referent power. These forms of power have a positive effect on the performance and satisfaction of those being influenced and are less costly to use. They are most likely to maintain a profitable relationship between leader and follower. Yet, effective leaders need access to all five types of power. Taking charge may require discipline through coercion, the judicious use of rewards and the power of position. In fact, a leader's impact is enhanced if, for example, she or he combines legitimate power with expert and referent power. A highly respected group member who is appointed the chair of a committee is in a very powerful position.

To summarize, group members seem to prefer leaders who rely on power associated with the unique characteristics of the person (expert and referent) rather than leaders who rely on power related to their position (coercion, reward, legitimate). Since effectiveness is more directly tied to personal performance than official position, we can manage our communication behaviors to increase our power which, in turn, can increase our ability to lead. Let's take a closer look at one cluster of communication behaviors—powerful forms of talk—that seem particularly well suited to building not only our expert power but also our referent power.

Powerful and Powerless Talk

Sociolinguists, anthropologists, communication specialists and others have long been fascinated with the two-way relationship between language and power. Viewed from the perspective of society, language is a mirror reflecting power differences. Every culture has a "standard language" that is spoken by the highest socioeconomic group in that society. Nonstandard languages are dialects spoken by less advantaged people.[7] Just as language provides a mirror of power, the use of language creates power differentials.[8] In fact, speakers are stereotyped as powerless or powerful based on their word choices.[9]

The fact that speakers are perceived as powerless or powerful based on the way that they talk means that language can be an important tool to use in building power bases. Conversely, inappropriate language can reduce perceived power and leadership potential. Over the past two decades, a number of language features have been identified as "powerful" or "powerless" by researchers (see Figure 4.2). Powerful talk makes speakers seem dominant and confident. Powerless talk is tentative and submissive. Most researchers have concentrated on identifying powerless speech forms. Powerful speech has often been treated as speech without powerless speech features. Here is a list of powerless types of talk:

1. *Hesitations* ("uh," "ah," "well," "um," "you know"). Hesitations are the most frequently used form of powerless talk and the least powerful speech feature. The characteristic that is most likely to clutter our talk is also the most likely to reduce our power.

2. *Hedges* ("kinda," "I think," "I guess"). Although hedging may occasionally be appropriate (when we truly are not sure of our facts, for example), it greatly reduces the impact of what we say. Compare "I think you should have that report in by Friday" to "Have that report in by Friday."

3. *Tag questions* ("It sure is a nice day, isn't it?"). The question tag on the end of a sentence ("isn't it?"; "wouldn't it?") is an indicator of uncertainty because this expression makes a declarative statement much less forceful.

4. *Disclaimers* ("Don't get me wrong, but;" "I know this sounds crazy, but"). Speakers use disclaimers when they are not sure if listeners will accept what they have to say. For instance: "Don't get me wrong, I'm not trying to be critical, but your speech was way too long." Like hedges, disclaimers can be a useful conversational tool. They should be used with caution, however, since they can signal that we lack confidence in our statements.

5. *Accounts* (excuses or justifications). Speakers employ accounts after they say or do the wrong thing. Those who use excuses deny responsibility for what happened ("It was an accident."). Those who use justifications accept full responsibility but claim that they had a good reason for what they did ("I wasn't ready for the test because

I stayed up all night helping my roommate with a problem."). A speaker who frequently excuses or justifies his/her behavior will be seen as inept or uncertain.

6. **Side Particles** ("like," "eh?"). The frequent use of irritating expressions such as "simply" or "that is" also detract from a powerful image.

Researchers report that the use of powerless speech significantly lowers source believability. (We'll have more to say about believability — what communication experts call credibility — in the next chapter.) Listeners consistently rate the knowledge and ability (competence) of powerless speakers lower than that of powerful speakers when both deliver the same message. In addition, they find such sources less trustworthy and dynamic. Powerless speech damages more than speaker credibility, however. Powerless speakers are also perceived as less attractive, and they are less persuasive. Audiences retain less information from a speech or lecture if the message is delivered in a tentative style.[10]

Language choices clearly have a strong influence on the two bases of power most easily controlled by the communicator: expert and referent power. Powerless speakers *appear* to be uninformed and unskilled even if they do, in fact, possess the necessary knowledge and abilities. Few listeners are drawn to tentative, uncertain sources. On the other hand, powerful speakers are seen as competent and attractive, and their messages have more persuasive and informational impact. Some evidence suggests that powerful talk can overcome the disadvantages that come from having low legitimate power.[11] It should be noted, however, that powerful speech is most effective when speakers are trying to be authoritative. There may be times, such as in a conversation between friends, when the use of powerless language is less damaging.[12]

Fortunately, we can eliminate powerless language features if we choose to do so. Lawyers report that they can teach clients to avoid powerless language. Public speaking instructors help their students eliminate powerless talk by noting powerless speech features on speech evaluation forms. To become a more powerful speaker, start by monitoring your powerless speech habits. Record a conversation and count the number of powerless speech features you use or have a friend give you feedback about your powerless speech patterns. Make a conscious effort to eliminate powerless language. Keep track of your progress using the recording and feedback methods described above. Another way to become a more powerful speaker is by noting the types

Figure 4.2   Research highlight

Powerful and Powerless Talk in the Courtroom

Forms of powerful and powerless talk were first identified by a group of scholars studying courtroom communication as part of Duke University's Law and Language program. Project leader William O'Barr and his associates were particularly interested in how women spoke on the witness stand. For years, law guides had instructed attorneys to treat female witnesses more cautiously than male witnesses. Previous research by Robin Lakoff had hypothesized that women use more language features like hedges, hesitations and tag questions which reflect their powerless position in society. The Duke researchers set out to determine if female witnesses really do use a different communication style than male witnesses.

After coding 150 hours of testimony from North Carolina courtrooms, O'Barr and his coworkers concluded that speech styles were status related, not sex related. Low status witnesses of both sexes used powerless forms of speech traditionally associated with females, while high status witnesses of both sexes avoided these features. They labeled speech high in hedges, hesitations and tag questions as the "powerless style" of speaking since such talk was associated with powerless people. Speech that avoided these features was called the "powerful style" since it was used by individuals with high standing in the community (physicians and other professionals) or high standing in the court (parole officers, police officers).

Once they had identified powerful and powerless speech styles, the Duke researchers tried to determine the impact of using one style or the other. In a series of studies they found that powerful witnesses were more credible and effective than powerless witnesses. In fact, juries in simulated trials were still swayed by differences in witness language patterns even when they were told to disregard how witnesses spoke. Disturbed by the implications of their findings, Conley, O'Barr and Lind wrote:

> . . . the law cannot be faithful to that [its] purpose if it ignores elements that, in the eyes of the jury, are as significant as factual reliability. Should a witness be held incompetent, for example, if he or she cannot present testimony in a style that will receive an unprejudiced hearing? (p. 1399)

Communication researchers later discovered that some of the elements of the original powerless style were not really powerless at all. Instead, they argued that each type of powerless speech should be examined individually to determine its impact. James Bradac and Anthony Mulac developed a hierarchy of powerful/powerless talk which demonstrated that 1) hesitations and hedges are the least powerful features and 2) speakers are typed as powerful or powerless based on their language choices. Thus, language not only *reflects* differences in power as the law and language researchers discovered, language can *create* perceptions of power or powerlessness.

Research into powerful/powerless talk has since expanded from the courtroom to the classroom, the public speech, the job interview, crisis counseling and other settings.

For further reading:

Bradac, J., & Mulac, A. (1984). A molecular view of powerful and powerless speech styles: Attributional consequences of specific language features and communicator intentions. *Communication Monographs, 51*, 307-319.

Conley, J., O'Barr, W., & Lind, E. A. (1978). The power of language: Presentational styles in the courtroom. *Duke Law Journal*, 1375-1399.

Erickson, B., Lind, E., Johnson, A., & O'Barr, W. (1978). Speech style and impression formation in a court setting: The effects of "powerful" and "powerless" speech. *Journal of Experimental Social Psychology, 14*, 266-279.

Johnson, C. (1987). An introduction to powerful and powerless talk in the classroom. *Communication Education, 36*, 167-172.

Lakoff, R. (1975). *Language and woman's place*. New York: Harper & Row.

Lind, E. A., & O'Barr, W. (1979). The social significance of speech in the courtroom. In H. Giles & R. St. Clair (Eds.), *Language and social psychology* (pp. 66-87). College Park, MD: University of Maryland Press.

O'Barr, W. (1982). *Linguistic Evidence: Language, power, and strategy in the courtroom*. New York: Academic Press.

of powerless speech features used by public speakers and others (including instructors). Evaluating what others do can help to improve your own performance.[13]

Four Reasons to Give Power Away

Up to this point, we have emphasized how power is the essential currency of leadership. There is no leadership without power, and some forms of power are more effective for leaders than others. However, there are times when a leader will want to distribute rather than to maintain power. Reducing power differentials often enhances group performance and may be the key to organizational survival. Paradoxically, leaders frequently gain more power by empowering others. There are four major reasons why leaders choose to share power.

Reason 1: Increased Task Satisfaction and Task Performance. In an organizational setting, distributing power increases the job satisfaction and performance of employees. Bernard Bass concludes that distributing power increases employee "job interest, concern with work innovation, and pride in work."[14] People like their jobs more and work harder when they feel that they have a significant voice in shaping decisions. Rosabeth Moss Kanter reports that withholding power has the opposite result.

"Powerlessness corrupts," reports Kanter, "and absolute powerlessness corrupts absolutely."[15] Those who feel powerless often respond by becoming cautious, defensive and critical.[16] To see how sharing power can benefit both employees and organizations, read the story of Max De Pree and the Herman Miller company in the case study in Figure 4.3.

Figure 4.3   Case Study

Empowerment in Action:
Max De Pree and the Herman Miller Company

Herman Miller, Inc. is one company that benefits from empowering employees. The Zeeland, Michigan commercial furniture manufacturer is a phenomenal success by any yardstick. Herman Miller was selected as one of America's "ten most admired companies" in 1988. The firm ranked seventh for total return to investors among the *Fortune* 500. Company stock rose at a compound annual rate of 41% between 1975 and 1986. After a brief dip in earnings, sales are up again.

Company chairman Max De Pree describes the leadership philosophy of Herman Miller in a book called *Leadership Is An Art*. At the heart of the Herman Miller corporation is the idea that power should be shared.

- The company allows every employee with over one year on the job to buy Miller stock. In the case of a hostile takeover, plant workers would receive large checks (called "silver parachutes") just like their managers. In addition, the salary of the chief executive officer is limited to twenty times the wage of the average line worker in the factory.

- Top executives report monthly to employees on company profits and productivity. These reports are part of the firm's program of "lavish communications" which ensures that everyone has access to important information. "Information is power," says De Pree, "but it is pointless power if hoarded. Power must be shared for an organization or a relationship to work."[1]

- Employees have a great deal of freedom to carry out their responsibilities. This freedom is reflected in the company's innovative products which are created by top designers who know that their designs will be manufactured without modifications.

- Workers are organized into work teams that evaluate their team leaders every six months.

Herman Miller's view of leadership and power is reflected in the terms that its chairman uses to describe leaders. To De Pree, the leader is a "servant" and a "debtor." The leader has a responsibility to help followers reach their full potential. He or she "owes" followers a clear statement of values and purpose, structure, and the creation of an atmosphere which encourages personal development and dignity. De Pree summarizes a leader's activities this way:

> The first responsibility of a leader is to define reality. The last is to say thank you. In between the two, the leader must become a servant and a debtor. That sums up the progress of an artful leader.[2]

Discussion Questions

1. What type of person would be most effective in the Herman Miller environment? Least effective?
2. Should leaders always be "servants"?
3. Are there any dangers in employee ownership plans like Herman Miller's?
4. What are the advantages and disadvantages of limiting the pay of top executives as Herman Miller does?
5. Should some forms of power be kept from employees?

[1] De Pree, M. (1989). *Leadership is an art*. New York: Doubleday, p. 92.
[2] De Pree, p. 9.

For more information on the Herman Miller company, see:

Labich, K. (1989, February 27). Hot company, warm culture. *Fortune*, pp. 74-78.
Wechsler, D. (1988, March 21). A comeback in cubicles. *Forbes*, pp. 54-56.

Reason 2: Greater Cooperation Among Group Members. Sharing power fosters cooperation. Cooperation, in turn, increases group accomplishment. The effectiveness of any group depends in large part on the cooperation of group members. For example, a small group cannot get an "A" on a class project if members withhold information from each other or if a number of members refuse to participate at all. The same is true for a sales team or computer project group. The genius of organizing lies in combining individual efforts in order to achieve goals that would be beyond the capability of any one person. The group advantage is lost or diluted when participation is only half-hearted. James Kouzes and Barry Posner report that enabling others is a key to leadership; accomplishment results from the efforts of many people, not just the leader. According to Kouzes and Posner: "After reviewing over 500 personal best cases, we have developed a simple one-word test to detect whether someone is on the road to becoming a leader. That word is *we*."[17]

Reason 3: Group Survival. Distributing power rather than concentrating it in the hands of one or a few people may mean that a group survives rather than fails. One of the best ways to stay competitive in a fast-paced environment is to develop a "flat" organizational structure.[18] Flat structures are decentralized and grant a great deal of decision-making authority to lower level leaders. For instance, branch managers in flat corporations control decisions affecting their operations. They do not have to check constantly with headquarters. In these companies, project groups blur traditional lines of authority in order to develop new ideas. Flat organizations offer two advantages: 1) they can move quickly to meet changing market conditions, and 2) they foster innovation—the development of new products on which a business ultimately depends.

Reason 4: Personal Growth and Learning. Effective leadership helps group members become more mature and productive than they were before. Empowerment is one way to stimulate growth. Sharing power with followers can help them tackle new challenges, learn new skills and find greater fulfillment. This personal learning and growth is a major source of satisfaction.[19] In the end, both the group member and the group are transformed when power is shared. Not only does the individual grow, but the collective gains a more committed and skilled member.

Summary

In this chapter, we examined the relationship between power and leadership. Power, the ability to influence others, is the "currency of leadership." Leadership is not possible without power, although not everyone who exercises power is a leader. There are five types of power: 1) coercive, 2) reward, 3) legitimate, 4) expert, and 5) referent. Personal forms of power (expert and referent) are less costly to use and generate higher task satisfaction and performance. Because expert and referent power are more tied to personal performance than position, developing our communication skills and abilities can increase these power bases and improve our leadership potential. Adopting powerful speech is one way to build expert and referent power. Powerful speakers avoid the use of such powerless speech features as hesitations, hedges, tag questions, disclaimers, accounts and side particles. As a result, they are seen as authoritative, persuasive and informative. There are times when a leader may want to give power away. Four reasons for empowering others are: 1) to increase follower task satisfaction and performance, 2) to foster greater cooperation in the group, 3) to ensure the survival of the group, and 4) to encourage the personal growth and learning of group members.

Application Exercises

1. Compare your power orientation with others in class or give the Power Orientation Scale to someone at work and compare your scores. Discuss how your orientation influences the following:
   - your conflict management style
   - your involvement in office or school "politics"
   - the types of power you seek
   - your view of the "goodness" or "badness" of power
   - how you feel about keeping power or giving it away

2. Create your own cost/benefit ratios for each type of power. Do you agree that leaders should strive for expert and referent power?

3. Develop a strategy for overcoming your powerless talk using the techniques discussed in the chapter. Report on your progress to another person in the class.

4. Power Use Case Study

   Laurie H. has just been appointed regional sales manager for the Heartfelt Candy Company. Laurie's top priority is to increase sales which have fallen dramatically over the past year. The decline does not seem to be due to changes in market conditions; instead, the number of sales calls is down. The sales force is paid both a salary and commissions. Laurie has been told that she has six months to increase sales to former levels or be returned to her previous position as a sales representative. She has been given the authority to make the changes she thinks are necessary to boost sales.

   1. Identify the potential causes for the sales decline.
   2. Identify the types of power Laurie might use in order to improve sales. In addition, list the potential costs and benefits of using each type of power in this situation.
   3. Identify the types of power that the sales force might use against Laurie in order to prevent change.
   4. Develop a strategy for Laurie based on your answers to the previous questions.

Endnotes

[1] Goldberg, A., Cavanaugh, M., & Larson, C. (1984). The meaning of power. *Journal of Applied Communication Research, 11*, 89-108.

[2] Bennis, W., & Nanus, B. (1985). *Leaders: The strategies for taking charge.* New York: Harper & Row, pp. 17-18.

[3] French, J. R. P., & Raven, B. (1959). The bases of social power. In D. Cartwright, *Studies in social power* (pp. 150-167). Ann Arbor: University of Michigan, Institute for Social Research. Although there are a number of power typologies, French and Raven's is the most widely used, generating research in such fields as management, communication and education.

[4] Glazer, M. P., & Glazer, P. M. (1989). *The whistleblowers*. New York: Basic Books.

[5] The most popular social exchange theory is that of Thibault and Kelley (*Interpersonal relations: A theory of interdependence*. New York: John Wiley, 1978.) For one application of social exchange theory to groups, see: Hollander, E. (1978). *Leadership Dynamics: A practical guide to effective relationships*. New York: The Free Press.

[6] Information on the costs and benefits of power types can be found in the following:
Bass, B. (Ed.) (1981). *Stogdill's handbook of leadership*. New York: The Free Press, Chs. 12 & 13.
Hersey, P., & Blanchard, K. H. (1988). *Management of organizational behavior: Utilizing human resources* (5th ed.). Englewood Cliffs, NJ: Prentice-Hall.
Baldwin, D. A. (1971). The costs of power. *Journal of Conflict Resolution, 15*, 145-155.
Yukl, G. (1981). *Leadership in organizations*. Englewood Cliffs, NJ: Prentice-Hall, Ch. 3.

[7] Giles, H., & Powesland, P. F. (1975). *Speech style and social evaluation*. London: Academic Press.

[8] O'Barr, W. (1984). Asking the right questions about language and power. In C. Kramarae, M. Schulz & W. O'Barr (Eds.), *Language and power* (pp. 260-280). Beverly Hills, CA: Sage.

[9] Bradac, J., & Mulac, A. (1984). A molecular view of powerful and powerless speech styles: Attributional consequences of specific language features and communicator intentions. *Communication Monographs, 51*, 307-319.

[10] Johnson, C., Vinson, L., Hackman, M., & Hardin, T. (1989). The effects of an instructor's use of hesitation forms on student ratings of quality, recommendations to hire, and lecture listening. *Journal of the International Listening Association, 3*, 32-43.

[11] Johnson, C., & Vinson, L. (1987). "Damned if you do, damned if you don't?": Status, powerful speech and evaluations of female witnesses. *Women's Studies in Communication, 10*, 37-44.

[12] Bradac & Mulac.

[13] Sorenson, R., & Pickett, T. (1986). A test of two teaching strategies designed to improve interview effectiveness: Rating behavior and videotaped feedback. *Communication Education, 35*, 13-22.

[14] Bass, *Stogdill's handbook of leadership*, p. 193.

[15] Kouzes, J. M., & Posner, B. Z. (1987). *The leadership challenge: How to get extraordinary things done in organizations*. San Francisco: Jossey-Bass, p. 162.

[16] Kanter, R. M. (1977). *Men and women of the corporation*. New York: Basic Books, Ch. 7.

[17] Kouzes & Posner, p. 10.

[18] Peters, T. J., & Waterman, R. H., Jr. (1982). *In search of excellence*. New York: Harper & Row, Ch. 11.; Peters, T. (1987). *Thriving on Chaos*. New York: Borzoi/Alfred A. Knopf.; Kanter, R. M. (1983). *The change masters: Innovation for productivity in the American corporation*. New York: Simon and Schuster.

[19] Bennis, W. (1976). *The unconscious conspiracy: Why leaders can't lead*. New York: AMACOM, p. 167.

5

Leadership and Influence

91

Exercising influence is the essence of leadership. Leading means influencing since leaders must shape the attitudes and behavior of others to help groups reach their goals. In the last chapter we examined the sources and uses of power. In this chapter we continue our discussion of influence by taking a closer look at how leaders modify the behavior of others through symbolic communication. Our focus will be on three sets of influence tools that are particularly significant to leaders: 1) credibility building behaviors, 2) compliance-gaining strategies, and 3) negotiation skills.

Credibility: The Key to Successful Influence

Credibility is the foundation for successful influence because the success or failure of a particular influence strategy ultimately depends on the credibility of the influencer. For example, promises or threats work only if recipients believe that influencers can and will deliver. The results of a survey of twenty-six hundred managers demonstrate just how important credibility is to leaders. When asked what they admired most in their leaders, the managers identified the following factors: 1) honesty, 2) competence, and 3) forward looking/inspiring. Taken together, these elements comprise what researchers label as believability or credibility.[1]

Credibility has always been central to the study of communication and leadership. The ancient Greeks studied the public speaking techniques of leaders and used the term "ethos" for what we now call credibility. To Plato, Aristotle and others, ethos consisted of high moral standards, intelligence and other speaker character traits.[2] An orator swayed an audience through logic (logos), emotion (pathos) and, most importantly, personal characteristics (ethos). Interest in credibility remains high today. After surveying thirty years of credibility research, James McCroskey and Thomas Young concluded that "few topics have gained as much attention from researchers in communication or speech as 'ethos,' or, more commonly 'source credibility.'"[3]

The strong tie between credibility and influence is the reason that scholars have been interested in ethos through the ages. No matter what the setting, credible sources are more effective. Consider the following:

- Highly credible public speakers are more likely to convince audiences to accept their arguments. By citing credible sources, speakers build their own credibility and generate greater attitude change.[4]

- Successful counselors first earn the trust of their clients.[5]
- Salespeople are more productive if they sell themselves (build their credibility) before they sell their products.
- Editorials are more persuasive if they come from highly credible newspapers like the *New York Times* or the *Chicago Tribune*.[6]

Dimensions of Credibility

Modern investigators no longer treat credibility as a set of speaker traits. Instead, they isolate factors that audiences use to evaluate the believability of speakers. The most significant elements or dimensions of credibility are:[7]

1. ***Competence.*** Competence can be defined as knowledge of the topic at hand, intelligence, expertise, skill or good judgment. James Kouzes and Barry Posner use the term "value-added" to describe the kind of competence that leaders need to demonstrate.[8] A leader must provide the skills that the group needs at a particular time. Often these skills have little to do with the technical requirements of a group or organization. For example, a new facilities manager may know little about carpentry, plumbing or painting. However, he/she can become an effective leader through using communication skills to build a cohesive work unit.

2. ***Trustworthiness (Character).*** Trustworthiness is another name for honesty and consistency.[9] This dimension of credibility is critical to effective leadership since the leader-follower relationship is built on trust. Managers rate honesty as the most important leader quality; the most influential public opinion leaders are also the most trustworthy. Paul Harvey's daily commentaries are the top rated radio programs in America. Harvey's ability to lead public opinion is based primarily on his sincerity. According to one analyst: "Paul Harvey is to listeners a real person, a touchstone of the real home-grown America. He engenders trust and affection."[10]

3. ***Dynamism.*** Dynamism refers to perceptions of a source's confidence, activity and assertiveness. Dynamic leaders communicate confidence in their visions for the future. They inspire others to work harder and to make greater sacrifices. Dynamism appears to be an integral part of what many people call charismatic leadership, a topic we will discuss in more detail in Chapter 8.

Leaders can rate highly on one or more dimensions of credibility while receiving low evaluations in another. Compare four recent presidents—Nixon, Ford, Carter and Reagan—to see how a leader can differ across credibility factors. Rate each of them on the three dimensions of credibility. When finished, turn to Figure 5.1 and check your answers with those given by other students.

Figure 5.1

Presidential Credibility Ratings

Richard Nixon

Competence:	high	Particularly strong in foreign policy, visiting both the Soviet Union and China.
Character:	very low	Even before Watergate, he had already earned the nickname "Tricky Dick." Low character cost him the presidency.
Dynamism:	low	His victory sign and facial expressions were often material for satirists. However, his dynamism never sank as low as his character evaluations.

Gerald Ford

Competence:	low	Often portrayed as bumbling and uncoordinated by cartoonists, comedian Chevy Chase and others.
Character:	high	Though his pardon of Nixon was controversial, he was considered to be an honest president.
Dynamism:	low/ moderate	Not particularly dynamic on television or in personal appearances.

Jimmy Carter

Competence:	high/ moderate	A good detail man with an engineering background. However, his failure to rescue the hostages in Iran made him appear ineffective.
Character:	moderate	Enjoyed a high degree of trust at first but appeared inconsistent toward the end of his term.
Dynamism:	low	Unable to rally the nation to save energy or to take any other major national effort.

Ronald Reagan

Competence:	low	Perhaps his greatest weakness as president. Not always aware of important details and sometimes quoted fiction as fact.
Character:	high	Many Americans disagreed with his specific policies but still liked him as a person. The Iran Contra Affair was damaging because he said he would never negotiate with terrorists while, at the same time, he appeared willing to trade arms for hostages.
Dynamism:	moderate/ high	Called "The Great Communicator." Not as forceful after the Iran Contra Affair. Yet, he was active enough to make many Americans forget that he was the oldest president in our nation's history.

Credibility Effects

Perceptions of credibility vary over time. Consider a typical college classroom. At the beginning of a course, students are most concerned about a teacher's competence. At the end of the quarter or semester, they are more interested in the instructor's character. They want to know if the professor will grade fairly.[11] Credibility evaluations also vary between situations. For instance, listeners hearing a speech to a social organization are likely to evaluate the presenter's competence. Those listening to a sermon put more emphasis on the speaker's trustworthiness.[12]

To have the greatest impact, highly credible communicators need to be identified at or near the beginning of messages. On the other hand, if a source with poor credentials is named first, then the audience is on guard against the message that the source will bring.[13] A message can change attitudes and behavior even if it comes from a source with low credibility, however. As time passes, the source is forgotten but the message is remembered and judged on its own merits. This is called the "sleeper effect."[14] The sleeper effect may explain the success of persuasive messages such as the advertising campaign for cough medicine in which an actor states "I am not a doctor, but I play one on TV." When you are in the supermarket shopping for cough medicine months after exposure to this commercial, you might select this product because you remember the message but not the source. You remember that "a doctor recommends this brand."

Building Your Credibility

Discovering how others assess your competence, trustworthiness and dynamism is an excellent way to begin to build your credibility. Rate yourself on the credibility scales found in Application Exercise 1. Then ask someone else to rate you and compare the responses. Like the presidents rated earlier, you will probably rank higher on one dimension of credibility than on others. In addition, your self-ratings might be either above or below the ratings you receive from your partner.

Once you've targeted the dimension(s) of credibility most in need of improvement, you can start to change your behaviors in order to generate more favorable impressions. In Chapter 1 we called this process impression management. Since initial impressions are largely based on nonverbal cues, pay particular attention to nonverbal behaviors such as appearance, voice, posture and eye contact. Nonverbal communication

authority Dale Leathers says that you can increase your credibility if you
follow these guidelines:[15]

- *Eye Contact.* Make sustained eye contact when communicating
with others. Avoid shifting the eyes, looking away, keeping your
eyes downcast or excessive blinking.

- *Gestures.* Use gestures to add emphasis to the points that you
make. Try to appear spontaneous and unrehearsed; let your gestures
convey the depth or intensity of your emotions. Handwringing,
finger-tapping, tugging at clothing and tentative movements
undermine credibility.

- *Posture.* Maintain an open, relaxed posture when talking with
others. Lean forward and smile when answering a question in order
to establish rapport. Use frequent and forceful postural shifts to
communicate responsiveness. Try to avoid those behaviors which
make you look timid or nonassertive—holding your body rigid,
keeping arms and hands crossed and close to the body and so on.

- *Voice.* Strive to sound confident by using a conversational
speaking style and vary your rate, pitch and volume. Sounding
nasal, tense or flat can make you appear significantly less credible.
In addition, frequent pauses, speaking too rapidly, repeating words,
and stuttering have a negative impact on credibility.

- *Clothing.* Dress to draw attention away from physical features
which are associated with negative stereotypes. For example, avoid
darkly tinted contacts or glasses. The stereotype holds that
untrustworthy people wear dark eyeglasses. Since the endomorphic
(round) body type is perceptually linked with low self-confidence
and low competence, wear neutral colors rather than bright colors
if weight is a problem. Bright colors draw attention to body size
while neutral colors do not.

In addition to the nonverbal behaviors listed above, there are many
other behaviors which can help build your credibility. Being prepared
for meetings, becoming an active listener, and following through on
promises and commitments are a few examples. Brainstorm a list of
additional credibility building behaviors (see Application Exercise 2).

Compliance-Gaining Strategies

Compliance-gaining strategies are the verbal tactics that leaders and
others use to get their way in face-to-face encounters. These strategies

are based on the types of power we described in Chapter 4. To identify some of the compliance-gaining strategies that you use, consider what you would do in the following situations:[16]

> Your best friend has the habit of borrowing money from you and not repaying it for long periods of time. Recently, your friend borrowed $25, and you need the money back quickly. You want to persuade your friend to repay the loan immediately.

> A close friend's birthday is next week. This friend has often admiringly described a rocking chair at a particular antique store. The owner of the store wants more money for the chair than you want to spend. You want to persuade the owner to lower the price.

Take a look at Figure 5.2 which describes popular compliance-gaining strategies. Match your tactics with those on the list. Did you choose a different approach to use with your friend than with the store owner?

Figure 5.2

Types of Compliance-Gaining Strategies

Categories of Tactics	Examples
1. Direct Requests	The actor asks the target to comply with a request in a direct manner. These messages do not contain any manipulation or motivation. • Can I borrow your notes until next period? • Will you have dinner with me tonight? • Dad, will you co-sign my note for the car?
2. Supporting Evidence	The actor utilizes one or more reasons why the target should comply—evidence, data, logic, reasoning, appeals to rules, fairness, etc. • I provided photocopies of the bills and cancelled checks. • I told him the procedures in this case were in my favor. • I thought about my arguments ahead of time and used them on her when she seemed annoyed.
3. Exchange	The actor attempts to gain the compliance of the target by offering to exchange things of value (money, services, favors, etc.). • I'll help you study if you'll go with me. • I'll agree to $1000 if you'll throw in a radio.

4. Face Maintenance	The actor uses indirect strategies such as ingratiation (flattery, favors, attractive self-presentation); or introduces topics so the target will infer or deduce the actor's goal.

- I was sweet to him and put him in a good mood.
- I told her how sad I was that I couldn't go with her.
- I mentioned to him how attractive he was and how cute we look together.

5. Distributive	The actor attempts to use coercive influence or attempts to make the target feel guilty, sad or selfish for not complying.

- I told him that I had never seen him act this way.
- I shouted at him for not agreeing to help.
- I started crying and told him that he was the only one who could help me.

6. Indirect Tactics	The actor requests compliance by initiating a conversation from which the target will infer or assume the actor's real intent.

- I'd hint about how much I wanted to go out with her.
- I would suggest how much I valued his help in the past.
- I would beat around the bush about how lonely I was.

7. Empathetic Understanding	Appeals to the target's love and affection for the actor are used.

- If you really loved me you wouldn't drink and drive.
- Dad, you know that we can't get along without you, and if you don't go for the treatment . . .
- I told him how I understood his situation but wanted him to help anyway.

8. Referent Influence	References to how similar target and actor are and how much each can identify with the other.

- Since we're in this boat together, why don't we join forces and . . .
- You and I have always thought alike, and it's only logical that we do this together.
- If you are going to be popular like me, you'll have to wear these clothes.

9. Other-Benefit	Tactics similar to supportive evidence, but the actor emphasizes how the target will benefit.

- I told her about the advantages of going to Europe alone.

> - I said to her that this car was just the right size for her.
> - I tried to convince her that going away to college was in her best interest.
>
> 10. Deceit   Use of dishonest means to secure compliance.
>
> - I lied and told her that I couldn't pay my tuition bill unless she paid me back.
> - I didn't exactly give him the whole story.
>
> Sources: Adapted from O'Hair, D., & Cody, M. J. (1987). Machiavellian beliefs and social influence. *Western Journal of Speech Communication, 51,* pp. 286-287. Copyright © 1987 by the Western Speech Communication Association. Reprinted with permission.

Michael Cody and Margaret McLaughlin report that compliance-seekers keep six situational variables in mind when selecting compliance tactics. These factors include 1) intimacy (acquaintance or friend, spouse or neighbor), 2) dominance (the amount of power each person has in the situation), 3) the likelihood that the receiver or target of the request will resist, 4) the compliance-seeker's right to make the request, 5) how much the persuader would gain from the request, and 6) the effects (consequences) that the compliance-gaining attempt might have on the future of the relationship.[17] The following chart highlights the impact these situational variables have on strategy selection.[18]

Variable	Strategy Selection
Intimacy	Supporting evidence and exchange tactics are popular in intimate relationships because they prevent relational damage.
Dominance	Direct requests are frequently made in equal power relationships while persuaders rely on supporting evidence when approaching supervisors and others of higher status.
Resistance	When the likelihood of resistance is high, actors rely heavily on supporting evidence.
Rights	Supporting arguments are offered when persuaders have the right to make requests. If actors in long term relationships have few rights to make requests, they are forced to rely on empathetic understanding tactics to overcome resistance.
Benefits	Indirect tactics are commonly chosen if persuaders personally have a lot to gain from compliance. In these situations, direct approaches make compliance-seekers appear selfish or power

hungry. If targets of requests will also benefit from compliance, persuaders are much more forceful and direct.

Relational   Exchange strategies preserve long term relationships because
Consequences   they make persuaders appear reasonable. Face maintenance and
                 distributive strategies are risky because they may offend targets
                 and damage relationships.

The presence of so many situational variables makes strategy selection quite complex. Relationships can be long term but not intimate; persuaders may have the right to make requests but face strong resistance from dominant targets, and so on. Assessing the emotional consequences of a compliance-gaining strategy can simplify the selection process. John Hunter, Franklin Boster and others suggest that persuaders select and reject compliance-gaining strategies based on the impact they have on the emotional state of both the actor and the target.[19] Compliance-gainers prefer "friendly persuasion"—messages which put both parties in a positive frame of mind.[20] Supporting evidence, exchange, referent influence and other-benefit tactics generally produce a positive emotional climate. Distributive and deceit strategies frequently create negative feelings. In Chapter 4 we developed a cost/benefit ratio for each of the five types of power. The same approach can be used to determine the best compliance-gaining strategy for a particular situation. Conduct an emotional cost/benefit analysis when choosing a compliance-gaining strategy. Whenever possible, select the strategy that is most likely to generate positive feelings for both you and the target of your request. (For a closer look at one group of leaders who rely heavily on friendly persuasion, see Figure 5.3.)

Overcoming Resistance to Compliance

When resistance is strong, you probably will need to use a series of compliance-gaining attempts rather than just one. One sequential approach to compliance-gaining is called Foot-In-The-Door (FITD). This strategy begins with a request for something small and then proceeds to larger requests. Those who agree to a small request (who let you get your foot in the door, so to speak) are often more likely to give in to later demands. One group of researchers asked Californians to put small "Keep California Beautiful" signs in their windows. Later they asked these homeowners to display large, poorly painted signs with the message "Be a Safe Driver" in their front yards. Those who had previously displayed the small sign were more likely to agree to display the larger sign.[21]

Figure 5.3

Compliance in the Classroom

Instructors are well aware of just how important influence is to successful teaching. In addition to creating a positive learning climate, a teacher must persuade students to focus attention on classroom activities, to turn assignments in on time, to enjoy the subject matter and to conform to classroom regulations. A teacher's choice of compliance-gaining tactics can have a significant impact on student learning as well as on the teacher's satisfaction with her or his job.

University of West Virginia professor James McCroskey and his associates measured teacher power strategies based on the power topology developed by French and Raven. They found that teachers rely most heavily on expert, reward and referent power. Instructor use of expert and referent power enhances student learning while the use of coercive and legitimate power has the opposite effect. Later McCroskey and his colleagues identified specific techniques and messages that teachers use to implement each type of power. For example, to employ reward power, a teacher might tell a student that he/she will enjoy doing an assignment (reward from behavior) or will get approval from classmates for complying (reward from others). Specific messages associated with expert and referent power (''You will feel good about yourself if you do.'' ''Because I need to know how well you understand this.'') are positively associated with learning. In addition, the researchers report that:

1. The most effective messages (labeled as prosocial by the investigators) are those that identify good reasons for compliance while the least effective messages (called antisocial) concentrate on the consequences of noncompliance. Students may see messages that emphasize negative consequences as a ''challenge'' and become more resistant.

2. Effective teachers use prosocial messages more frequently than poor teachers.

3. Experienced teachers use a wider variety of compliance-gaining techniques than inexperienced teachers.

4. Those teachers who use nonverbal communication behaviors which reduce physical and psychological distance—frequent head nods, close distance and open posture—face less resistance from students no matter what type of verbal message they use.

5. Teachers are most likely to use antisocial tactics like punishment or relying on authority in response to active misbehaviors (talking frequently, disrupting the class); they will also respond more forcefully to frequent misbehaviors. In addition, male teachers rely more heavily on punishment techniques.

6. Teacher job satisfaction is directly related to instructor choice of classroom influence strategies. College instructors are more satisfied with teaching and with students if they rely on prosocial influence techniques. Among secondary and elementary teachers, those who use antisocial messages are less content with their professional careers.

Sources:

Kearney, P., Plax, T. G., Richmond, V. P., & McCroskey, J. C. (1985). Power in the classroom III: Teacher communication techniques and messages. *Communication Education, 34*, 19-28.

Kearney, P., Plax, T. G., Smith, V. R., & Sorensen, G. (1988). Effects of teacher immediacy and strategy type on college student resistance to on-task demands. *Communication Education, 37*, 54-67.

Kearney, P., Plax, T. G., Sorensen, G., & Smith, V. R. (1988). Experienced and prospective teachers' selections of compliance-gaining messages for "common" student misbehaviors. *Communication Education, 37*, 150-164.

McCroskey, J. C., & Richmond, V. P. (1983). Power in the classroom I: Teacher and student perceptions. *Communication Education, 32*, 175-184.

McCroskey, J. C., Richmond, V. P., Plax, T. G., & Kearney, P. (1985). Power in the classroom V: Behavior alteration techniques, communication training and learning. *Communication Education, 34*, 214-226.

Plax, T. G., Kearney, P., & Downs, T. M. (1986). Communicating control in the classroom and satisfaction with teaching and students. *Communication Education, 35*, 379-388.

Plax, T. G., Kearney, P., & Tucker, L. K. (1986). Prospective teachers' use of behavior alteration techniques on common student misbehaviors. *Communication Education, 35*, 32-42.

Plax, T. G., Kearney, P., McCroskey, J. C., & Richmond, V. P. (1986) Power in the classroom VI: Verbal control strategies, nonverbal immediacy and affective learning. *Communication Education, 35*, 43-55.

Richmond, V. P., & McCroskey, J. C. (1984). Power in the classroom II: Power and learning. *Communication Education, 33*, 125-136.

Richmond, V. P., McCroskey, J. C., Kearney, P., & Plax, T. (1987). Power in the classroom VII: Linking behavior alteration techniques to cognitive learning. *Communication Education, 36*, 1-12.

The second sequential compliance-gaining strategy has been labeled the Door-in-the-Face technique (DITF). This technique reverses the strategy used in the Foot-In-The-Door method. The DITF approach starts with a large demand and follows with smaller requests. People are more likely to comply to follow-up requests after rejecting an initial request. They may view a smaller follow-up request as a concession and be more willing to offer their own concession (acceptance of the request) in return. This procedure was first tested by investigators who asked strangers to make a two year commitment as youth volunteers. The researchers then followed up their initial request by asking these same individuals to take children to the zoo for two hours. To create a comparison group, they approached a separate group of strangers with only the second request. Those who had first been asked to make the long term commitment were more likely to agree to go to the zoo.[22]

Keep your initial demand within rational limits when using the DITF approach. You'll seem unreasonable if your initial request is too large. In addition, your second request should be made immediately after your first one is rejected. Both Door-In-The-Face and Foot-In-The-Door work best when they are used to gain compliance on important issues like protecting the environment. Neither strategy is as effective if you use it for a self-serving concern like requesting a day off for a long weekend.[23]

The Leader as Negotiator

Leaders often must influence those who actively disagree with them. Whenever conflict becomes a significant part of the influence situation, leaders must negotiate in order to achieve their goals. A number of leadership and organizational scholars emphasize the important role that negotiation plays in leadership. For instance, Peter Smith and Mark Peterson define leadership, in part, *as* negotiation.[24] The significance of negotiation to organizations is underscored by the number of popular books on negotiation (i.e. *You Can Negotiate Anything, The Complete Negotiator*) that fill the business sections of bookstores.

Negotiation consists of back and forth communication aimed at reaching a joint decision when people are in disagreement. Negotiation isn't the only way to handle conflict. One person could make a unilateral decision or coerce the other, for example. But negotiation offers the best chance of reaching a solution that satisfies both parties. After surveying the alternatives to negotiation, negotiation expert Dean Pruitt notes that "one often hears a sigh of relief when negotiation substitutes for harsher struggles."[25]

A mix of compatible and incompatible interests marks all negotiation situations. Negotiators must have some common goal or they wouldn't negotiate. On the other hand, at least one issue must divide them or they wouldn't need to negotiate to reach an agreement. Negotiation is a common occurrence in organizational life. Consider the relationship between members of the production and marketing departments. While both share a common interest in seeing company sales increase, marketing wants fast product turnaround to capture a new market while production wants to minimize costs while maintaining quality. These departments must resolve their differences through negotiation in order to be successful. Similar disagreements can be found in small groups. Everyone working in your class project group probably wants a high grade. However, some group members may want to spend their time relaxing or studying for other classes instead of meeting with the group or gathering research. The amount of work each does for the group then becomes a matter for negotiation.

The significance of negotiation to leading becomes particularly apparent when a leader introduces change. Take the case of a law originated in the House of Representatives. The author of the legislation may have to negotiate for cosponsors and then negotiate passage through one or more committees and the House. Once the bill passes, any differences in the House version of the bill must be reconciled with the Senate's version in another committee. Changes must be ratified by both bodies before the bill goes to the President who may or may not sign the legislation. A presidential veto may mean further negotiations as the House and Senate try to enact the bill without a presidential signature. To complicate matters, this whole process takes place under the scrutiny of special interest groups, the media and the public who may try to negotiate their own changes to the bill.

Creating a Cooperative Climate

Our discussion of compliance-gaining emphasized the activities of the persuader. The outcome of the negotiation process depends on the **joint** efforts of the parties involved. As we indicated earlier, negotiators have compatible and incompatible goals. Since they have similar and different interests, the two parties simultaneously possess the incentive to cooperate *and* to compete. Participants must foster cooperation and reduce competition if they are to reach a mutually satisfying solution. According to conflict expert Morton Deutsch, there are sharp differences between cooperative and competitive negotiation climates:[26]

Cooperation	Competition
Open and honest communication	Very little communication, messages often negative and misleading
An emphasis on similarities	An emphasis on differences
Trusting, friendly attitudes	Suspicion, hostility

| Mutual problem solving | One party wins over the other |
| Reduction of conflicting interests | Escalation of conflict and negative emotions |

Those who want others to cooperate act in a cooperative manner. Conversely, those who compete meet with resistance. Both cooperation and competition get "locked in" to a negotiation relationship at an early stage and persist throughout the negotiation process.[27] One way to foster cooperation is by using the Tit for Tat strategy. The three rules of Tit for Tat are 1) Be Nice, 2) Be Provokable, and 3) Be Forgiving. Begin the negotiation by offering to cooperate. If the other negotiator tries to take advantage of you, respond in kind. When he or she switches to a cooperative approach, begin to cooperate again.[28]

Promises and concessions are two ways to signal that you are willing to cooperate. Offer to share important information, for example, or back away from one of your initial demands. If the other party responds in kind, make further concessions. However, if your concession is not matched by the other party, he or she may be looking to compete rather than to cooperate. In this case, follow the rules of the Tit for Tat strategy and make no further concessions until the other negotiator becomes more conciliatory.

Threats hinder the development of cooperation. Threats gain compliance but they intensify the conflict because they invite retaliation. A threat puts both the threat maker and the recipient in a bad position. The negotiator who makes a threat gives up other options and must be willing to carry out the threat. The recipient of the threat may not want to retaliate but failure to do so signals weakness.[29]

Perspective Taking Skills

Understanding the other negotiator's perspective is a valuable negotiating tool. A negotiator with high perspective taking ability anticipates the goals and expectations of the other party. He/she can encourage concessions that lead to agreement. Perspective taking reduces the defensiveness of the other negotiator and makes him/her more conciliatory. The result is faster, more effective negotiations.[30] However, trying to see the other person's point of view in a negotiation is difficult for these reasons:

- strong emotions like anger may be aroused
- both parties may be highly committed to their positions

- negotiators may have significantly different values, beliefs, and experiences
- time that should be spent listening is spent, instead, on developing counterarguments

Perspective taking begins before any actual negotiation. Start by gathering information about the issues and individuals involved in the future negotiation. For example, if you want to negotiate for more funding for your organization from the student government, find out the amount of money available, past grants to your group and other campus organizations, the interests of those serving on the funding committee and so on. In addition, identify the negotiating style of the other party. Interpersonally oriented negotiators are sensitive to relational aspects of the negotiation. They want to get to know the other negotiator before they do business. In contrast, high task negotiators do not want coffee, doughnuts or small talk but will attack the issues right away. Cooperative negotiators have an interest in others while competitive bargainers only seek benefits for themselves. Knowing where the other party falls on these orientations can help you target your approach more effectively. A high task/competitive negotiator will want to focus solely on task issues and may try to intimidate you at first. A cooperative/high interpersonal/high task bargainer will expect you to be enthusiastic and highly involved.[31]

Once you've gathered as much information as you can, role play the negotiation by taking the part of the other negotiator. This should give you a greater understanding of that person's vantage point. For instance, if you are a manager preparing for labor negotiations, act out the role of the union negotiator. Do symbolic role playing if you can't physically role play. Imagine how the other party thinks and feels in the situation. As a manager in contract negotiations, consider the relationship between the union negotiator and the union membership. This person may have to make unreasonable demands at first in order to satisfy the rank and file.

Active listening skills are critical once the negotiation begins. Ask for clarification when needed and paraphrase the speaker's comments. By making an effort to listen actively to the other negotiator, you demonstrate that you want to understand his or her point of view. This makes conciliation more likely.[32]

Negotiation as Joint Problem Solving

As we've seen, effective negotiators create a cooperative atmosphere and take the perspective of others. The most productive approaches to negotiation incorporate these two elements by viewing negotiation as a problem solving process rather than as a competitive tug of war. In contrast to the win-lose approach, problem solving negotiation fosters cooperation and focuses on generating solutions that will meet the interests of both sides. Perhaps the best known example of the problem solving style of negotiation is the Principled Negotiation Model developed by Roger Fisher, William Ury and associates of the Harvard Negotiation Project.[33] Following the four steps of Principled Negotiation will help you reach a solution that is satisfactory to both you and the other party.

1. *Separate the people from the problem*   Avoid defining the situation as a test of wills. Focus instead on working side by side on a common goal—resolving the issues at hand. Build trust to defuse strong emotions and to keep conflict from escalating. The case of Frank Lorenzo and Eastern Airlines is a vivid example of how making personalities the issue can cause negotiations to break down. (See Figure 5.4.)

2. *Focus on interests, not positions*   A negotiating position is the negotiator's public stance (i.e. "I want $40,000 a year in salary from the company."). An interest, on the other hand, is the reason *why* the negotiator takes that position ("I need to earn $40,000 so that I can save the downpayment for a house."). Focusing on positions can blind you and the other negotiator to the fact that there may be more than one way to meet the underlying need or interest. The company in the example above might pay less in salary and yet meet the employee's need for housing by offering a low cost home loan. The Camp David peace treaty between Egypt and Israel demonstrates how making a distinction between interests and positions can generate productive settlements. When the two nations first sat down to negotiate with the help of President Carter in 1978, they argued over the return of the Sinai Peninsula which had been seized by Israel from Egypt during the Six Day War in 1967. Egypt took the position that all occupied lands should be returned while Israel took the position that only some of the Sinai should be returned to Egyptian control. As a result, the talks stalled. However, once the negotiators realized that Israel's real interest was national security and Egypt's interest lay in regaining sovereignty over her land, an agreement was reached. Israel gave back the occupied territory in return for pledges that Egypt would not use the Sinai for military purposes.[34]

3. *Invent options for mutual gain*.   Spend time brainstorming solutions that can meet the needs of both negotiators. Obviously, this is impossible unless you first separate the people from the problem and

Figure 5.4   Case Study

When the Negotiator *is* the Issue:
Frank Lorenzo and Eastern Air Lines

   Conflict between Eastern Air Lines president Frank Lorenzo and Eastern employees began almost immediately after Lorenzo bought Eastern in 1986. The new owner angered machinist president Charles Bryan and other union leaders by transferring and selling assets to other airlines while insisting on wage concessions. Consultants urged machinists to make Lorenzo the issue in negotiations by painting him as an unscrupulous takeover artist out to make a fast buck. After a year of federally mediated negotiations, Eastern machinists and pilots went on strike and the rhetoric on both sides escalated. The president of the Air Line Pilots Association called Lorenzo "the Gordon Gekko of airlines, with a mind that would make Machiavelli look like Gomer Pyle." Machinist Bryan claimed that the battle between management and employees was "the purest case of evil vs. good." Pickets walked the lines with placards featuring a bull's eye over Lorenzo's face. For his part, Eastern's president called the pilots' role in the strike "suicidal" and compared their actions to the Jonestown tragedy. According to Lorenzo, "They (the pilots) did a pretty good job of drinking Kool-Aid together."
   With the focus on the clash of personalities rather than on problem solving, no settlement was reached. Eastern filed for bankruptcy and over thirty-two thousand jobs were put in jeopardy. The fate of the company is still uncertain. While each side can take satisfaction in the damage it did to the other, both parties were losers. Mixing people with problems is a no-win negotiation strategy.

Discussion Questions

   1. As a federal mediator, what strategies would you have used to get the negotiations between Eastern and its employees back on track?
   2. Is there any hope of generating creative solutions if both parties distrust one another?
   3. Identify the characteristics of successful union management negotiations. What elements contribute to satisfactory outcomes?

Sources:
Bolte, G., & McCarroll, T. (1989, March 20). Eastern goes bust. *Time*, p. 53.
Schwartz, J. (1989, March 20). A boss they love to hate. *Newsweek*, pp. 20-23.

focus on interests rather than on negotiating positions. Fisher and Ury offer the following example of a creative solution which met the interests of both parties:

Consider the story of two men quarreling in a library. One wants the window open and the other wants it closed. They bicker back and forth about how much to leave it open: a crack, halfway, three quarters of the way. No solution satisfies them both. Enter the librarian. She asks one why he wants the window open: "To get some fresh air." She asks the other why he wants it closed: "To avoid the draft." After thinking a minute, she opens wide a window in the next room, bringing in fresh air without a draft.[35]

4. *Insist on objective criteria*.   Find a set of criteria that you both can agree on when determining the terms of the settlement. This reduces the possibility that one party will force the other into accepting an unsatisfactory solution. In most cases, negotiators will be comfortable with an agreement that corresponds to widely accepted norms. Such standards can range from used car price books to legal precedents for insurance settlements to industry standards for wages.

Summary

In this chapter, we examined some of the ways that leaders exert influence. We began with a look at credibility, the key to any successful influence attempt. Credibility is built on perceptions of competence, trustworthiness, and dynamism. These perceptions, in turn, can be modified by adopting credibility-building behaviors. Next we identified verbal compliance-gaining strategies used to make requests in face-to-face encounters. Compliance-gainers keep these factors in mind when choosing a compliance-gaining tactic: 1) relational intimacy, 2) the relative power or dominance of the compliance-seeker and target, 3) the likelihood of resistance, 4) rights to make the request, 5) possible benefits to both parties from compliance, and 6) relational consequences. Strategies which put the compliance-seeker and target in a positive frame of mind are most popular. Making a sequence of compliance-gaining requests increases the likelihood of compliance when resistance is strong. The Foot-in-the-Door sequence uses a series of small requests while the Door-in-the-Face approach begins with a large request which is followed by smaller demands.

In the final section of the chapter we identified skills that are essential to effective negotiation. Negotiation involves back and forth communication aimed at reaching an agreement that is satisfactory to both parties when they disagree on one or more issues. Successful negotiators build a cooperative atmosphere, take the perspective of the other person and work together to reach a joint solution. Joint problem-solving negotiation involves separating the people from the problem, identifying the interests of each party, brainstorming options for mutual gain, and basing the settlement on objective criteria.

Application Exercises

1. Evaluate Your Credibility

   Rate your credibility on Form 1 below which consists of items taken from the Berlo, Lemert and Mertz (1969) and McCroskey and Young (1983) credibility scales.* You may want to evaluate yourself based on your image in a particular situation. For example: how competent, trustworthy and dynamic do you appear in class or at your job? Next, have someone else rate you on Form 2 while you evaluate that person. After you have finished your evaluations, discuss your reactions to this exercise. Were you surprised at how your partner rated you? Pleased? Displeased? Why did you rate yourself as you did? Would others rate you the same way?

Form 1: Self-Analysis

Competence

Experienced	___ ___ ___ ___ ___ ___ ___	Inexperienced
Informed	___ ___ ___ ___ ___ ___ ___	Uninformed
Skilled	___ ___ ___ ___ ___ ___ ___	Unskilled
Expert	___ ___ ___ ___ ___ ___ ___	Inexpert
Trained	___ ___ ___ ___ ___ ___ ___	Untrained

Trustworthiness

Kind	___ ___ ___ ___ ___ ___ ___	Cruel
Friendly	___ ___ ___ ___ ___ ___ ___	Unfriendly
Honest	___ ___ ___ ___ ___ ___ ___	Dishonest
Sympathetic	___ ___ ___ ___ ___ ___ ___	Unsympathetic

Dynamism

Assertive	___ ___ ___ ___ ___ ___ ___	Hesitant
Forceful	___ ___ ___ ___ ___ ___ ___	Meek
Bold	___ ___ ___ ___ ___ ___ ___	Timid
Active	___ ___ ___ ___ ___ ___ ___	Passive

Form 2: Partner Rating

Competence

Experienced	—	—	—	—	—	—	—	Inexperienced
Informed	—	—	—	—	—	—	—	Uninformed
Skilled	—	—	—	—	—	—	—	Unskilled
Expert	—	—	—	—	—	—	—	Inexpert
Trained	—	—	—	—	—	—	—	Untrained

Trustworthiness

Kind	—	—	—	—	—	—	—	Cruel
Friendly	—	—	—	—	—	—	—	Unfriendly
Honest	—	—	—	—	—	—	—	Dishonest
Sympathetic	—	—	—	—	—	—	—	Unsympathetic

Dynamism

Assertive	—	—	—	—	—	—	—	Hesitant
Forceful	—	—	—	—	—	—	—	Meek
Bold	—	—	—	—	—	—	—	Timid
Active	—	—	—	—	—	—	—	Passive

* Adapted from DeVito, J. (1980). *The interpersonal communication book* (2nd ed.). New York: Harper & Row.

---

2. Brainstorm a list of behaviors that can strengthen the credibility of communicators. Which of the behaviors given in the text or in your list would be most useful to you. Why?

3. Analyze your effectiveness as a compliance-gainer. Describe a recent situation in which you were the persuader. What compliance-gaining strategy did you select and why? What elements of the situation did you consider? What emotions were created by your strategy? How successful was your effort? What would you do differently next time?

4. Prepare for an upcoming negotiation using the principles presented in this chapter. Describe how you will build a cooperative atmosphere, take the perspective of the other person and try to reach solutions through joint efforts. Write up your plan of action.

Endnotes

1 Kouzes, J. M., & Posner, B. Z. (1987). *The leadership challenge: How to get extraordinary things done in organizations.* San Francisco: Jossey-Bass.

2 Sattler, W. M. (1947). Conceptions of ethos in ancient rhetoric. *Speech Monographs, 14,* 55-65.

3 McCroskey, J. C., & Young, T. J. (1981). Ethos and credibility: The construct and its measurement after three decades. *Central States Speech Journal, 32,* p. 24.

4 Haiman, F. S. (1949). An experimental study of the effects of ethos in public speaking. *Speech Monographs, 16,* 190-202.; Warren, I. D. (1969). The effects of credibility in sources of testimony and audience attitudes toward speaker and topic. *Speech Monographs, 36,* 456-458.

5 Strong, S. R., & Schmidt, L. D. (1970). Expertness and influence in counseling. *Journal of Counseling Psychology, 17,* 81-87.; Strong, S. R., & Dixon, D. N. (1971). Expertness, attractiveness, and influence in counseling. *Journal of Counseling Psychology, 18,* 562-570.

6 Hovland, C. I., & Weiss, W. (1951). The influence of source credibility on communication effectiveness. *Public Opinion Quarterly, 15,* 635-650.

7 Brembeck, W. L., & Howell, W. S. (1976). *Persuasion: A means of social influence* (2nd ed.). Englewood Cliffs, NJ: Prentice Hall.

8 Kouzes & Posner, p. 19.

9 Carl Hovland, a pioneer in credibility research, was among the first to argue that a distinction should be made between competence and trustworthiness. He pointed out that a message from a competent source will be rejected if hearers believe that this person is lying. See: Hovland, C., Janis, I., & Kelley, H. H. (1953). *Communication and persuasion.* New Haven: Yale University Press.

10 Aufderheide, P. (1986, July). Paul Harvey, good day!. *The Progressive,* p. 20.

11 McGlone, E. L., & Anderson, L. J. (1973). The dimensions of teacher credibility. *Communication Education, 22,* 196-200.

12 Applbaum, R. L., & Anatol, W. E. (1972). The factor structure of credibility as a function of the speaking situation. *Speech Monographs, 39,* 216-222.

13 Ward, C. D., & McGinnies, E. (1974). Persuasive effects of early and late mention of credible and non-credible sources. *Journal of Psychology, 86,* 17-23.; O'Keefe, D. J. (1987). The persuasive effects of delaying identification of high and low-credibility communicators: A meta-analytic review. *Central States Speech Journal, 38,* 63-72.

14 Kelman, H. C., & Hovland, C. I. (1953). "Reinstatement" of the communicator in delayed measurement of opinion change. *Journal of Abnormal and Social Psychology, 48,* 327-335.

15 Leathers, D. G. (1986). *Successful nonverbal communication: Principles and applications.* New York: Macmillan, Chs. 8, 11. See also: McMahan, E. M. (1976). Nonverbal communication as a function of attribution in impression formation. *Communication Monographs, 43,* 287-294.

16 These situations are used in a number of compliance-gaining studies, including: Cody, M. J., & McLaughlin, M. L. (1980). Perceptions of compliance-gaining situations: A dimensional analysis. *Communication Monographs, 47,* 132-148.

17 Cody & McLaughlin.

[18] Goss, B., & O'Hair, D. (1988). *Communicating in interpersonal relationships*. New York: Macmillan, Ch. 12. For more information on the relationship between situational variables and compliance-gaining strategy selection, see:

Sillars, A. L. (1980). The stranger and the spouse as target persons for compliance-gaining strategies: A subjective utility model. *Human Communication Research, 6*, 265-279.

Cody, M. J., & McLaughlin, M. L., & Schneider, M. J. (1981). The impact of relational consequences and intimacy on the selection of interpersonal persuasion tactics: A reanalysis. *Communication Quarterly, 29*, 91-106.

Miller, G., Boster, F., Roloff, M., & Seibold, D. (1977). Compliance-gaining message strategies: A typology and some findings concerning effects of situational differences. *Communication Monographs, 44*, 37-51.

Boster, F. J., & Stiff, J. B. (1984). Compliance-gaining message selection behavior. *Human Communication Research, 10*, 539-556.

Dillard, J. P, & Burgoon, M. (1985). Situational influences on the selection of compliance-gaining messages: Two tests of the predictive utility of the Cody-McLaughlin typology. *Communication Monographs, 52*, 289-304.

[19] Hunter, J. E., & Boster, F. J. (1987). A model of compliance-gaining message selection. *Communication Monographs, 54*, 63-84.

Vinson, L. (1988, November). *An emotion-based model of compliance-gaining message selection*. Paper presented at the Speech Communication Association convention, New Orleans, LA.

[20] Marwell, G., & Schmitt, D. (1967). Dimensions of compliance-gaining behavior: An empirical analysis. *Sociometry, 30*, p. 350-364. Some researchers use the terms prosocial and antisocial to distinguish between friendly and unfriendly types of compliance-gaining. For more information on the differences between pro and antisocial tactics, see:

Falbo, T. (1977). Multidimensional scaling of power strategies. *Journal of Personality and Social Psychology, 35*, 537-547.

Kearney, P., Plax, T. G., Sorensen, G., & Smith, V. R. (1988). Experienced and prospective teachers' selections of compliance- gaining messages for "common" student misbehaviors. *Communication Education, 37*, 150-164.

Roloff, M. E., & Barnicott, E. F. (1978). The situational use of of pro- and antisocial compliance-gaining strategies by high and low Machiavellians. In B. Ruben (Ed.), *Communication Yearbook 2* (pp. 193-208). New Brunswick, NJ: Transaction Books.

[21] Freedman, J. L., & Fraser, S. L. (1966). Compliance without pressure: The foot-in-the-door technique. *Journal of Personality and Social Psychology, 4*, 195-202.

[22] Cialdini, R., Vincent, J., Lewis, S., Catalan, J., Wheeler, D., & Darby, B. (1975). Reciprocal concessions procedure for inducing compliance: The door-in-the-face technique. *Journal of Personality and Social Psychology, 31*, 206-215.

[23] Dillard, J. Hunter, J., & Burgoon, M. (1984). Sequential-request persuasive strategies: Meta-analysis of foot-in-the-door and door-in-the-face. *Human Communication Research, 10*, 461-488. Cantrill, J. G., & Seibold, D. R. (1986). The perceptual contrast explanation of sequential request strategy effectiveness. *Human Communication Research, 13*, 253-267.

[24] Smith, P. B., & Peterson, M. F. (1988). *Leadership, organizations and culture*. London: Sage, Ch. 9.

[25] Pruitt, D. G. (1981). *Negotiation behavior*. New York: Academic Press, p. 6.

[26] Deutsch, M. (1973). *The resolution of conflict*. New Haven: Yale University Press.

[27] Rubin, J. Z., & Brown, B. R. (1975). *The social psychology of bargaining and negotiation*. New York: Academic Press.

[28] An impressive demonstration of the effectiveness of the Tit for Tat strategy is found in: Axelrod, R. (1984). *The evolution of cooperation*. New York: Basic Books. Axelrod set up a tournament using a computerized version of the Prisoner's Dilemma game. The Tit for Tat strategy beat all other entries.

[29] Putnam, L. L., & Jones, T. S. (1982). The role of communication in bargaining. *Human Communication Research, 8*, 262-280.

[30] Neale, M. A., & Bazerman, M. H. (1983). The role of perspective taking ability in negotiating under different forms of arbitration. *Industrial and Labor Relations, 36*, 378-388.; Bazerman, M. H., & Neale, M. A. (1983). Heuristics in negotiation: Limitations to effective dispute resolution. In M. H. Bazerman & R. J. Lewecki (Eds.), *Negotiating in organizations* (pp. 51-67). Beverly Hills: Sage.

[31] An excellent demonstration of negotiator styles can be found in the videotape *Negotiation and bargaining skills* (1984) produced by Alvin Goldberg and Carl Larson of the University of Denver. Dr. Goldberg is also our source for the three rules of the Tit for Tat negotiation strategy.

[32] For more information on how to increase perspective taking skills in interpersonal encounters, see Kogler Hill, S. E. (1982). The multistage process of interpersonal empathy. In S. E. Kogler Hill (Ed.) *Improving interpersonal competence: A laboratory approach* (pp. 83-89). Dubuque, IA: Kendall/Hunt.

[33] Fisher, R., & Ury, W. (1981). *Getting to yes*. New York: Penguin Books.

[34] Fisher & Ury, pp. 42-43.

[35] Fisher & Ury, p. 41.

Part II

Leadership Contexts

6

Leadership in Groups

Small groups play a major role in all of our lives. Every week we're part of planning committees, dorm councils, social clubs, condominium associations and countless other groups. Often our most enjoyable memories are of group experiences like playing on a winning softball team or developing a new product on a task force. Yet, at the same time, some of our greatest frustrations arise out of group interaction. Many classroom project groups, for example, get low grades because group members dislike one another. In other instances, members fail to show up for meetings, leaving one person to do most of the work on the project at the last minute.

The purpose of this chapter is to improve your chances of having a successful group experience by building your understanding of group leadership. There are no formulas that we know of which guarantee that you will become a group leader or that your group will be successful. However, learning about how group leadership works can increase the likelihood that both will happen. We'll start by looking at some fundamentals of group behavior. With these basics out of the way, we will then talk about emergent leadership, leading meetings, and the essentials of team performance.

Fundamentals of Group Interaction

Viewing Groups From a Communication Perspective

As you read this book (particularly if you have not taken a communication class before) you may be learning a number of new terms or you may be discovering new meanings for familiar terms. The symbols we master during our academic training focus our attention on some parts of the world and away from others. Kenneth Burke calls this focusing influence of language the "terministic screen." [1] Phillip Tompkins describes the following case of terministic screens in action:

> For example, suppose we assemble an economist, a psychologist, and a sociologist in the college cafeteria and ask each to give explanations of food choices made by a customer. Suppose further that the customer we observe happens to select custard rather than either cake or pie. The economist might explain that, because custard is less "labor intensive" and therefore cheaper than the other desserts, it was the only dessert the customer could afford. The psychologist might explain the choice by means of the customer's history; for instance, he or she might say that the customer's "past reinforcement schedule" provides the answer. The sociologist might

explain the choice by pointing to the "ethno-social background" of the customer and showing how different classes of people favor different desserts. . . . Thus, the terministic screen of vocabulary causes each to focus on elements and interpretations of the situation to the exclusion of others.[2]

The terministic screens of academic languages also operate when scholars from different fields study groups. Psychologists, for example, are often interested in the "personalities" of group members and focus on how these characteristics shape group behaviors and outcomes. Sociologists pay attention to other factors like the "social status" of group members. Communication scholars, however, are most interested in the communication that occurs within groups, what they label as "interaction." They argue that group success or failure often rests most heavily on what group members say and do when the group is together rather than on what group members bring with them to the discussion.

Supreme Court decisions are good examples of how group outcomes can't necessarily be predicted by knowing the characteristics of members. Presidents often try to influence Supreme Court decisions by appointing justices who favor either a conservative or liberal point of view. They are often surprised when their appointees violate their expectations after deliberating with other justices. In your own experience, there probably have been times when you went into a group meeting with your mind made up only to change your opinion as a result of the discussion. From a communication perspective, then, any definition of a group must take into account that communication is a group's "essential characteristic."[3] A survey of small group communication texts reveals that the following elements define small groups:[4]

1. *A common purpose or goal*.   A group is more than a collection of individuals. Several people waiting for a table at a restaurant would not constitute a group. Group members have something that they want to accomplish together—whether it is to overcome drug dependency, to decide on a new site for a manufacturing plant or to study for an exam. As an outgrowth of this common goal and participation in the group, a sense of belonging or identity emerges. One group of strangers, for example, was placed into an evening class that met weekly. Seven months later class members felt such a strong sense of group identity that they bought shirts with the name of the class imprinted on the back. (See Figure 6.1 for a closer look at how group identity emerges.)

2. *Interdependence*.   The success of any one member of the group depends on everyone doing his or her part. When student group members fail to do their fair share of the work, the grade of even the brightest individual goes down.

3. *Mutual influence*.   Not only do group members depend on each other, they influence each other through giving ideas, challenging opinions, listening, agreeing and so on.

4. *Face-to-Face Communication*.   In order for a group to exist, members must engage in face-to-face communication. For example, although individuals working on an assembly line share the common goal of producing a product, they do not constitute a group unless they interact with one another.[5]

5. *Specific Size*.   Groups range in size from 3 to 20 people. The addition of a third person makes a group more complex than a dyad. Group members must manage many relationships, not just one. They develop coalitions as well as sets of rules to regulate group behavior. The group is also more stable than a dyad. While a dyad dissolves when one member leaves, the group (if large enough) can continue if it loses a member or two. Twenty is generally considered the maximum size for a group because group members lose the ability to communicate face-to-face when the group grows beyond this number.

One definition that summarizes the five elements described above was developed by John Brilhart. He defines a group as "a small group of persons talking with each other face-to-face in order to achieve some interdependent goal, such as increased understanding, coordination of activity, or a solution to a shared problem."[6]

Task and Social Dimensions

Most groups must deal with both the task or "business" of the group and the social relationships between group members. (For more information on task and interpersonal communication, refer back to Chapter 2.) Robert Bales, a pioneer in the interactional approach to small groups, developed a guide for analyzing group behaviors which highlights these task and social dimensions.[7] In the Bales Interaction Process Analysis System, comments of group members fall into one of twelve categories (see Figure 6.2). Categories 1-3 and 10-12 deal with the group's social dimension. As you can see from the table, comments from categories 1-3 indicate that members have positive feelings toward others in the group while those from categories 10-12 reflect negative emotions. Statements that fall into categories 4-9 are concerned with the group's task.

According to Bales, groups must establish an equilibrium or balance between task and relational demands. Too much time on the task takes away from social concerns while a group that concentrates too heavily

Figure 6.1   Research Highlight

Building Group Identity Through Fantasy

It doesn't take long for a group to create its own identity. Established groups have inside jokes, nicknames for members, rules about who sits where, moral standards, plans for the future and so forth. Though group members take these elements for granted, they can bewilder outsiders who, for instance, can't figure out why everyone is laughing at something that doesn't seem at all funny.

According to Ernest Bormann, group members build a common ground both directly and indirectly. In the direct approach, group members clearly state what they think the group should do, what they believe and so on. In the indirect approach, group members express their attitudes and values through jokes, anecdotes, and stories. Members of classroom groups, for example, frequently reveal their feelings by telling stories about the strengths or failings of their instructors. This approach to identity building is called dramatizing.[1]

In their studies of group behavior at the University of Minnesota, Bormann and his colleagues noticed that some dramatic communication attempts captured the imagination of the entire group. At these moments, members became excited and the tempo of the conversation picked up. Bormann called these successful dramatic efforts "group fantasy chains." Fantasy chains tap into needs, attitudes and ideas shared in common by group members. The content of a message that successfully chains out is called a fantasy theme. When several fantasy themes are woven together, they form a group's rhetorical vision — a symbolic portrait of reality. Bormann went on from his small group studies to demonstrate how rhetorical visions motivate larger society. One such motivating vision was developed by the Puritans. The Puritans saw themselves as God's holy people destined to set up an ideal religious society in the New World. Their vision sustained them through many physical hardships and drove them to achieve in order to demonstrate that they had received God's forgiveness.[2]

Fantasy themes are powerful tools for shaping group norms, values and behaviors. They demonstrate right and wrong behavior, reflect strong emotions, bond members together and give meaning to the group's experience. Effective group leaders must shape group identity both directly and indirectly. Along with making direct suggestions and comments, they need to participate in group fantasies. In fact, leaders may want to start fantasy chains of their own. To be effective, however, they must deliver stories in a dramatic style and do so when the group is receptive.[3]

[1] Bormann, E. G. (1972). Fantasy and rhetorical vision: The rhetorical criticism of social reality. *Quarterly Journal of Speech, 58*, 396-407.

[2] Bormann, E. G. (1985). *The force of fantasy: Restoring the American dream.* Carbondale, IL: Southern Illinois University Press.

[3] Bormann, E. G. (1975). *Discussion and group methods: Theory and practice* (2nd ed.). New York: Harper & Row.

Figure 6.2

Bales' Interaction Process Analysis Categories

Category	Description
1. Seems friendly	Cooperation, harmony, praise, encouragement, admiration, laughter
2. Dramatizes	Images, emotional symbols, dramatic delivery, fantasy
3. Agrees	Recognition, understanding, agreement
4. Gives Suggestion	Takes initiative in the task dimension
5. Gives Opinion	Interpretation, evaluation, thinking out loud
6. Gives Information	Statements of fact and experience
7. Asks for Information	Requests objective, factual answers
8. Asks for Opinion	Encourages statements or reactions of all kinds (not limited to facts)
9. Asks for Suggestion	Turns initiative over to another, may reflect confusion about which direction to take
10. Disagrees	Mild disagreement with what someone else has said
11. Shows Tension	Hesitation, surprise, alarm, stammering
12. Seems Unfriendly	Negative feelings, controlling, interrupting, attacking, boasting, correcting, indifference, noncompliance, blaming self, coolness, unhappiness

Source: Bales, R. F. (1970). *Personality and interpersonal behavior.* New York: Holt, Rinehart and Winston. Used by permission.

on interpersonal needs may neglect its job. Bales initially believed that one leader emerges to take charge in task matters while another takes the lead in improving relationships. Later researchers, however, found that the same person could lead in both areas. The Bales system also overlooks the fact that messages can deal with both tasks and relationships at the same time. Even a message that seems to relate directly to the task carries important information about the relationship between the sender and receiver. For example, a group member can offer an opinion (Category 5 in the Bales system) which also reflects hostility toward the other group members (Category 12).

Despite its shortcomings, the Bales model is significant because it draws attention to the twin, interdependent concerns of every group. In most cases, groups perform best when meeting both task and relational needs. Most people need to feel good about their relationships with others in the group before they are willing to work hard on the group's behalf.

Group Evolution

Using the Bales system and other methods to analyze group communication reveals that groups change and mature over time. A number of models that describe the evolution of groups, particularly the development of decision-making groups, have been offered. One early model was developed by Thomas Scheidel and Laura Crowell.[8] These two researchers suggested that group decisions are not made through a linear, step by step process. Instead, an idea is introduced, discussed and then dropped. Later that same idea is reintroduced and developed further. After several such starts and stops, agreement is reached and the decision emerges. This process is called the Spiral Model because the discussion spirals in greater and greater loops as the discussion continues.

B. Aubrey Fisher relied heavily on the Spiral Model when developing his influential Decision Emergence Theory of group decision making.[9] As they listened to groups communicate, Fisher and his coworkers noted what each group member said (labeled a speech act) and how the next person responded. This pairing of speech acts is called an interact. A group interact might look something like this:

Kathy: I think we ought to get away from the office for a day and do some planning for next year.

Tim: I don't think we can cover everything in one day.

By looking at series of interacts, Fisher discovered four phases in group decision making.

1. *Orientation Phase.* Members are uncertain and tentative when groups first get together. They are not sure how to tackle the group's task or what kind of behavior will be accepted in the group. Individuals may be asking themselves such questions as "What kinds of jokes can I tell?" or "What happens when I disagree with the rest of the group?" In this initial stage, statements about what the group should do are ambiguous and members try hard not to offend others.

2. *Conflict Phase.* In the second phase, members are no longer tentative and ambiguous. Instead, they express strong opinions about decision proposals and provide evidence to support their positions. Members who support the same ideas band together. Interacts frequently reflect disagreement in this stage. A statement of support for an idea, for example, will often be followed by a negative opinion.

3. *Emergence Phase.* At this point the group begins to rally around one solution or decision. Coalitions formed during the second phase disband while dissent and social conflict die out.

4. *Reinforcement Phase*.   Consensus develops during the final stage. Interacts are positive in nature, reflecting support for other group members and for the solution which emerged in phase three. Tension is gone and the group commits itself to implementing the decision.

Not everyone is convinced that groups develop through a single series of phases. For example, Marshall Scott Poole argues that groups go through multiple stages of development.[10] Poole suggests that at any given time a group may be at one point in its social development and at another in its task development. One group might start by proposing solutions and stop later to socialize while another group might build relationships before tackling the task. Important moments of change in a group's development are called "breakpoints." These breakpoints can involve naturally occurring topic changes, moments of delay or, most seriously, disruptions caused by conflict or failure. Consensus about who the leader is will result in fewer delays and disruptions in the group's decision making process.

Though scholars may describe the process in different ways, the concept of group evolution has important implications. First, because groups develop over time, timing is critical. It's not just what you say, it's when you say it. A good proposal made too early in the discussion, for instance, may not be accepted. Second, since groups take time to develop successfully, any attempt to rush a group's development is likely to meet with failure. Third, high success groups are characterized by a high degree of cohesion and commitment. Consensus both speeds the development of groups and is the product of effective group interaction. Finally, the evolution of groups suggests that group leadership also develops in stages or as a process. This concept, called emergent leadership, is the subject of the next section.

Emergent Leadership

Ernest Bormann and others at the University of Minnesota studied emergent or "natural" leadership in small groups.[11] These researchers found that, "*the group selects its leader by the method of residues*." Instead of choosing a leader immediately, the group eliminates leader contenders until only one person is left. This procedure is similar to what happens in the presidential primary system. Many candidates begin the race for their party's presidential nomination; gradually the field shrinks as challengers lose the primaries, run out of money, get caught in ethics violations and so forth. Eventually only one candidate remains.

This same principle of selection by elimination operates in the small group. Although all members enter the group as potential leaders, contenders are disqualified until only one leader emerges.

According to Bormann and others, the elimination of potential leaders occurs in two phases. In the first phase, those deemed unsuitable for leadership are quickly removed from contention. Unsuitable candidates may be too quiet or they may be too rigid and aggressive. Many would-be leaders stumble because they appear to be unintelligent and uninformed. Once these cuts have been made, the group then enters the second phase. At this point, about half the group is still actively contending for leadership. Social relations are often tense during this stage. Communication behaviors that lead to elimination in phase two include dominating other group members and talking too much. Such factors as social standing outside the group and gender may be used to eliminate other aspiring leaders.

Four major patterns of leader emergence were found in the Minnesota studies. In the first pattern, the ultimate winner recruits an ally or "lieutenant" who helps him/her win out over another strong contender. In the second pattern, each of the remaining contenders has a lieutenant and, as a result, the leadership struggle is prolonged or no strong leader emerges. In the third pattern, a crisis determines leader emergence. The successful leader is the person who helps the group handle such traumatic events as unruly members or the loss of important materials. In the fourth pattern, no one emerges as a clear leader. The result is a high level of frustration. Bormann says that people find such groups to be "punishing."[12]

Communicating Your Way to the Top

If you are like most people, you generally hope to emerge as a leader in a group. In one study, seventy-eight out of the eighty group members surveyed said they wanted to become leaders.[13] We've already seen how such negative behaviors as failing to participate, talking too much, and seeming rigid and uninformed can eliminate leader contenders. The more difficult task is to isolate positive behaviors that are essential to leadership emergence. Here is a list of communication strategies that can increase your chances of emerging as a group leader:

1. *Participate early and often*.   The link between participation and leadership is the most consistent finding in small group leadership research.[14] While high participation does not guarantee a leadership role, failure to participate will nearly always keep you from being considered

as a potential leader. Participation demonstrates both your motivation to lead and your commitment to the group. Impressions about who would and would not make a suitable leader begin to take shape almost immediately after a group is formed.[15] Therefore, you must start to contribute early in the group's first session.

2. *Focus on communication quality as well as quantity*. High participation earns you consideration as a leader but communicating the wrong messages can keep you from moving into the leadership position. For example, one study examined 108 three-man groups and found that one third of the high participators were not viewed as group leaders. According to the researchers, "these subjects were seen as argumentative, disruptive, critical, and inconsiderate."[16] Communication behaviors which are positively correlated with emergent leadership include setting goals, giving directions, managing tension and conflict, and summarizing.[17] Not only is quality communication essential to becoming a leader, but effective leadership communication helps the group as a whole. Groups are most likely to make good decisions when their most influential members facilitate discussion by asking questions, challenging poor assumptions, clarifying ideas and keeping the group on track.[18]

3. *Demonstrate your competence*.   Not surprisingly, the success of would-be leaders depends heavily on their ability to convince others that they can successfully help the group complete the job at hand. Doing your homework in preparation for a project, for example, gives your leadership bid a major boost. Along with competence, you will also need to demonstrate your character and dynamism. Group members want to know that the leader candidate has the best interests of the group in mind and is not manipulating the group for personal gain. Being enthusiastic and confident makes other members more receptive to your suggestions and ideas. As we noted in Chapter 5, nonverbal communication plays an important role in building perceptions of all three dimensions of credibility. One study of the nonverbal behaviors of emergent small group leaders found that they gestured frequently, established good eye contact, and expressed agreement through nodding and facial expressions.[19]

4. *Help build a team*.   You must also demonstrate that you want to work with others in a cohesive unit if you want to become a group leader. Successful leader candidates work to build the status of others and don't claim all the credit for decisions. This critical element of leader emergence will be discussed in more detail later in the chapter.

Idiosyncratic Credits

Another useful tool to use in understanding group leadership is Edwin Hollander's notion of idiosyncratic credits. The process of accumulating idiosyncratic credits is similar to starting an account at a bank. Members generate positive impressions in the group called idiosyncratic credits which then are deposited in their "accounts."[20] Those with the highest credit levels or balances emerge as leaders. Credits are accumulated two ways. The first and most important way to build credits is by contributing to the completion of the group's task. The second is by conforming to group expectations. These expectations involve 1) general group norms (not being rude or overly emotional, for example), and 2) role expectations for a leader (such as representing the group well in front of other groups). Idiosyncratic credits are lost through incompetence and norm violations.

Leaders, because they have accumulated a large number of idiosyncratic credits, have greater freedom to deviate from group norms than other group members. However, the right to deviate is granted only after leadership has been achieved. To demonstrate the important relationship between timing and the acceptance of deviance, one group of researchers planted confederates in groups who would either support or violate such group norms as speaking in turn and majority rule. Those confederates who deviated early in the group process had more trouble convincing others to accept their opinions than those who deviated later in the session.[21] Group leaders have more freedom to disobey rules that apply to everyone. They should not, however, violate expectations associated with the leader role. A group leader may get away with being late to meetings or interrupting. She or he probably will not be able to act unfairly or selfishly.[22]

Appointed vs. Emergent Leaders

By this time you may wonder if anyone has paid any attention to groups who have appointed rather than emergent leaders. In many cases, a leader is assigned to a group before it meets for the first time. As you may have discovered from personal experience, groups are often successful in spite of, not because of, their official leaders. Not only do many appointed leaders fail to function as leaders, but assigning an incompetent leader actually slows group progress since members must spend additional time and energy developing alternative leadership. Groups spend less time on leadership issues if the appointed leader earns the leader label by doing an effective job.[23]

Researchers comparing the impact of assigning or choosing leaders have discovered that followers expect more from natural leaders than appointed leaders. Since they have more invested in leaders that they have selected for themselves, members have higher expectations and tolerate less failure. Yet, at the same time, group members give natural leaders more room to operate. Emergent leaders have greater freedom to make decisions on behalf of the group.[24]

One of the most common assignments for appointed group leaders is to plan and to preside over meetings. Effective leadership in meetings is the subject of the next section.

Leadership in Meetings

For many people, the thought of attending a meeting conjures up images of long, boring sessions spent doodling on a note pad while endless amounts of useless information are presented. The reason for this common attitude about meetings is simple: most meetings are poorly planned and ineptly led. Effective meeting leaders plan and prepare before a meeting to be certain that content is both informative and useful. Adopting the following guidelines can help to insure that your meetings are successful.

1. *Determine if a meeting is necessary before calling people together*.   The first step before calling a meeting is to determine if you are justified in taking people away from other activities. Bert Auger, a supervisor with the 3M corporation for over thirty years, provides a checklist outlining when you should and should not call a meeting.[25]

When to Call a Meeting

- When organizational goals need clarification.
- When information that may stimulate questions or discussion needs to be shared.
- When group consensus is required regarding a decision.
- When a problem needs to be discovered, analyzed or solved.
- When an idea, program or decision needs to be sold to others.
- When conflict needs to be resolved.
- When it is important that a number of different people have a similar understanding of the same idea, program or decision.
- When immediate reactions are needed to assess a proposed problem or action.
- When an idea, program or decision is stalled.

When Not to Call a Meeting

- When other communication networks, such as telephone, facsimile machine, letter or memo will transmit the message as effectively.
- When there is not sufficient time for adequate preparation by participants or the meeting leader.
- When one or more of the key participants are not available.
- When issues are personal or sensitive and could be handled more effectively by talking with each person individually.

2. *Have a clear agenda*.   A leader should outline the items he or she wishes to address before a meeting begins. A copy of this agenda should be circulated in advance of the meeting. Participants should be encouraged to add items to the agenda (within reason) which they feel are important. The agenda should be constructed with time constraints in mind. Additions which greatly increase the number of topics to be discussed should be tabled or scheduled for a separate meeting. Remember, it is the leader's responsibility to decide how much meeting time is available and to keep the meeting on schedule. As with writing a report or delivering a presentation, a meeting leader should always have a clear purpose and a plan for achieving his or her goals. Always ask: "Why are we having this meeting?"

3. *Maintain focus on the agenda throughout the meeting*.   Unless leaders maintain sharp focus, meetings have a tendency to drift away from the intended agenda. When the meeting digresses significantly, the leader needs to redirect the group. "I think we're getting away from the real issue here. Sam, what do you think about. . ." can serve to reinforce the original agenda. A meeting leader must engage in communication behaviors that help to stimulate and to maintain group interest and attention. Effective meeting leaders use language that is precise yet understandable. They speak loudly and clearly (not in a mumble), and they avoid distracting gestures or movements.

4. *Listen to others*.   Effective meeting leaders are active, attentive listeners. Listening involves more than merely hearing what others say; it involves incorporating the meaning of messages. University of Minnesota professor Ralph Nichols pioneered the research on effective listening. Nichols suggests several strategies for improving listening skills.[26]

- *Focus on the content of the message, not the speaker's delivery*. Information is contained in the symbols the speaker uses.

Although certain habits or mannerisms such as pacing, pushing up eyeglasses repeatedly, or the excessive use of powerless forms of language such as "ah" or "um" can be distracting, the content of the message should be the most important focal point. Effective listeners focus on the information that is important and useful while ignoring distracting elements of delivery.

- *Listen for ideas, not just facts.* Good listeners focus on the big picture. Effective listeners don't just collect facts; they listen for concepts. If you miss some of the facts but understand the main idea, it is easy to conduct research to fill in the missing details. On the other hand, a listener who tries to incorporate all the facts may miss the larger and more important issues being addressed. It's always much more difficult to fill in the big picture later.

- *Don't let yourself get distracted.* Avoid distractions by any means possible. If you are distracted by a talkative group member, get up and move. If you are hungry, bring a snack with you to the meeting. Don't let external or internal distractions get in the way of your listening. One of the most common distractions experienced in meetings is complex or technical information. Many listeners simply tune out when information becomes difficult to comprehend; effective listeners concentrate even harder. A good listener works to avoid all forms of distraction that interfere with effective listening.

- *Be open minded.* Most of us respond instantly when someone says something we disagree with. We may not blurt out our rebuttal immediately, but we almost always begin thinking of our response. The problem with this habit is that it interferes with our ability to listen intently to the other person's point of view. Effective listeners are open minded and don't overreact to divergent points of view.

- *Use thought speed to your advantage.* Various researchers have suggested that we think from four to twenty times as fast as we speak.[27] This capability sometimes causes us to lose concentration while listening—everyone daydreams! Effective listeners use the ability to think more rapidly to their advantage. They use internal thought processes to anticipate the next point, to summarize or paraphrase information that has already been presented, or to focus on nonverbal behaviors such as facial and body movements that help to illustrate key ideas.

5. ***Involve all participants***. Effective meeting leaders encourage the involvement of all participants. Meetings are designed as a forum for the exchange of information and ideas. Remember, a leader calls a meeting because he or she is eager to receive immediate information. Don't stifle participants. Always encourage an atmosphere in which discussion flourishes.

Developing Team Building Skills

As we noted earlier, two of the distinguishing features of groups are commonality of purpose and interdependence. Effective groups function as a team. A team is much more than a collection of individuals; it is an entity, in and of itself. Successful group leaders work to build a team climate.

Carl Larson and Frank LaFasto spent nearly three years studying more than seventy-five diverse teams.[28] Larson and LaFasto interviewed key members of these teams including the leader of the Boeing 747 project, a person who served on several presidential cabinets, members of cardiac surgery teams, the founder of the U. S. Space Command, a member of a Mount Everest climbing expedition, and several players from the 1966 Notre Dame championship football team. From their interviews, Larson and LaFasto identified the following eight strategies which they believe are essential to effective team performance.

1. ***Establish clear and inspiring team goals***. Effective teams are clearly focused on goals which maximize team outcomes. Further, these goals serve to inspire the team to perform at peak levels. The team leader is primarily responsible for defining and articulating goals and for motivating followers. Team failure can be caused by a lack of clarity in the identification of a team agenda, the loss of focus from the agenda, or from distractions associated with individual demands at the expense of the group.

2. ***Maintain a results-oriented team structure***. Within effective teams, each member clearly understands his or her role in the overall successful functioning of the group. Further, team members are accountable for their behavior in all situations. Every member of a successful team knows what is expected and takes responsibility for making sure tasks are done correctly. Members of a surgical team, for example, all play an important role in the overall success of an operation. The anesthesiologist monitors the patient's breathing, the nurse prepares the instruments, and the surgeon performs the procedure. Each member of the team must

perform his or her task in concert with others in order to achieve a successful outcome.

Communication within results-oriented teams is open and honest. Effective team leaders communicate in a highly democratic manner. (You may want to refer back to Chapter 2 to reacquaint yourself with the qualities of the democratic leadership communication style.) Information is easily accessible and questions and comments are always welcomed from all members of the group.

Effective team leaders provide frequent evaluation and feedback to members. Identifying strengths and weaknesses of group members is necessary in order to reward excellence and to suggest strategies for improving deficiencies.

Finally, results-oriented teams base their decisions on sound factual data. Although "gut" feelings and hunches may produce positive results on occasion, successful decision making is based on objective criteria.

3. *Assemble competent team members*. Effective teams are comprised of competent team members. Both technical and interpersonal competencies are essential to team success. Technical competence refers to the knowledge, skills, and abilities relevant to the team's goals. Interpersonal competence relates to the ability of team members to communicate feelings and needs, to resolve conflict, and to think critically. Hewlett Packard has a reputation as one of the most innovative organizations in the electronics industry. One reason for the company's success is that Hewlett Packard hires only the most highly regarded research and development engineers.

4. *Strive for unified commitment*. The members of successful teams are wholly committed. Members feel an almost spiritual bond with the team. In many cases, team goals rate as the highest priority of team members, even coming before family for some. Leaders seeking this type of unified commitment must work to create a team identity. Team identity is enhanced when team members are involved in decision-making, policy implementation, and analysis. Indeed, involvement begets commitment. The President's Cabinet and staff are examples of unified teams with a collective identity. Members of these groups feel such a strong sense of duty that they are literally on-call to handle any crisis which may arise.

5. *Provide a collaborative climate*. Cooperation and teamwork are essential to allow teams to function smoothly. Teams that work well together perform most effectively. Trust is the key ingredient in teamwork. An open, honest environment in which team members trust and respect one another promotes collaboration.

6. ***Encourage standards of excellence***. Successful teams have high expectations regarding outcomes. These standards of excellence define acceptable performance. High standards mean hard work, and top performing teams spend a great deal of time preparing and practicing. They are ready for virtually any contingency.

The cockpit crew of United Airlines Flight 232 performed an almost impossible task in July, 1989. Although over one hundred passengers died during the crash landing at the Sioux City, Iowa airport, aviation experts lauded the crew for maneuvering the plane under the most extreme emergency—a complete failure of the hydraulic system. Fortunately for the surviving 185 passengers, the crew expected that they could do the impossible.

Standards of excellence are found everywhere within successful teams. Individual team members expect excellence from themselves and others. Perhaps most importantly, the leaders of highly effective teams demand that a standard of excellence be upheld. They will accept nothing less from themselves or the team.

7. ***Furnish external support and recognition***. External support in the form of material or social rewards is important to the success of teams. These rewards alone do not guarantee success, but the absence of any form of external recognition or support appears to be detrimental to a team's overall effectiveness. According to Larson and LaFasto, recognition and support are most critical when the team is performing either extremely well or extremely poorly.

8. ***Apply principled leadership***. The leaders of effective teams employ transformational leadership techniques. As discussed in Chapter 3, the transformational leader is creative, interactive, visionary, empowering, and passionate. Larson and LaFasto found that three qualities seemed most important to effective team leadership: (a) establishing a vision; (b) creating change; and (c) unleashing talent.

Effective team leaders have a clear vision for the team. The specific actions required to achieve this vision are clearly presented to team members. Further, this vision represents an inspiring and desirable goal for the group.

Effective leaders also create change. Change is essential to improving and progressing. Effective team leaders encourage team members to seek out new and better ways to perform tasks and solve problems. Successful team leaders are not completely satisfied with the present level of achievement; they are always looking to the next challenge. (For one example of a team with principled leadership, see Figure 6.3.)

Figure 6.3   Case Study

Teamwork in Action—the Rogers Commission

The January 28, 1986 explosion of the Challenger space shuttle which killed six astronauts and schoolteacher Christa McAuliffe was one of the most traumatic events in recent American history. Millions (including many children who wanted to see the first teacher launched into space) watched the accident on live television; millions more saw tapes of the crash replayed over and over on local and national news broadcasts. Shortly after the tragedy, President Reagan appointed a commission to determine the cause of the explosion and to suggest ways to prevent future accidents. Former secretary of state William Rogers headed the thirteen member task force which was given four months to complete its task.

During the course of its investigation, the Rogers Commission compiled fifteen thousand pages of transcript and sixty-three hundred documents. After shifting through the evidence, the team concluded that failure of the 0-ring seals on the rocket booster caused the crash. The seals were identified as a serious safety risk long before the crash occurred and engineers at Morton Thiokol, the manufacturer of the rocket booster, recommended against the Challenger launch because they weren't sure that the rings would seal in temperatures below 53 degrees Fahrenheit. To prevent future tragedies, the task force recommended that astronauts and contractors play a more important role in launch decisions and that astronauts have an escape system in case of accident. The work of the Commission was well received. One senator called the report "a model for presidential commissions for years to come."[1]

Many factors contributed to the team's success. First, team members were highly competent. Each was selected because of his/her scientific and technical expertise. The task force included two astronauts, a Nobel Laureate in physics and the developer of the Boeing 747. Second, group members put aside other commitments during the investigation and made the commission's work top priority. Third, the commission received widespread publicity and support for its efforts. Finally, William Rogers provided principled leadership for the team. Rogers never let the commission stray from its goal of finding the cause of the crash, and he believed that the future of the US space program depended on the work of the team. In addition, he empowered others by letting team members write the commission's final report. According to Rogers: "We called on everyone. We listened to everybody. And they wrote the report."[2]

Unfortunately, many of the factors that made the Rogers Commission so successful were missing from National Aeronautics and Space Administration prior to the Challenger accident. Once NASA had landed astronauts on the moon (the group's original goal), the space administration lost its sense of purpose. Lines of communication between engineers and managers broke down. Few agency directors stayed in office long enough to give the space program clear direction. NASA began exaggerating its accomplishments while underestimating the dangers of manned space flights in order to justify its budget requests. In the end, the agency's failure to work effectively as a unit led to the decision to launch the Challenger despite concerns about the 0-ring seals.

Discussion Questions

1. What problems did the Rogers Commission face in completing its investigation? How many of these problems are common to all teams?

2. What factor was most critical to the Commission's success?

3. What would you do to encourage effective teamwork at NASA?

[1] Magnuson, E. (1986, June 23). NASA takes a beating. *Time*, p. 32.
[2] Sidey, H. (1986, June 9). We have to be in space. *Time*, p. 18.

Additional Sources:

Eberhart, J. (1986, June 14). Challenger disaster: 'Rooted in history.' *Science News*, p. 372.

Feynman, R. P. (1988, February). An outsider's inside view of the Challenger inquiry. *Physics Today*, pp. 26-40.

Greenberg, D. (1986, September). Shuttle lessons. *Science Digest*, p. 18

Larson, C. E., & LaFasto, F. M. J. (1989). *Teamwork: What must go right/What can go wrong.* Newbury Park, CA: Sage.

Powell, S. (1986, June 16). Military agenda for NASA. *U.S. News and World Report*, pp. 14-16.

Finally, effective team leaders empower their followers by unleashing the talent of all members of the team. To use the words of Larson and LaFasto:

> The most effective leaders, as reported by our sample, were those who subjugated their ego needs in favor of the team's goals. They allowed team members to take part in shaping the destiny of the team's effort. They allowed them to decide, to make choices, to act, to do something meaningful. The result of this approach was the creation of the "multiplier effect." It created a contagion among team members to unlock their own leadership abilities.[29]

Summary

To start our study of group leadership, we defined a group from a communication perspective. Communication scholars are more interested in the interaction between group members than in the characteristics that members bring with them to the group. From a communication viewpoint, a small group has five essential elements: 1) a common purpose or goal, 2) interdependence, 3) mutual influence, 4) face to face communication, 5) a size of 3 to 20 members. Most groups deal with both the task of the group and the relationships between group members.

Groups evolve over time. Both group decisions and group leaders emerge as the group changes and matures. Natural group leaders (leaders who aren't appointed by someone outside the group) emerge by a process of elimination—the "method of residuals." Leader contenders are eliminated until only one remains. Ineffective groups have long struggles for leadership or never select a leader at all. To emerge as a leader, participate frequently in the group discussion, help keep the group on track, demonstrate your competence and help build a team. Another way to think of establishing leadership credentials is through idiosyncratic credits. Potential leaders build their credits in the eyes of other group members by demonstrating that they can help the group complete its task. They also conform to group norms. Followers expect more from natural than from appointed leaders. On the other hand, they are willing to give emergent leaders more freedom to act on behalf of the group.

Leading meetings is an important task for both emergent and appointed leaders. To provide effective leadership in meetings: 1) determine if a meeting is necessary before calling people together; 2) have a clear agenda; 3) maintain focus on the agenda throughout the meeting; 4) listen to others; and 5) involve all participants.

We ended the chapter by noting eight characteristics that researchers have identified as essential to effective team performance. These include: 1) clear and inspiring team goals; 2) results oriented team structure (clear roles and responsibilities, an effective communication network, frequent feedback, objective criteria); 3) competent team members; 4) unified commitment; 5) a collaborative climate; 6) standards of excellence; 7) external support and recognition; and 8) principled (transformational) leadership.

Application Exercises

1. Tape record a short segment of a group discussion. Then use the Bales IPA system to chart the task and social dimensions of the group's interaction.

2. Brainstorm a list of possible group norms. What norms do leaders always have to follow? Which can they violate?

3. Discuss the pattern of leadership emergence in a group to which you belong. First, describe the communication patterns that eliminated members from leadership contention. Next, describe the communication behaviors of the leader (if one emerged) that contributed to that person's success. Evaluate your own performance. Why did you succeed in your attempt to become the leader or why did you fail? Finally, choose the leadership pattern that describes your group from the four identified in the Minnesota studies. Write up your findings.

4. Add to the list of reasons why you should or should not hold a meeting. What happens if you have a meeting when there isn't a valid reason for doing so?

5. Think about groups with which you have been affiliated in the past. Which of these groups functioned as teams and which did not? Why?

Endnotes

[1] Burke, K. (1968). *Language as symbolic action*. Berkeley: University of California Press.

[2] Tompkins, P. K. (1982). *Communication as action: An introduction to rhetoric and communication*. Belmont, CA: Wadsworth, p. 8.

[3] Littlejohn, S. (1989). *Theories of human communication* (3rd ed.). Belmont, CA: Wadsworth, p. 202.

[4] Books surveyed include:

Beebe, S. A., & Masterson, J. T. (1986). *Communicating in small groups: Principles and practices* (2nd ed.). Glenview, IL: Scott Foresman.

Brilhart, J. K. (1982). *Effective group discussion* (4th ed.). Dubuque, IA: Wm. C. Brown.

Cragan, J. F., & Wright, D. W. (1980). *Communication in small group discussion: A case study approach*. St. Paul: West Publishing.

Fisher, B. A. (1980). *Small group decision making* (2nd ed.). New York: McGraw-Hill.

Patton, B. P., Giffin, K., & Patton, E. N. (1989). *Decision-making group interaction* (3rd ed.). New York: Harper & Row.

Wilson, G. L., & Hanna, M. S. (1986). *Groups in context: Leadership and participation in small groups*. New York: Random House.

[5] Patton, Giffin, & Patton, p. 4.

[6] Brilhart, p. 8.

[7] Bales, R. F. (1970). *Personality and interpersonal behavior*. New York: Holt, Rinehart and Winston; Bales, R. F., & Cohen, S. P. (1979). *Symlog: A system for the multiple level observation of groups*. London: Collier.

[8] Scheidel, T. M., & Crowell, L. (1964). Idea development in small discussion groups. *Quarterly Journal of Speech, 50*, 140-145.

[9] Fisher, B. A. (1970). Decision emergence: Phases in group decision making. *Speech Monographs, 37,* 53-66.

[10] Poole, M. S. (1983). Decision development in small groups II: A study of multiple sequences in decision making. *Communication Monographs, 50,* 206-232.; Poole, M. S. (1983). Decision development in small groups III: A multiple sequence model of group decision development. *Communication Monographs, 50,* 321-341.

[11] A summary of the results of these studies can be found in Bormann, E. G. (1975). *Discussion and group methods* (2nd ed.). New York: Harper & Row, Ch. 11. Leader emergence findings from this research program are also reported in Mortensen, C. D. (1966). Should the discussion group have an assigned leader? *The Speech Teacher, 15,* 34-41; and Geier, J. G. (1967). A trait approach to the study of leadership. *Journal of Communication, 17,* 316-323.

[12] Bormann, p. 261.

[13] Geier.

[14] See, for example:

Stang, D. J. (1973). Effect of interaction rate on ratings of leadership and liking. *Journal of Personality and Social Psychology, 27,* 405-408.

Regula, C. R. & Julian, J. W. (1973). The impact of quality and frequency of task contributions on perceived ability. *Journal of Social Psychology, 89,* 115-122.

Riecken, H. (1975). The effect of talkativeness on ability to influence group solutions of problems. In P. V. Crosbie (Ed.), *Interaction in small groups* (pp. 238-249). New York: Macmillan.

Daly, J. A., McCroskey, J. C., & Richmond, V. P. (1980). Relationship between vocal activity and perception of communication in small group interaction. *Western Journal of Speech Communication, 41,* 175-187.

[15] Schultz, B. (1980). Communicative correlates of perceived leaders. *Small Group Behavior, 11,* 175-191.

[16] Morris, C. G., & Hackman, J. R. (1969). Behavioral correlates of perceived leadership. *Journal of Personality and Social Psychology, 13,* 350-361. See also Ginter, G., & Lindskold, S. (1975). Rate of participation and expertise as factors influencing leader choice. *Journal of Personality and Social Psychology, 32,* 1085-1089.

[17] Schultz, B. (1979). Predicting emergent leaders: An exploratory study of the salience of communicative functions. *Small Group Behavior, 9,* 109-114.; Knutson, T. J., & Holdridge, W. E. (1975). Orientation behavior, leadership and consensus: A possible functional relationship. *Speech Monographs, 42,* 107-114.

[18] Hirokawa, R., & Pace, R. (1983). A descriptive investigation of the possible communication-based reasons for effective and ineffective group decision making. *Communication Monographs, 50,* 363-379.

[19] Baird, J. E. (1977). Some nonverbal elements of leadership emergence. *Southern Speech Communication Journal, 42,* 352-361.

[20] Hollander developed the idea of idiosyncratic credits over three decades. A summary of this research is found in *Leadership Dynamics: A practical guide to effective relationships.* New York: Free Press, 1978.

[21] This study is described in Jacobs, T. O. (1970). *Leadership and exchange in formal organizations.* Alexandria, VA: Human Resources Research Organization, Ch. 3.

[22] Hollander, p. 42.

[23] Poole, Decision development III.

[24] Hollander, pp. 60-64.

[25] Auger, B. Y. (1972). *How to run better business meetings*. New York: AMACOM.

[26] Nichols, R. G. (1961). Do we know how to listen? Practical helps in a modern age. *The Speech Teacher, 10*, 120-124.

[27] See, for example:

Foulke, E. (1971). The perception of time compressed speech. In D. L. Horton & J. J. Jenkins (Eds.), *The perception of language* (pp. 79-107). Columbus, OH: Charles E. Merrill.

Korba, R. J. (1986). *The rate of inner speech*. Unpublished doctoral dissertation, University of Denver.

Landauer, T. J. (1962). Rate of implicit speech. *Perceptual and Motor Skills, 15*, 646.

[28] Larson, C. E., & LaFasto, F. M. J. (1989). *Teamwork: What must go right/What can go wrong*. Newbury Park, CA: Sage.

[29] Larson & LaFasto, p. 128.

7

Leadership in Organizations

Leaders and organizations. It's hard to talk for very long about either topic without mentioning the other. Although this chapter is devoted to a discussion of leadership in organizations, we've already talked at length about organizational leadership in this book. Most of the leadership theories presented in Chapters 2 and 3, for example, were developed by organizational scholars. Blake and Mouton's Managerial Grid, Path-Goal Theory and Situational Leadership Theory, to name a few, have their origins in the study of organizational leadership behavior. Interest in organizational leadership is not surprising when you consider that leaders are extremely important to the health of organizations and that we spend a good deal of our time in organizations. Amitai Etzioni sums up the importance of organizations this way:

> We are born in organizations, educated by organizations, and most of us spend much of our lives working for organizations. We spend much of our leisure time paying, playing, and praying in organizations. Most of us will die in an organization and when the time comes for burial, the largest organization of all — the state — must grant official permission.[1]

In the pages that follow we will focus, first of all, on the nature of organizations and symbolic leadership. Then we'll examine the special challenges faced by females who seek to be organizational leaders. We'll end the chapter by exploring the ways that leader expectations can either increase or decrease follower performance.

Symbolic Leadership in the Organization

Communicating and Organizing

To understand the role of the leader in the organization, we first need to understand what organizations are from a communication standpoint. Organizational experts have traditionally taken a "container approach" to organizational life. Viewed this way, communication is something that takes place within an organization which acts as a container.[2] When the organization is seen as a container, communication then becomes only one of many variables which determine the health of the organization. Textbooks written from this perspective talk about how leaders design organizational structures, manage information, oversee tasks and relationships, use technology and so forth.

The container approach understates the role of communication in organizing. Communication is not contained within the organization.

Instead, communication **is** the organization. Earlier we noted that humans have the ability to create reality through their use of symbols. Nowhere is this more apparent than in the organizational context. Organizations are formed through the process of communication. As organizational members meet and interact, they develop a shared meaning for events. In recent years communication scholars and others have borrowed the idea of culture from the field of anthropology to describe how organizations create shared meanings. From a cultural perspective, the organization resembles a tribe. As the tribe meets together it develops its own language, hierarchy, ceremonies, customs and beliefs. Because each organizational tribe shares different experiences and meanings, each develops its own unique way of seeing the world or culture.[3] The perspective of every organization is different; anyone who joins a new company, governmental agency or nonprofit group quickly recognizes unique differences. New employees often undergo culture shock as they move into an organization with a different language, authority structure and attitude towards work and people.

   Core values—important convictions that shape organizational decisions and actions—are at the heart of the organizational culture. Values are often reflected in such slogans as "Like a Good Neighbor, State Farm Is There," "Own A Piece of the Rock" (Prudential Insurance), or "Fly the Friendly Skies" (United Airlines).[4] These highly publicized corporate philosophies merely reflect deeply rooted, less visible beliefs about what the organization thinks is important, how it views employees and so forth. In a fascinating analysis of the corporate culture of General Motors, Joanne Martin and Caren Siehl demonstrate how important values guide organizational behavior.[5] They identify three core values that shape life at General Motors. The first is respect for authority which leads top managers to treat executive assistants like servants. The second important value involves fitting in. Employees are nearly invisible as individuals, dressing alike and occupying offices of the same size and decor. The third core value is being loyal to the boss and the company as a whole. As a result, subordinates rarely challenge the decisions of their superiors.

Organizational Symbols

   To gain a clearer understanding of organizations as the product of communication, we first need to identify the functions of organizational symbols. According to Thomas Dandridge, organizational symbols serve the following functions:[6]

1. *Descriptive*. Symbols answer such questions as: "What's this organization like?" or "What's it like to work here?" Callous acts, such as firing employees without notice, describe organizations that are uncaring; considerate gestures like recognizing employees on their birthdays describe organizations that value their members.

2. *Energy Controlling*. Symbols play an important role in increasing, decreasing or channeling the energy of organizational participants. Effective leaders use slogans, meetings, conventions, promotions and other symbols to inspire members to reach goals such as higher sales quotas, reducing factory rejects or delivering pizzas in a half-hour or less. Other symbols may be used to discourage people, as in the case of the Marines who hope to screen out applicants by accepting only "a few good men." Organizational symbols also help vent strong emotions. For instance, teachers and students may release their anger towards each other through the annual faculty/student softball game.

3. *System Maintenance*. Often symbols create a sense of order and stability, as in the case of the annual sales banquet which "justifies" the organization's emphasis on sales contacts by honoring high sales producers. Rituals like passing basic training, fraternity pledging or the retirement party provide acceptable ways for individuals and the organization to change. Such tangible symbols as office location and size differentiate between the status of organizational members. In some companies, promotions mean moving up in the building as well as the organizational chart. A step up in rank in these organizations means a move to a more spacious office on a higher floor.

A single symbol can perform more than one function. Consider the faculty tenure process, for example. The granting of tenure designates what is important to the college and indicates what kinds of activities will be rewarded at the institution. Some schools reward teaching, others put more emphasis on research or service. Tenure can either increase or decrease the motivation of faculty. Faculty members may become discouraged, for instance, if tenure is given only to a few outstanding candidates. The tenure process reinforces the stability of the college by differentiating between high and low performers and by serving as a rite of passage from one organizational status to another. The fact that a symbol serves more than one function is a reminder that organizational symbols both reflect reality and create reality. Symbols are the tools that members use to generate the organization; they are also the visible outcomes or products of the organizing process.

Now that we've identified their functions, let's take a closer look at key organizational symbols. Experts pay particularly close attention to the following symbols when they analyze organizational culture.

1. *Language*. A good way to determine how an organization views itself and the world is by listening carefully to the language that organizational members use. Word choices both reflect and reinforce working relationships and values. One of the most revealing word choices is the selection of the simple word "we." The use of "we" reflects a willingness to share power and credit and to work with others (see Chapter 4). Terms that describe followers also provide important insights into organizational life. For example, using the term "associates" rather than "employees" suggests that all organizational participants are important members of the team. Workers at Disneyland are called "cast members" to emphasize that they have significant roles to play in the overall Disneyland performance for visitors. Contrast these positive labels to the term "dog robber" that describes some executive assistants at General Motors. These subordinates are named after household servants who clean up scraps and thus rob family dogs of extra meals.[7]

Language serves all three of the functions we talked about earlier. Not only can we learn a lot about an organization by the way it talks, but that talk also directs energy and maintains the system. Language is a powerful motivator which focuses attention on some aspects of experience and away from others. Those who speak of customer service or quality workmanship ("At Ford, Quality Is Job 1") are generally more likely to provide good service and quality products. In addition, a common language binds group members together. To demonstrate this fact, brainstorm a list of terms that you frequently use at school and on the job. Many verbal symbols like "student union" or "all nighter" that you take for granted as a student might not be familiar to those at your workplace. On the other hand, some of the terms you use at work might be new to other students.

2. *Stories*. Organizational stories carry multiple messages. They reflect important values, inspire, vent emotions, describe what members should do and so forth. (For more information on how stories build group identity, refer back to the discussion of fantasy building in Chapter 6.) In many cases, organizational members are more likely to believe the stories they hear from coworkers than the statistics they hear from management.[8] Often stories deal with the actions of prominent people. For example, stories at the Fred Meyer company, a large food and merchandise retailer in the Northwest, center around the founder's frugality and commitment to customer service. One story describes how

Fred Meyer called a company distribution center to complain that employees were extravagant because they had placed an old couch, lamp and end table in the warehouse entryway. In another instance, employees tell of Meyer's visit to a store where he found jars of coffee stacked over six feet high on a shelf. This violated company policy which prohibited high stacks because they made products hard for customers to reach. The elderly Meyer used his cane to sweep all the jars on the top shelf to the floor where they shattered. This story had a great impact on employees because Meyer was so frugal. If Meyer was willing to lose money by breaking jars of coffee to make his point, then employees figured that he really must be serious about customer service.

3. ***Rituals, Rites and Routines***. Rituals, rites and routines involve repeated patterns of behavior like saying "hello" in the morning to everyone on the floor, an annual staff retreat or disciplinary procedures. Harrison Trice and Janice Beyer identify these common organizational rites:[9]

- *Rites of Passage*. These events mark important changes in roles and statuses. When joining the army, for instance, the new recruit comes in as a civilian but is stripped of past identity and converted into a soldier with a new haircut, uniform, and prescribed ways of speaking and walking. Sorority and fraternity pledges endure rites of passage in the form of initiation nights and hazing.

- *Rites of Degradation*. Some rituals are used to lower the status of organizational members, such as when a coach or top executive gets fired. These events are characterized by degradation talk which is aimed at discrediting the poor performer. Critics may claim, for example, that the coach couldn't get along with his players or that the executive was overly demanding.[10]

- *Rites of Enhancement*. Unlike rites of degradation, rites of enhancement raise the standing of organizational members. Giving medals to athletes, listing faculty publications in the college newsletter, and publicly distributing sales bonuses are examples of such rituals. The Mary Kay Cosmetic Company is one organization that makes effective use of enhancement rituals. At Mary Kay seminars, high performers are rewarded with jewelry, fur stoles and pink Cadillacs in front of cheering audiences. The pink Cadillac is a clear symbol of high status for the Mary Kay salesforce since this is the type of car that Mary Kay herself drives.

- *Rites of Renewal*. These rituals strengthen the current system. Many widely used management techniques like Management by

Objectives and Organizational Development are rites of renewal because they serve the status quo. Such programs direct attention toward employee evaluation, goal setting, long range planning and other areas that need improvement.

- *Rites of Conflict Reduction*. Organizations routinely use collective bargaining, task forces, and committees to resolve conflicts. Even though committees may not make important changes, their formation may reduce tension since they signal that an organization is trying to be responsive.

- *Rites of Integration*. Rites of integration tie subgroups to the large system. Annual stockholder meetings, professional gatherings and office picnics all integrate people into larger organizations.

The Nature of Symbolic Leadership

Viewing organizations as the product of symbol using suggests that organizational leaders play an important role in the creation of organizational meaning or culture. In particular, the organizational leader is actively involved in "symbolic leadership" by using symbols to determine the direction of the organization. In the first chapter we argued that there are important distinctions between managers and leaders, including the fact that leaders focus on the future while managers maintain the status quo. Many organizational leadership theories derived from the container approach to communication seem to prescribe managerial behaviors rather than leadership behaviors. The Path-Goal model is a case in point. According to this theory, leaders adopt directive, supportive, participative or achievement-oriented communication styles in order to increase the effectiveness of the group. We would argue that while the group may perform efficiently when the leader uses the right communication style, this efficiency could be wasted if the leader simply focuses on the status quo. What good is increasing production, for example, if there is no market for the product?

In contrast to the manager, the effective symbolic leader never loses sight of the fact that he or she is in the business of directing people's attention to future goals. At any given time, an organization can veer in many different directions. Even a successful company must decide on new products and services, react to new government regulations, decide to maintain or to change production methods and so on. Rosabeth Moss Kanter calls these choices "action possibilities."[11] A successful leader guides the organization down one particular path or, to use

Kanter's words, to one particular action possibility that meets both individual and collective needs.

Symbolic leaders concern themselves with much more than organizational charts, information management systems and all the other traditional subjects of management training. They also pay close attention to the key organizational symbols we described earlier—language, stories, and rituals—which play an important part in creating and reflecting organizational culture. Organizational psychologist Edgar Schein highlights the significant role that leaders play in the creation of organizational culture:

> Organizational cultures are created by leaders, and one of the most decisive functions of leadership may well be the creation, the management, and—if and when that may become necessary—the destruction of culture. Culture and leadership, when one examines them closely, are two sides of the same coin, and neither can really be understood by itself. In fact, there is a possibility—underemphasized in leadership research—that the *only thing of real importance that leaders do is to create and manage culture* and that the unique talent of leaders is their ability to work with culture.[12]

Schein notes that the responsibilities of symbolic leaders shift as the organization matures. The founder/owner of the organization is a "risk absorber" who provides stability and reduces the anxiety people feel when an organization is just starting out. A new organization often struggles with meeting payroll, developing a market niche, managing growth, etc. Founders also have the greatest impact on the values that an organization develops. The values they impart often stick with the organization throughout its life. Followers have a good deal of influence on the direction an organization takes, but "the initial shaping force" is the belief system and personality of the founder.[13] The seeds of future problems are often sown during the organization's initial stage of development. Not all cultures are consistent. For example, a founder/leader might emphasize teamwork but continue to make all major decisions. Other founders, like Steven Jobs who started Apple Computer, do not perform as effectively as leaders once the organization has been firmly established. Founder/leaders often lay the groundwork for future change by promoting people who will share some, but not all, of their values. Once the organization reaches its midlife and maturity, leaders (frequently someone other than the founder) become change agents who intervene to challenge cultural assumptions, reinforce key values, or create new symbols.

Becoming a Symbolic Leader

The type of symbolic leadership you provide will depend in part on your organization's stage of development. Since most of us join established organizations, we'll concentrate on your role as a symbolic change agent. There are three major reasons why you may need to introduce cultural change.

1. There is evidence to suggest that organizations with strong cultures, cultures that are widely known and shared by group members, are more productive. Tom Peters, Terrence Deal, Allen Kennedy, and others argue that members of organizations with widely recognized cultures are more committed, are more likely to make extra efforts to reach goals, and enjoy higher job satisfaction. These writers also suggest that if members understand the philosophy of the organization, they can quickly make decisions based on whether or not their actions will help their company or nonprofit group. In Chapter 1 we cited the example of the Procter and Gamble employee who bought all the mislabeled Jif peanut butter jars he found at the store. This worker bought the peanut butter because he knew that this would be the right thing to do according to the values of Procter and Gamble.

2. New values and practices may make the organization more productive. A number of companies have made dramatic turnarounds after adopting new values and procedures. Take the case of Harley Davidson, for example. The firm nearly went out of business because its motorcycles were so poorly made. The manufacturer regained its market share after giving product quality top priority and involving every employee in the quality control process. Gib Akin and David Hopelain contend that there is a "culture of productivity" that permeates successful companies of all kinds. Members of such organizations identify strongly with their jobs, work well in teams and feel that their efforts are important. In these settings, effective managers keep their focus on the job to be done and spell out the parts that workers play in the "drama" of work.[14]

3. Organizational survival may depend on cultural change. Many organizations need to develop cultures that foster innovation in order to remain competitive as the pace of change increases (see Figure 7.1). AT & T, for example, had to learn how to be a competitive communications company rather than a service oriented phone monopoly. Other organizations must cope with the forced integration of cultures brought about by mergers and acquisitions. The merger of the North American and Rockwell companies demonstrates just how difficult cultural integration can be. The companies appeared to be a perfect match.

Rockwell wanted new technology and products from research-oriented North American which, in turn, wanted Rockwell's manufacturing and marketing capabilities. The companies had trouble blending together at first. Rockwell's short term, profit/cost control orientation clashed with the relaxed atmosphere at North American. At North American, engineers concentrated on the long term development of ideas rather than quarterly profits. As a result, they paid less attention to controlling costs which was a major concern of Rockwell's management.[15]

Figure 7.1	Research Highlight

Innovation in the Organization

In his 1987 book, *Thriving on Chaos*, Tom Peters notes that some companies like People Express that were featured in his earlier books on organizational excellence have gone out of business. Others, such as IBM, have lost their competitive edge only to regain it in a matter of a few years. The pace of change is accelerating with the growth of international markets, the spread of the mass media and rapid technological developments. To survive, many organizations need to foster cultures that encourage innovation and change. This is not only true for businesses but also for nonprofit groups. Churches and synagogues frequently disband or move when one racial group moves out and another moves in. More effective congregations develop new ministries to serve the needs of new residents.

One extensive investigation of innovations in organizations was conducted by Rosabeth Moss Kanter of Harvard. Kanter looked at how 115 innovations ranging from x-ray machines to new office procedures developed in ten firms. In a book called *The Change Masters: Innovation for Productivity in the American Corporation* she summarizes her findings, describing both the characteristics of innovative organizations and the skills of successful organizational innovators.

Kanter classifies firms according to their degree of innovativeness. She labels innovative firms like Hewlett Packard, Polaroid, Wang and Honeywell as Integrative Action companies. She uses the term Segmentalist to describe less innovative corporations. The characteristics of each type of company are summarized below.

Segmentalist	Integrative Action
many separate departments	overlapping departments and functions
vertical communication	lateral communication
low trust	high trust
isolate problems in one division	problems and solutions cross divisional lines
oriented toward the past	future oriented

fear failure	expect future success based on past success
middle and upper managers maintain power	employees given freedom and power to tackle projects and problems
financial and informational resources centralized	money, space and information decentralized

In addition to a culture that fosters innovation, organizations need effective innovators. According to Kanter, successful innovators have a clear vision of what they would like the organization to do or be in the future. "Entrepreneurs are, above all, visionaries," she says. "They are willing to continue the single-minded pursuit of a clearly articulated vision, even when the line of least effort or resistance would make it easy to give up." (p. 239) Having a vision is not enough to make the innovation become a reality, however. Change masters are able to convince others to get behind something new, a product or procedure that may be very different from what the organization has known in the past. Kanter found that effective innovators employ participative/collaborative skills to shepherd the development of their ideas. They convince others to part with resources, build coalitions and teams, and are willing to share information and credit for their innovations.

Kanter pays particular attention to the role of symbols in innovation. At one point she notes:

> Innovation and change, I am suggesting, are bound up with the meanings attached to events and the action possibilities that flow from those meanings. But that very recognition—of the symbolic, conceptual, cultural side of change—makes it more difficult to see change as a mechanical process and extract the "formula" for producing it. (p. 281)

Kanter examines the changes that occur in stories about important organizational innovations to emphasize that innovation is a symbolic process. As an innovation progresses through the organization, the history of that innovation becomes distorted. The idea's originator becomes less important in the story and the group gains prominence because more people share in the ownership of the project. Many of the early actors and events are replaced by later figures and actions. Conflicts and other choices disappear from the narrative and the accidents and uncertainties which surround the origin of any innovation suddenly become clear strategies. In sum, the story changes to reflect what the organization wants to preserve. According to Kanter:

> Organizational change consists in part of a series of emerging constructions of reality, including revisions of the past, to correspond to the requisites of new players and new demands. . . . The art and architecture of change, then, also involves *designing reports about the past to elicit the present actions required for the future*. . . . (pp. 287-88)

Sources:
Kanter, R. M. (1983). *The change masters: Innovation for productivity in the American corporation*. New York: Simon and Schuster.
Peters, T. (1987). *Thriving on chaos*. New York: Borzoi/Alfred A. Knopf.

Although cultural change is often necessary, it is far from easy. Some organizational consultants suggest that changing organizational culture is an orderly, step by step process. This is not the case. Change is difficult because cultures are organized around deeply rooted beliefs and values. Innovation of any kind can be threatening since current symbols provide organizational and individual stability. However, following these four suggestions can help you guide the cultural change process.

1. *Begin With a Vision or Agenda*. By articulating vision, leaders begin to transform key values and assumptions and to create a strong organizational culture. This is a crucial first step because failure to articulate a realistic yet challenging vision can damage both leaders and followers. As Tom Peters and Nancy Austin point out, "Nothing is more demoralizing and ultimately useless than an unachievable vision."[16]

Warren Bennis and Burt Nanus suggest that vision development begins with listening.[17] Good leaders are great listeners. They are in constant touch with employees, scholars, planners, customers and others. The creation of visions also involves looking at the organization's past, present and future. Knowing your organization's past is important because it gives you a picture of the group's cultural development. You can save yourself a good deal of frustration by knowing the successes and failures of your predecessors. Having a clear grasp of your organization's present status will reveal strengths, resources and weaknesses and help you determine your organization's niche in the marketplace. Making projections into the future can identify changing market conditions, likely competitors, and economic and population trends.

2. *Focus Attention on Key Values*. Although organizational values are hard to change, leaders can often accomplish a great deal by persistently emphasizing those values that undergird the company philosophy or plan. If your vision emphasizes customer service, for example, then you need to focus the organization's attention on service activities. This focus begins with what you pay attention to, measure and control.[18] Your claim that service should be the company's first priority will not be taken seriously unless you as a leader perform service, honor good service and penalize those who fail to respond to customer needs. In this way, others are encouraged to act as you do, to share your meaning that good service is important and that service activities are critical. Some, like Ren McPherson of Dana Corporation, argue that paying attention is the key activity of leader/managers. In McPherson's words: "When you assume the title of manager, you give up doing honest work for a living. You don't make it, you don't sell it, you don't service it. What's left? Attention is all there is."[19] Compensation

programs also play an important role in reinforcing values. The best systems reward behaviors like quality workmanship and service which contribute to company goals.

3. ***Recreate Your Vision and Values in Others***. Effective leaders work to develop others who share the vision. Become a coach and teacher to followers, particularly to those who are directly underneath you on the organizational ladder. You can also instill organizational philosophy through formal training programs. Hewlett Packard estimates that one-third of its initial training session is devoted to discussing the "Hewlett Packard Way." Employee evaluation is partially based on how well workers adhere to the HP philosophy.

4. ***Make Maximum Use of Important Symbols***. Since language, stories and rituals all play a significant role in organizational culture, pay close attention to these elements. Start by changing the way that you and those around you talk. Begin with the terms that describe work and status relationships. Do you and your organization use the word "we" when discussing tasks and accomplishments? Are followers called subordinates/contingents or associates/team members/coworkers?

Next, consider creating new stories and changing old ones. John DeLorean was one leader who created a story as a way to bring about cultural change. DeLorean headed the Chevrolet division at General Motors before he started a controversial car company of his own. DeLorean objected to the deference to authority at GM. Organizational status at General Motors was measured in part by how many employees came to meet company executives at airports. DeLorean flew to New York and drove himself to a speaking engagement in order to demonstrate that followers needed to put less emphasis on status.[20] If you are faced with a negative story that is already part of the organizational culture (perhaps a tale of how management is insensitive to worker needs), try to determine the message of the story ("management doesn't care about workers") and work to change the behaviors that make the story believable.

Finally, focus on rituals. Nonessential rituals (those with little meaning for participants) can be dropped, essential rituals can be adapted to new purposes and new rituals can be created. For instance, the annual Christmas party that has been a source of discomfort can become an annual banquet in which the organization promotes cooperation and teamwork. Harrison Trice and Janice Beyer suggest that rites of passage and enhancement are the best ways to encourage change. Develop new ways to help organizational members pass from one status to the next and publicly celebrate the accomplishments of those who meet the new standards.[21]

The Gender Leadership Gap

Over the past century, the number of women occupying leadership positions in organizations has risen dramatically. In 1900, only one out of every twenty-five managerial positions was held by a woman. By 1987 one out of every three managers was female. The total number of women in the workforce has also increased significantly. When the century began, only 19% of all women were employed outside of the home. This percentage had tripled by the mid 1980s and will continue to increase throughout the 1990s.[22]

Despite these gains, a gender leadership gap still exists. Women at every level of the organization are at a disadvantage, earning 70 cents for every dollar earned by men. Males in the same occupations earn more than their female counterparts, and male dominated occupations have higher pay scales. Two-thirds of all managerial positions are still held by males and very few women have moved into top management jobs. In 1986, for example, only two of the top one thousand industrial and service companies had a woman chief executive. Many managerial women are close to the top positions in their organizations but can't reach them, creating what some researchers have labeled as the Glass Ceiling Effect.[23] (For another example of how the gender leadership gap has limited the influence of female organizational leaders, see Figure 7.2.)

The existence of the gender leadership gap raises a number of significant questions: 1) Are there differences in how males and females lead? 2) What factors hinder the emergence of women as organizational leaders? 3) How can the gender leadership gap be narrowed? To answer these questions, we'll begin by taking a look at what researchers have discovered about female and male leadership behavior.

Male and Female Leadership Behavior: Is There a Difference?

Some researchers report that male leaders receive higher leadership ratings than females. However, these investigators study gender leadership differences in organizational simulations or in other experimental settings. In such short term, artificial situations, gender differences are overstated because participants rely heavily on stereotypes which cast males in the leader role. The bias against female leaders breaks down when information about their performance in actual leadership situations becomes available. In studies of cadet leaders at the Air Force Academy, for example, cadets rated female leaders less favorably before they saw these women in action. After they had served with women leaders over

Figure 7.2   Case Study

The Gender Leadership Gap in Action

For the centennial edition of the *Wall Street Journal*, writers and editors compiled a list of outstanding business leaders in an article entitled "Ten for the Textbooks." To make the list, leaders had to meet two criteria: 1) they had to have transformed the way that America does business, and 2) their impact would have to be felt in the year 2089, the date of the paper's bicentennial. No women or minorities appear on the list, although Katherine Graham of the *Washington Post*, designer Liz Claiborne, Berry Gordy of Motown Records and An Wang of Wang Laboratories make honorable mention. The result is a list of white, largely middle-aged males. In alphabetical order, the Ten for the Textbooks are:

1. Lee Iacocca (Chrysler Corporation)
Iacocca is the best known business leader in America. He is always ready to face the public, whether it be through the press, on company advertising or before Congress. He takes personal responsibility for all of the successes and failures of the Chrysler Corporation. Prior to coming to Chrysler, Iacocca developed the Mustang at Ford.

2. Steven Jobs (Next Inc.)
Jobs and Steven Wozniak developed the Apple computer which brought computer technology within reach of the individual. Now at Next Inc., Jobs continues to emphasize that computers should be user friendly.

3. Henry Kravis (Kohlberg Kravis Roberts & Co.)
Kravis and his company pioneered leveraged buyouts in which firms use debt to buy control from their stockholders. Not only has this practice generated huge debts for companies involved in the buyouts, but a number of other companies have restructured to avoid such takeovers.

4. Peter Lynch (Fidelity Magellan Fund)
The Fidelity Magellan Fund grew to be the largest mutual fund in the world ($10 billion in assets) when it was directed by Lynch. He helped change the way that Americans invest their money. Now 25% of all U.S. families invest in mutual funds (up from 8% in 1980).

5. William G. McGowan (MCI Communications Corp.)
McGowan challenged the AT & T telephone monopoly and helped create competition in long-distance phone services. Under his leadership, MCI has become a major force in the long distance market.

6. Michael Milken
Milken was the first to use risky but high yielding junk bonds to help companies raise money for takeovers and other activities. While at Drexel Burnham Lambert Inc. he was instrumental in the merger or private takeover of such companies as Gulf Oil, Crown Zellerbach and Beatrice.

According to *Journal* writer Peter Steiger, "Not since J. P. Morgan has any financier influenced Wall Street and the nation the way Michael Milken has." He is now under indictment for securities crimes.

7. Frederick W. Smith (Federal Express Corp.)
Smith is credited with creating the air-express delivery industry. His company, Federal Express, handles a million shipments per day. Competitors have sprung up in Europe and Japan as well as in the United States.

8. Ted Turner (Turner Broadcasting System Inc.)
The owner of the most successful cable television programming company, Turner opened up competition in the broadcast television industry. The first national "superstation," the Cable News Network and Turner Network television are among his creations.

9. P. Roy Vagelos (Merck & Co.)
Dr. Vagelos (a physician) joined the Merck company and developed a line of drugs which slow the progress of disease by blocking enzymes. Other companies have adopted a similar approach which has made drug research more productive. Vagelos is representative of those who are able to use technology to create successful commercial products.

10. Sam Walton (Wal-Mart Stores Inc.)
Most retailers ignored smaller towns, but not Walton. He built a $25 billion a year retailing business by concentrating on smaller rural markets and by emphasizing employee teamwork.

Discussion Questions
1. Using the same criteria as the *Journal* editors, whom would you include on a list of outstanding business leaders?
2. If you were to compile a similar list of women and minority leaders, whom would you name? Why?

Source: Steiger, P. E. (1989, Centennial Edition). Ten for the textbooks. *Wall Street Journal*, p. B1.

a period of time, cadets gave females and males equal evaluations.[24] One review of seventeen gender leadership/management studies concluded that males and females engage in the same amount of consideration and task behavior and that they have equally satisfied subordinates.[25]

Perhaps the largest comparison of female vs. male managers and leaders was conducted by Susan Donnell and Jay Hall. These researchers surveyed 950 female and 966 male managers and matched them based on age, rank, organizational type and number of people supervised.[26] In a series of five studies they found only minor differences between women and men in managerial roles. According to Donnell and Hall: 1) males and females share the same managerial philosophies; 2) females have a higher motivational profile, seeking more opportunities for growth and challenge; 3) males and females employ the same participative leadership techniques; 4) females are less likely to share data with colleagues; 5) men and women have similar leadership styles.

Judging by the results of studies of women leaders serving in organizational positions, female leadership behavior does not significantly contribute to the creation of the gender leadership gap. To discover the origins of this gap, we must look elsewhere.

Creating the Gap: Barriers to Female Leaders

One way to visualize the development of the gender leadership gap is to think of women and men competing against each other on a track. Women run the 440 hurdles while the men run the 440 dash. With each hurdle, more women fall behind and the gap between male and female leadership aspirants widens. Most of the female competitors have been eliminated from contention by the time both genders reach the highest levels of leadership at the finish line. Here's a list of some of the hurdles that aspiring female leaders must overcome:

1. *Socialization*. Through the process of socialization some learn to see leadership as the province of males. Others learn that some professions are open to men but not women.

2. *Low self-confidence*. Low self-esteem makes some women reluctant to take risks and to strive for leadership positions.[27]

3. *Gender role stereotypes*. In the absence of other evidence, evaluators tend to give males higher leadership ratings. In addition, management positions are often defined in masculine terms. Employers tend to prefer males for these positions and male interviewers are more likely to hire males. The self-reinforcing nature of gender bias has prompted one expert on gender differences in management to conclude that "it is a wonder that change occurs in the level of segregation in any organization."[28]

4. *Tokenism*. If there are only a few women in the workplace, they face difficulties common to all who act as token representatives of their social groups.[29] Tokens are highly visible so they try hard to fit in, tend to be isolated and play stereotyped roles. Female tokens may even turn against other females as a result of adopting the views of the dominant male culture.

5. *Biased Evaluation*. When women succeed, their success is attributed to their effort, high motivation or luck. In contrast, evaluators attribute successful male performance to high ability. As a result, females often don't receive as much credit for good performance as men.[30]

6. *A Mentor Shortage*. Those women who finally make it to the top levels of management generally receive help in the form of sponsorship and tutoring. Unfortunately, there are few female mentors available to guide the development of prospective female leaders. While males can serve as mentors for females, they are frequently reluctant to do so. Those males who do sponsor females often have less power in their organizations and therefore they are less helpful to their proteges.[31]

Narrowing the Gap: Building Communication Competencies

Because women must overcome many hurdles in order to achieve leadership equality with men, a single strategy will not be sufficient to bridge the gender leadership gap. Changing perceptions about the roles of men and women in society, hiring larger numbers of women for leadership positions, breaking down gender segregation by occupation, using objective performance criteria, and developing mentor programs for women are just a few of the steps that can be taken. Yet, these strategies overlook the important role that communication competencies play in the organizational advancement of both women and men. In Chapter 1 we cited a survey in which personnel managers rated communication skills as the most important factors for gaining employment, performing successfully on the job and managing effectively. Women must develop these communication skills if they want to emerge as organizational leaders. In addition, superiors must recognize that women possess these skills.

In a pair of studies, Pamela Shockley-Zalabak and Constance Staley surveyed female professionals and their immediate supervisors to determine 1) the relationship between communication competence and organizational achievement and 2) if women professionals and their supervisors agree as to how competent they really are.[32] The investigators found a strong correlation between communication competencies and career success. When supervisors gave high marks to professional women on such skills as exhibiting leadership and diagnosing organizational problems, these women were promoted more often. However, the professionals and their supervisors did not agree on which skills the professionals possessed and which they needed to develop.

The professionals gave themselves higher marks than did their bosses on skills ranging from listening and interviewing to delegating authority and managing conflict. These findings suggest that while women may see themselves as competent, their supervisors (the people most directly responsible for judging their performance and recommending promotion) may evaluate their abilities much differently. Developing communication competencies is one way to overcome the hurdles that create the gender leadership gap. For this strategy to succeed, women must make sure that their superiors acknowledge their communication abilities.

The Power of Expectations: The Pygmalion Effect

What a leader expects is often what a leader gets. This makes the communication of expectations one of a leader's most powerful tools. Our tendency to live up to the expectations placed on us is called the Pygmalion Effect after a prince in Greek mythology. Prince Pygmalion created a statue of a beautiful woman whom he named Galatea. After the figure was complete, he fell in love with his creation. The god Venus took pity on the poor prince and brought Galatea to life. The Pygmalion Effect has been studied in a number of settings. Consider the following examples of the power of expectations in action:

- Patients often improve when they receive placebos because they believe they will get better.
- The expectations of teachers can influence the test and IQ scores of students. The most widely publicized investigation of the Pygmalion Effect in education was conducted by Robert Rosenthal and Lenore Jacobson who randomly assigned students in a San Francisco area elementary school to a group labeled as intellectual "bloomers." These investigators told teachers to expect dramatic intellectual growth from these students during the school year. The "bloomers" made greater gains on intelligence tests and reading scores than the other children.[33]
- Military personnel perform up to the expectations of their superiors. At an Israeli army training base, for example, instructors were told that trainees had high, regular or unknown command potential. The high potential soldiers (who really had no more potential than the other trainees and who were *not* told that they were superior) outperformed the members of the other groups, were more satisfied with the training course, and were more motivated to go on for

further training.[34] In another investigation conducted in the US Navy, the performance of problem sailors improved significantly after they were assigned to mentors and given a special training seminar designed to promote personal growth.[35]

- The expectations of researchers can influence animal behavior. In one experiment, students were told that half of the rats were "maze bright" while the other half were "maze dull." The allegedly dull rats refused to start the maze 29% of the time while the supposedly smart rats only refused 11% of the time. The explanation? Experimenters who anticipated better performance from their bright rats got what they expected because they were more relaxed and thus handled their animals more often and with more care.[36]

As we can see, expectations can be powerful motivators no matter what the specific context. In addition, patterns created through expectations tend to persist. David Berlew and Douglas Hall examined the careers of two groups of AT & T managers and found that new managers performed best if they worked for supervisors who had high but realistic expectations.[37] These new employees internalized positive attitudes and standards and were entrusted with greater responsibilities. Six years later they were still highly productive. On the other hand, managers who worked for bosses who expected too much or too little performed poorly throughout the test period. These workers either failed to develop high standards or didn't get recognition for the work that they did complete. As a result, they may have decided to perform at minimal levels. Berlew and Hall conclude that the first twelve to eighteen months are critical to the career success of any new employee. Patterns set during this initial period often continue throughout an employee's tenure at a company.

Two important variables appear to moderate the impact of leader expectations. The first is the self-esteem of the leader. Even when placed with subordinates with superior abilities, some leaders fail to communicate positive expectations because they lack confidence in their own abilities. One study of sales managers at a Metropolitan Life Insurance agency demonstrates the important relationship between leader self-confidence and the Pygmalion Effect. Sales agents were randomly divided into high, average, and poor performance groups. Sales of the high performer unit dramatically increased while sales of the weakest unit declined and members dropped out. Significantly, the performance of the "average" group went up because the leader of this group refused to accept the fact that he or his sales force were any less capable than the supposedly outstanding sales unit. In summarizing the results of this study, J. Sterling Livingston (who appears to think of managers as males) writes:

> . . . superior managers have greater confidence than other managers in their own ability to develop the talents of their subordinates. Contrary to what might be assumed, the high expectations of superior managers are based primarily on what they think about themselves — about their own ability to select, train, and motivate their subordinates. . . . If he [the manager] has confidence in his ability to develop and stimulate them to high levels of performance, he will expect much of them and will treat them with confidence that his expectations will be met. But if he has doubts about his ability to stimulate them, he will expect less of them and will treat them with less confidence.[38]

A second variable that moderates the influence of the Pygmalion effect is the level of expectations. As we saw in the case of the AT & T managers, expectations must be high but realistic. Setting standards too low does not challenge the abilities of followers since there is little satisfaction to be gained by fulfilling minimal expectations. Yet, setting expectations too high guarantees failure and may start a negative self-fulfilling prophecy. Having failed once, the organizational member expects to fail again. Some theorists suggest setting goals that have a 50/50 chance of being met. That way success is not guaranteed nor is it out of reach.[39]

To summarize, followers often perform up to expectations, whether it be in the classroom, the military or the corporation. Leaders must have confidence in their own abilities and set realistic goals for followers in order for the positive Pygmalion Effect to operate. However, the confidence that leaders have in themselves and their followers will have no impact on group behavior unless group members know that this confidence exists. Leaders must clearly communicate their expectations to followers. With this in mind, we turn now to a description of how expectations are communicated.

The Communication of Expectations

Telling others that they have ability, offering them compliments and saying that you expect great things from them are some direct ways to communicate high expectations. Subordinates also get the message that leaders have high or low expectations of them even when expectancies are not explicitly stated, however. Expectations are communicated through four important channels.[40]

1. *Climate*. Climate refers to the type of social and emotional atmosphere leaders create for followers. When dealing with people whom they like, leaders act in a supportive, accepting, friendly and encouraging manner. Nonverbal cues play a major role in creating climates. Communication experts John Baird and Gretchen Wieting recommend that organizational managers use nonverbal behaviors that emphasize concern, respect, equality and warmth while avoiding behaviors that communicate coolness, disinterest, superiority and disrespect.[41] See Figure 7.3 for a summary of nonverbal cues that communicate positive expectations.

2. *Input*. In an organizational setting, positive expectations are also communicated through the number and type of assignments and projects given employees. Those expected to perform well are given more responsibility which creates a positive performance spiral. As employees receive more tasks and complete them successfully, they gain self-confidence and the confidence of superiors. As a result, these star performers are given additional responsibilities and are more likely to meet these new challenges as well.

3. *Output*. Those expected to reach high standards are given more opportunities to speak, to offer their opinions or to disagree. Superiors pay more attention to these employees when they speak and offer more assistance to them when they need to come up with solutions. This is similar to what happens in the classroom where teachers call on "high achievers" more than "low achievers," wait less time for low achievers to answer questions, and provide fewer clues and follow-up questions to low achievers.[42]

4. *Feedback*. Supervisors give more frequent positive feedback when they have high expectations of employees, praising them more often for success and less often for failure. In addition, managers provide these subordinates with more detailed feedback about their performance. However, superiors are more likely to praise minimal performance when it comes from those labeled as poor performers. This reinforces the perception that supervisors expect less from these followers.

The Galatea Effect

Our focus so far has been on the ways that leaders communicate their expectations to followers. Once communicated, these prophecies can have a significant impact on subordinate performance. The same effects can be generated by expectations that followers place on themselves, however. Earlier we noted the example of Israeli army trainees who performed up to instructor expectations. In a follow up

Figure 7.3

Nonverbal Cues Which Communicate Positive Expectations

Nonverbal Category	Positive Behaviors
Time	Don't keep employees waiting, give adequate time, make frequent contacts.
Setting	Meet in pleasant, attractive surroundings and avoid using furniture as a barrier.
Physical Proximity	Sitting or standing close to an employee promotes warmth and decreases status differences.
Gestures	Make frequent use of open palm gestures.
Head Movements	Use head nods, but do not indicate suspicion by cocking the head or tilting it backward while the other person is speaking.
Facial Expression	Smile frequently.
Eye	Make frequent, direct eye contact.
Voice	Combine pitch, volume, quality and rate to communicate warmth. Avoid sounding bored or disinterested.

Source: Baird, J., & Wieting, G. K. (1979, September). Nonverbal communication can be a motivational tool. *Personnel Journal*, pp. 607-610 + .

experiment, a psychologist told a random group of military recruits that they had high potential to succeed in a course. These trainees did as well as those who had been labeled as high achievers by their instructors. In this case, the trainees became their own "prophets."[43] The power of self-expectancies has been called the Galatea Effect in honor of Galatea, the statue who came to life in the story of Pygmalion.

A model of the relationship between supervisor and self-expectations is found in Figure 7.4. In the Pygmalion Effect, the chain starts with the supervisor's expectancy which influences his/her leadership behavior (Step 1). These behaviors then shape the expectations that followers have of themselves (Step 2), resulting in either higher or lower motivation and performance (Steps 3 and 4). Subordinate performance then completes the chain because employee behavior raises or lowers the supervisor's expectations for future assignments (Step 5). However, stages 1 and 2 are eliminated in the Galatea Effect. Subordinates perform better if they set high standards for themselves. When they reach their goals, they expect to achieve even more in the future (Step 6).

There are other possible variations of the expectation model. For example, leaders (like the psychologist in the army experiment described above) may create self-expectancies in followers which continue without further reinforcement from leaders. Leaders may also reinforce the Galatea Effect. Take the case of the supervisor who is new to the group. He or she may note the superior performance of employees who set high standards for their own work and treat those individuals as high potential employees.

Conclusions: Putting Pygmalion to Work

Since expectations have such a powerful influence on performance, we need to know how to put the power of Pygmalion to work. As leaders, we often aren't conscious of the expectations we have for others or we don't realize how we communicate these expectations. We may assume that we treat all followers alike. Nevertheless, we've already noted that there are significant differences in how managers, teachers and others treat high and low performers. Take inventory of how you communicate expectations using the four channels we discussed earlier: climate, input, output, and feedback. Analyze your nonverbal communication according to the chart in Figure 7.3. Then take a look at how assignments are distributed, how frequently some employees are given the opportunity to offer their opinions, whom you help most often and the type of feedback you provide. Finally, identify the steps that you can take to communicate high expectations to your subordinates and try to put these behaviors into action.

In addition to taking steps as an individual leader to "harness" the power of Pygmalion, there are strategies that your organization can use to institute a positive expectation-performance cycle. Because the patterns of high expectations/high success and low expectations/low success are established early in organizational careers, try to insure that new employees work under effective managers. Often new subordinates are exposed to the worst leadership the organization has to offer—inexperienced supervisors or those who are trapped in low level management positions because of poor past performance. Try instead to place new workers with the best leaders in the organization, those with high self-confidence who set stringent yet realistic goals. The positive patterns new subordinates establish under the guidance of these

Figure 7.4

A Model of the Self-Fulfilling Prophecy at Work

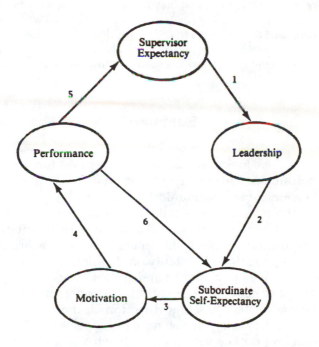

Source: Eden, D. (1984). Self-fulfilling prophecy as a management tool: Harnessing Pygmalion. *Academy of Management Review, 9*, 64-73. Used by permission.

supervisors will pay off for both the individual and the organization for years to come. Consider moving established low performers to new situations where they can break the influence of old, negative self-fulfilling prophecies.

We can also put the power of Pygmalion to work as followers. Dov Eden argues that as subordinates we can protect ourselves from the force of negative leadership expectations by being aware of how such expectancies operate. We can also encourage supervisors to have high expectations of us by meeting and exceeding standards. In essence, this approach uses the Galatea Effect to create positive expectations in leaders. Eden summarizes subordinate use of expectations this way:

Subordinates could be taught how to behave in a manner that would evoke more effective leadership from their supervisors. This would be harnessing Pygmalion in reverse, subordinates "treating" their supervisors in such a way that they mold their supervisory behavior in accordance with subordinate desires. Similarly, awareness of interpersonal expectancy effects might help immunize certain subordinates against the debilitating effects of poor leadership from supervisors who harbor low expectations toward them.[44]

Summary

In this chapter we looked at leaders in the organizational context. We began by defining organizations as the product of communication. As organizational members communicate, they develop shared meanings which form the organization's unique way of seeing the world—an organization's culture. Organizational symbols help describe the nature of the organization, control the energy levels of organizational participants, and maintain stability and order. Key organizational symbols include language, stories and rituals. Since the organization is the product of symbol using, organizational leaders are really symbolic leaders who use symbols to set the direction for the group. If you want to exercise symbolic leadership you need to: 1) create a vision or agenda, 2) focus attention on key values through what you do, measure and control, 3) recreate your vision and values in others by coaching and teaching, and 4) make effective use of important organizational symbols.

We focused next on female organizational leaders. The percentage of women in leadership positions shrinks with every step up the organizational ladder, creating a gender leadership gap. This gap is not the result of differences in male and female leadership behavior, but stems from a series of hurdles which eliminate women from leadership contention. These barriers include the socialization process, low self-confidence, gender role stereotypes, tokenism, biased evaluation practices, and a lack of mentors. The development of communication competencies is one way to narrow the gender leadership gap. However, these competencies must be recognized by superiors if they are to help women advance.

In the final section we described how expectations shape motivation and performance. The Pygmalion Effect refers to our tendency to live up to the expectations of others. Generally, the higher the expectancy, the higher the performance. Leaders communicate expectations through 1) climate (social and emotional atmosphere); 2) input (the number and type of assignments they give to employees); 3) output (the number of opportunities that followers have to voice opinions); 4) feedback (the frequency of praise or criticism). To create a high expectations/high performance cycle, effective leaders build a warm climate, delegate important responsibilities, solicit ideas and provide frequent positive feedback. Self-expectations (called the Galatea Effect) also influence performance. Followers who set high standards for themselves are more productive.

Application Exercises

1. Write a one sentence statement that summarizes the vision/goal/ plan you have for your life and/or career. Now evaluate the vision or philosophy of your school or employer. How well does your vision match the organization's? What changes would you suggest for the direction of the organization or for your group (division, department, etc.) within the organization? Share your vision statement and evaluation in a group.

2. As a major research paper, conduct your own organizational culture analysis. Be sure to identify the following:
   - the role of the founder and current leadership
   - core values
   - language
   - myths and stories
   - rituals
   - tangible symbols
   - efforts at change

   After summarizing the organization's culture, analyze its strengths and weaknesses. Is there a good match, for example, between the organization and its business environment? How productive are members? Will attempts at change be successful?

3. Some scholars are optimistic that the gender leadership gap will diminish as more women enter the workforce and move up the organizational ladder. Others are more pessimistic, believing that the number of women in leadership positions has stabilized and that gender stereotypes will keep women from progressing further. What do you think?

4. Form a small group and brainstorm ways that teachers, managers and others communicate both low and high expectations. Report your findings during class discussion.

5. Develop a strategy for communicating high expectations to someone you lead but do not like. Analyze what expectations you have for that person now and how you communicate these expectancies. Identify steps that you can take to create a positive Pygmalion Effect. Is it possible to modify your expectations? To mask your negative feelings? Write up your conclusions.

Endnotes

[1] Etzioni, A. (1964). *Modern organizations*. Englewood Cliffs, NJ: Prentice-Hall, p. 1.

[2] Hawes, L. C. (1974). Social collectivities as communication: Perspectives on organizational behavior. *Quarterly Journal of Speech, 60,* 497-502.

[3] Pacanowsky, M. E., & O'Donnell-Trujillo, N. (1983). Organizational communication as cultural performance. *Communication Monographs 50,* 126-147.

[4] Deal, T. E., & Kennedy, A. A. (1982). *Corporate cultures: The rites and rituals of corporate life.* Reading, MA: Addison-Wesley.

[5] Martin, J., & Siehl, C. (1983). Organizational culture and counterculture: An uneasy symbiosis. *Organizational Dynamics, 12,* 52-64.

[6] Dandridge, T. C. (1983). Symbols' function and use. In L. R. Pondy, P. J. Frost, G. Morgan, & T. C. Dandridge (Eds.), *Organizational symbolism* (pp. 69-79). Greenwich, CT: JAI Press.; Dandridge, T. C., Mitroff, I., & Joyce, W. (1980). Organizational symbolism: A topic to expand organizational analysis. *Academy of Management Review, 5,* 77-82. Many of the examples used in this section of the chapter come from the work of Dandridge and his associates.

[7] Martin & Siehl.

[8] Martin, J., & Powers, M. E. (1983). Truth or corporate propaganda: The value of a good story. In L. R. Pondy, P. J. Frost, G. Morgan, & T. C. Dandridge (Eds.). *Organizational Symbolism* (pp. 93-107). Greenwich, CT: JAI Press.

[9] Trice, H. M., & Beyer, J. M. (1984). Studying organizational cultures through rites and ceremonials. *Academy of Management Review, 9,* 653-669.

[10] For an in-depth look at how managers use degrading talk, see:
O'Day, R. (1974). Intimidation rituals: Reactions and reforms. *Journal of Applied Behavioral Science, 10,* 373-386.

[11] Kanter, R. M. (1983). *The change masters: Innovation for productivity in the American corporation.* New York: Simon and Schuster, p. 281.

[12] Schein, E. H. (1985). *Organizational culture and leadership.* San Francisco: Jossey Bass, p. 2.

[13] Schein, p. 320. For additional information on the role of organizational founders, see: Schein, E. H. (1983). The role of the founder in creating organizational culture. *Organizational Dynamics, 12,* 13-28; and Pettigrew, A. M. (1979). On studying organizational cultures. *Administrative Science Quarterly, 24,* 570-582.

[14] Akin, G., & Hopelain, D. (1986). Finding the culture of productivity. *Organizational Dynamics, 14*, 19-32.

[15] Schwartz, H., & Davis, S. (1981). Matching corporate culture and business strategy. *Organizational Dynamics, 10*, 30-48.

[16] Peters, T., & Austin, N. (1985). *A passion for excellence: The Leadership Difference.* New York: Warner Books, p. 312.

[17] Bennis, W. & Nanus, B. (1985). *Leaders: The strategies for taking charge.* New York: Harper & Row.

[18] Schein. *Organizational culture and leadership*, Ch. 10.

[19] Peters & Austin, p. 337.

[20] Martin & Siehl.; For more information on the relationship between stories and cultural change see: Wilkins, A. L. (1984). The creation of company cultures: The role of stories and human resource systems. *Human Resource Management, 23*, 41-60.

[21] Trice, H. M., & Beyer, J. M. (1985). Using six organizational rites to change culture. In R. H. Kilmann, M. J. Saxton, & R. Serpa (Eds.). *Gaining control of the corporate culture* (pp. 370-399). San Franciso: Jossey Bass.; See also: Knittel, R. E. (1974). Essential and nonessential ritual in programs of planned change. *Human Organization, 33*, 394-396.

[22] Statistics on women in the workforce are taken from Powell, G. N. (1989). *Women and men in management.* Beverly Hills, CA: Sage.; and Sabin, R. (1989, November 20). Women's growing role in the workplace. *San Francisco Chronicle*, p. C1 +

[23] Morrison, A. M., White, R. P., & Van Velsor, E. (1987). *Breaking the glass ceiling: Can women reach the top of America's largest corporations?* Reading, MA: Addison Wesley.

[24] Adams, J., Rice, R., & Instone, D. (1984). Follower attitudes toward women and judgments concerning performance by female and male leaders. *Academy of Management Journal, 27*, 636-643.

See also:

Osborn, R. N., & Vickers, W. M. (1976). Sex stereotypes: An artifact in leader behavior and subordinate satisfaction analysis? *Academy of Management Journal, 19*, 439-449.

Magaree, E. I. (1969). Influence of sex roles on the manifestation of leadership. *Journal of Applied Psychology, 53*, 377-382.

[25] Dobbins, G., & Platz, S. (1986). Sex differences in leadership: How real are they? *Academy of Management Review, 11*, 118-127.

[26] Donnell, S. M., & Hall, J. (1980). Men and women as managers: A significant case of no significant difference. *Organizational Dynamics, 8*, 60-77.

[27] Instone, D., Major, B., & Bunker, B. B. (1983). Gender, self-confidence, and social influence strategies: An organizational simulation. *Journal of Personality and Social Psychology, 44*, 322-333. For related findings, see: Andrews, P. (1984). Performance, self-esteem and perceptions of leadership emergence: A comparative study of men and women. *Western Journal of Speech Communication, 48*, 1-13.

[28] Powell, p. 99. See also: Massengill, D., & DiMarco, N. (1979). Sex-role stereotypes and requisite management characteristics: A current replication. *Sex Roles, 5*, 561-570.;

[29] Kanter, R. M. (1977). Some effects of proportions on group life: Skewed sex ratios and responses to token women. *American Journal of Sociology, 82*, 965-990.

[30] See, for example:

Powell, G. N., & Butterfield, A. D. (1982). Sex, attributions, and leadership: A brief review. *Psychological Reports, 51*, 1171-1174.

Deaux, F., & Emswiller, T. (1974). Explanations of successful performance on sex-linked tasks: What is skill for the male is luck for the female. *Journal of Personality and Social Psychology, 29*, 80-85.

31 See, for example:

Stewart, L., & Gudykunst, W. B. (1982). Differential factors influencing the hierarchical level and number of promotions of males and females within an organization. *Academy of Management Journal, 25*, 586-597.

Kogler Hill, S. E., Bahniuk, M. H., & Dobos, J. (1989). The impact of mentoring and collegial support on faculty success: An analysis of support behavior, information adequacy, and communication apprehension. *Communication Education, 38*, 15-33.

32 Staley, C. C., & Shockley-Zalabak, P. (1986). Communication proficiency and future training needs of the female professional: Self-assessment vs. supervisors' evaluations. *Human Relations, 39*, 891-902.; Shockley-Zalabak, P., Staley, C. C., & Morley, D. D. (1988). The female professional: Perceived communication proficiencies as predictors of organizational advancement. *Human Relations, 41*, 553-567.

33 Rosenthal, R., & Jacobson, L. (1968). *Pygmalion in the classroom*. New York: Holt, Rinehart and Winston.

34 Eden, D., & Shani, A. B. (1982). Pygmalion goes to boot camp: Expectancy, leadership, and trainee performance. *Journal of Applied Psychology, 67*, 194-199.

35 Crawford, K. S., Thomas, E. D., & Fink, J. J. (1980). Pygmalion at sea: Improving the work effectiveness of low performers. *Journal of Applied Behavioral Science, 16*, 482-505.

36 Rosenthal, R., & Fode, K. L. (1963). The effect of experimenter bias on the performance of the albino rat. *Behavioral Science, 8*, 183-189.

37 Berlew, D., & Hall, D. (1966). The socialization of managers: Effects of expectations on performance. *Adminstrative Science Quarterly, 2*, 208-223

38 Livingston, J. S. (1969). Pygmalion in management. *Harvard Business Review, 47*, p. 85. For another discussion of self- esteem and expectations, see: Hill, N. (1976, August). Self-esteem: The key to effective leadership. *Administrative Management*, pp. 24-25, 51.

39 Atkinson, J. W. (1957). Motivational determinants of risk-taking behavior. *Psychological Review, 64*, 359-372.

40 Sandler, L. (1986, February). Self-fulfilling prophecy: Better management by magic. *Training*, pp. 60-64.

41 Baird, J., & Wieting, G. K. (1979, September). Nonverbal communication can be a motivational tool. *Personnel Journal*, pp. 607-610 + .

42 Good, T., & Brophy, J. (1980). *Educational psychology: A realistic approach*. New York: Holt, Rinehart and Winston.

43 Eden, D., & Ravid, G. (1982). Pygmalion vs. self-expectancy: Effects of instructor and self-expectancy on trainee performance. *Organizational Behavior and Human Performance, 30*, 351-364.

44 Eden, D. (1984). Self-fulfilling prophecy as a management tool: Harnessing Pygmalion. *Academy of Management Review, 9*, 64-73.

8

Public Leadership

The Power of Public Leadership

Public leadership is one of the most visible and dynamic forms of social influence. Religious and political authorities, educators, social activists and other public leaders attempt to modify the attitudes and behaviors of mass audiences. The influence of public leaders on the course of history is a matter of conjecture. Some scholars adopt the viewpoint of Scottish historian Thomas Carlyle, suggesting that history is essentially the story of "heroic" leaders.[1] Others agree with the British philosopher Herbert Spencer, claiming that no single leader is capable of changing the evolutionary development of history.[2]

Conventional wisdom supports Carlyle's notion that powerful leaders shape history. Many public leaders have had a profound effect on human affairs. Robert Tucker, a Princeton University political scientist, argues that the atrocities which transpired under the leadership of Adolph Hitler in Nazi Germany and Joseph Stalin in the Soviet Union were directly attributable to the "paranoid" personalities of these two ignoble public leaders.[3]

Public leadership is not limited to nationally known politicians or major religious or social figures. Public leaders like student body officers, protest organizers and union officials are found at every level of society. John Gardner, former Secretary of Health, Education and Welfare in the Johnson administration and the founder of Common Cause, uses the term "dispersed leadership" to describe how leaders are found at all levels, including social agencies, universities, the professions, businesses, and minority communities. Gardner believes that dispersed leadership is essential to the health of complex organizations and societies. Lower level leaders can deal more effectively with local problems. When local leaders take initiative, they encourage higher level leaders to do the same.[4]

Every public leader, from the President of the United States down to the president of a local chamber of commerce, must influence the attitudes and behaviors of groups within a social system. This process of influence is called opinion leadership. Since public leaders deal with large audiences, they often use different tactics than leaders in other contexts. In an interpersonal encounter, for example, a leader can target a persuasive message to the special needs of one follower. In a public setting, a leader must address messages to what groups of people have in common—health and financial worries, political beliefs, age, ethnic heritage and so on. Effective public leaders shape public opinion through public speaking and persuasive campaigns. In this chapter we will examine these two important leadership tools. We'll conclude our discussion of public leadership with a look at the characteristics of those extraordinary leaders we call "charismatic."

Public Address: A Key Leadership Tool

To command a public audience is to have influence. Just by listening to a public figure we acknowledge his or her leadership. Public speaking is a significant tool for all types of public leaders. Lee Iacocca, for example, receives over three thousand speaking invitations each year (he accepts forty-five). Candy Lightner, founder of Mothers Against Drunk Driving, gives over 150 speeches annually.[5] Billy Graham has delivered sermons to ninety million people. Perhaps the most dramatic demonstration of the important relationship between public speaking and public leadership can be seen in the exercise of the presidency (see Figure 8.1).

For further evidence that public address is essential to public life and public leadership, clip out all the news stories about public speakers from an edition of your newspaper (see Application Exercise 2). The stories described below appeared in just one issue of a major metropolitan daily.[6]

1. A rally in support of timber workers made headline news. Ten thousand demonstrators gathered to hear a US Senator, gubernatorial candidate, industry leaders and others protest plans to set aside additional timber lands for the northern spotted owl.

2. In a speech to the South African Youth Congress, Nelson Mandela warned the South African government against shooting black protestors.

3. Leaders of a coalition of black and white churches congratulated the city council for giving more public works jobs to poor, inner-city residents and minorities.

4. At a business club luncheon, three scientists predicted that biotechnology would play an important role in the state's economic growth.

5. The vice-chairman of the transportation commission announced that the state would spend between five and seven million dollars a year in local highway improvements at a speech before a regional planning group.

Figure 8.1   Research Highlight
When the President Speaks. . .

In a comprehensive, eight-year study, University of Texas political communication expert Roderick Hart analyzed the 9,969 public speeches delivered by United States presidents between 1945 and 1985.[1] Hart's conclusion after looking at forty years of presidential communication was that although a president's message may soon be forgotten, his presence as a speaker is memorable. As Hart explains, public communication is "the primary means of *performing the act* of presidential leadership."[2] Speaking is equated with action. Presidents, as well as the public, seem to operate under the illusion that talking about a particular issue is the same as doing something about it.

According to Hart, presidents deliver the number of public speeches they do because audiences are willing to listen. Although no relationship between how often a president speaks and how well he does in opinion polls was discovered, Hart notes that the frequency of presidential speechmaking increased significantly over the forty-year period he studied. Presidents Truman and Eisenhower rarely spoke in public. Truman averaged about fifteen speeches a month during his presidency while Eisenhower averaged only about ten speeches per month. (October, 1955 — shortly after Dwight Eisenhower's coronary — was the only month between 1945 and 1985 when no presidential speeches were delivered.) Presidents Kennedy, Johnson, and Nixon spoke almost twice as often as their post World War II predecessors. (Nixon's average would have been even higher without the Watergate scandal.) Presidents Ford, Carter and Reagan substantially surpassed earlier speechmaking totals. Gerald Ford averaged a dizzying forty-two speeches a month. Over his twenty-nine-month term of office he delivered an average of one speech every six hours. Even Ronald Reagan, criticized by some as being inaccessible, averaged over twenty-seven speeches a month during his eight years in office.

Hart's research suggests that the link between public speaking and presidential leadership is inexorable. To be president is to have a public willing to listen to your message. No matter what it is.

[1] Hart, R. P. (1987). *The sound of leadership: Presidential communication in the modern age.* Chicago: University of Chicago Press.
[2] Hart, p.46.

6. One community calendar announcement described an upcoming rally against the sexual abuse of children. Another gave the time and date for a speech by a counsel general of Israel.

Because public address is such an important skill for public leaders, we need to understand the key elements that go into an effective public message. To learn more about how to put together a successful speech or presentation, turn to Appendix A.

Leading Public Opinion: Persuasive Campaigns

Characteristics of Successful Campaigns

As we've seen, public speaking is an important tool for public leaders. However, a single speech, like a single television advertisement or newspaper editorial, does not always change the attitudes or behaviors of large numbers of people. For this reason, public leaders frequently put together persuasive campaigns in order to influence public opinion. Persuasion expert Herbert Simons defines a campaign as an "organized, sustained attempt at influencing groups of people through a series of messages."[7] Campaigns use both the mass media and interpersonal communication networks to achieve their goals. There are four types of persuasive campaigns: 1) political (electing candidates to office and implementing political policy), 2) product (selling goods and services), 3) image (building positive images for individuals or organizations), and 4) cause (promoting ideas, beliefs, values and practices).[8]

Not all campaigns are successful. Consumer rejection of the New Coke and the failure of Burger King's "Where's Herb?" advertising blitz demonstrate that even well planned and well financed product campaigns can go astray. Other types of campaigns often suffer the same fate. Organizers of one image campaign wanted to make the people of Cincinnati more aware of the United Nations. They used sixty weekly radio spots, sixty thousand pieces of literature, and twenty-eight hundred presentations to flood Cincinnati with the message that "Peace Begins with the United Nations—and the United Nations Begins with You." Before the campaign started, 70% of those surveyed knew something about the main purpose of the UN. When the campaign was over, this percentage had only risen by 2%.[9]

While many campaigns fail, others meet their objectives. For example, in 1988 The American Association of Retired Persons and other groups convinced Congress to pass the Medicare Catastrophic Coverage Act. This piece of legislation put limits on how much retirees had to pay out of their own pockets for hospital charges, drug and doctor bills, and nursing home costs. To fund the expanded coverage, Congress imposed a four dollar charge on all Medicare recipients and added a surcharge to the bills of wealthier senior citizens. These better-off seniors rebelled against paying higher Medicare premiums and started a second campaign aimed at repealing the Catastrophic Care Act. Led by James Roosevelt, son of Franklin Roosevelt and the head of the National Committee to Preserve Social Security and Medicare, they persuaded Congress to revoke the legislation a year later.[10]

Why do some campaigns have a significant impact on public attitudes and behavior while others have little influence at all? In order to answer this question, Everett Rogers and Douglas Storey surveyed forty years of campaign research.[11] Rogers and Storey identified the following as characteristics of successful campaigns.

Pretest messages and identify market segments. Organizers of effective campaigns rely on research to help them shape their messages. The producers of Sesame Street, for instance, pretest their programs to determine how they will be received by preschool audiences. Doing market research prior to a campaign reveals what audiences currently believe, if receivers understand campaign advertisements and slogans, and which messages are best suited to particular segments of the market. The US Committee for Energy Awareness (USCEA) is one industry group that uses research to identify important audiences. This association argues that nuclear energy is a safe source of power which cuts dependence on foreign oil and helps meet the demand for electricity. To overcome resistance to nuclear power plants, the USCEA targets messages to media reporters, government officials, and college educated adults between the ages of twenty-five and sixty-four who earn over $33,000 a year. The USCEA image campaign apparently is a success. In one survey of legislators, 94% reported that the campaign was informative and 73% reacted favorably to USCEA objectives.[12]

Expose a large segment of the audience to clear campaign messages. Message exposure is a prerequisite for campaign success. Audiences must be aware of campaign messages before they can act on the information contained in those messages. Similarly, it is important that messages be clear. The UN persuasive campaign mentioned earlier failed, not because planners didn't get their messages out, but because many Cincinnatians had a hard time figuring out just what the project's slogan—"The United Nations Begins With You"—really meant.[13]

Use media which are most accessible to target groups. Successful campaigns utilize those media which are most accessible to audiences. In some countries few people have access to either television or newspapers. In these situations, campaign organizers must rely on radio and other media. The timing of messages is also critical. Effective campaigns reach audiences when they are most receptive. For example, when the Olympic Games are in session (and public interest in the

Olympics is at its peak), corporations use media spots to trumpet the fact that their products are endorsed by the US Olympic Committee.

Use the media to raise awareness. The media are most effective when they are used to provide important information, stimulate interpersonal conversations, and recruit additional people to participate in the campaign. Media messages raise awareness and get people talking about the merits of politicians, products, organizations and causes. In addition, many people volunteer for food drives, fund raisers, clean up campaigns and other projects after hearing about them through advertisements or news stories. The media play such an important role in shaping public opinion that almost all organizations, from community hospitals to multinational corporations, hire public relations specialists to help them place stories in newspapers and magazines and on radio and television broadcasts.

Rely on interpersonal communication, particularly communication between people of similar social backgrounds, to lead to and reinforce behavior change. Interpersonal communication networks play a particularly important role in persuasive campaigns which are designed to change people's behaviors. Behavioral change is more likely when the desired behaviors are modeled by others. Rogers and Storey note, "While the mass media may be effective in disseminating information, interpersonal channels are more influential in motivating people to act on that information." [14] The national crime prevention campaign that urges listeners and viewers to "Take a Bite Out of Crime" is one example of how media and interpersonal channels can complement each other. Although many people learn about crime prevention behaviors through the campaign's media spots, listeners put these behaviors into action only after they become involved in neighborhood watch groups. Neighborhood watch groups provide additional information about crime prevention and demonstrate that crime prevention activities are socially acceptable.

Certain individuals—called opinion leaders—play a major role in convincing others to adopt new products, techniques or ideas. Enlisting the participation of these individuals greatly increases a campaign's chances of success. Opinion leaders share four characteristics: 1) they have greater exposure to the media, outside change agents and other key external communication sources; 2) they participate in a variety of social networks and rapidly spread new ideas to others; 3) they generally have higher socioeconomic status than opinion followers; 4) they are more innovative when the norms of the social system favor change. [15]

Use high credibility sources. Successful campaigns use highly credible representatives. (Refer back to Chapter 5 for more information on the dimensions of credibility.) For instance, many people criticized the Nestle company for taking advantage of the credibility of medical personnel by using women dressed as nurses to promote the use of infant formula in Third World countries. Infant formula is extremely expensive in developing areas and is unsafe when mixed with dirty water. Audiences keep the motives of sources in mind when evaluating their credibility. An actor who promotes AIDS prevention is often seen as more credible than an actor who promotes a product because those who advertise goods and services are paid for their efforts.

Direct messages at the individual needs of the audience. Audiences are most influenced by messages aimed directly at personal needs. Effective political campaigns emphasize how the candidate will help the voter by lowering taxes, providing more jobs, building better roads, lowering crime and so on. Campaigns for popular products link the purchase of the item with a specific need felt by the audience. One product that failed because it didn't meet a need was Mennen E deodorant. A major promotional campaign could not convince the American public that Vitamin E (the product's unique ingredient) served any useful purpose in a deodorant.

Emphasize positive rewards rather than prevention. Many campaigns (such as one urging us to wear our seat belts) try to help audiences avoid future, unwanted events. These campaigns often fail because the consequences of noncompliance are uncertain. In the case of safety belts, many of us drive without them because we believe that we will never be in a serious auto accident. Effective campaigns emphasize the immediate positive rewards that come from adopting a value, belief or behavior. Campaign planners may use our fear of suffering a heart attack to encourage us to start a regular exercise program. However, we are more likely to adopt a regular exercise routine if campaign messages emphasize weight loss, stress reduction and other *immediate* benefits.

Campaign Stages

Even with an understanding of the factors which contribute to successful campaigns, organizing a campaign can seem like an overwhelming task. Successful campaigns involve research, the careful construction of messages, and effective use of both the media and interpersonal networks. To make the campaign process more manageable, Gary Woodward and Robert Denton suggest that you follow the six steps described below and in Figure 8.2.[16]

Figure 8.2

Campaign Implementation Overview

Stage	Components
1. Situation analysis	target audience
	product/issue/idea
	competition or opponent
2. Objectives	mission
	goals
	outcomes
3. Strategies	messages
	media
	presentation activities
4. Budget	labor
	material
	media
	talent
	production
5. Implementation	timing
	follow-up
6. Evaluation	what people say
	what people think
	what people do

Source: Woodward, G. C., & Denton, R. E. Jr. (1988) *Persuasion & Influence in American Life.* Prospect Heights, IL: Waveland Press, Inc. Used by permission.

Stage 1: Situation Analysis. Situation analysis is the foundation for the rest of the campaign. Begin by identifying key audience characteristics. These include: 1) demographic variables (age, education, occupation), 2) geographic variables (urban vs. suburban, West vs. Midwest), and 3) psychographic variables (lifestyle, interests, activities and opinions). If your campaign is product oriented, then size up the competition and determine attitudes toward your product. Your research can be both informal and formal. Informal research is the process of gathering information from libraries, personal contacts, industry publications and other sources. Formal research is based on the statistical analysis of data collected through surveys and interviews.

Stage 2: Objectives. Once the preliminary research is complete, goals should be set. Objectives can center on increased awareness, attitude change, or changes in behavior. Many campaigns fail because they are too ambitious. When you seek significant behavioral change, set more modest goals. For example, you might be able to convince a large percentage of your audience that recycling reduces our dependence on landfills. Yet, only a portion of those who believe in recycling will actually take items to a recycling center.

Stage 3: Strategies. This stage of the campaign is concerned with how to get things done. Structure messages to appeal to market segments, determine how you will use the media to reach audiences, and plan presentational activities like press conferences, rallies, and conventions.

Stage 4: Prepare a Budget. Financial resources will frequently determine the scope of your campaign. Labor, material, media, talent, and production costs must all be taken into consideration.

Stage 5: Implementation. The campaign goes into action during this stage. Monitor your progress and determine the timing of messages through ongoing research. Poll voters, test product attitudes and so forth. By periodically gathering data, you will know if your campaign is on target and if you should modify your campaign messages and strategies.

Stage 6: Evaluation. The evaluation stage completes the ongoing campaign and lays the groundwork for future projects. In order to determine if you reached the campaign objectives you set earlier, you will need to survey target audiences, measure sales and so on. What you learn from the successes and failures of one persuasive campaign can serve as the foundation for the next.

Perspectives on Charisma

Charismatic leaders are the "superstars" of leadership. We usually reserve the label "charismatic" for leaders like Mahatma Gandhi, Winston Churchill and Lee Iacocca who have a dramatic impact on others. Identifying the characteristics of charismatic leaders can provide us with important insights into leadership behavior. By discovering how charismatics communicate, we can increase our effectiveness as leaders. In this section of the chapter, we'll summarize major approaches to the study of charismatic leadership and offer our own communication-based perspective.

Sociological Origins

German sociologist Max Weber was one of the first scholars to use the term charisma to describe secular leaders. The word charisma, which Weber borrowed from theology, means "gift" in Greek.[17] Early Christians believed that God gave special gifts or abilities to church leaders. Weber expanded the definition of gifted leadership to include all leaders, both religious and nonreligious, who attract devoted followers through their extraordinary powers. In summarizing the nature of the charismatic leader, Weber said:

> . . . he is set apart from ordinary men and treated as endowed with supernatural, superhuman, or at least specifically exceptional powers or qualities. These are such as are not accessible to the ordinary person, but are regarded as of divine origin or as exemplary and on the basis of them the individual concerned is treated as a leader.[18]

According to Weber, a leader retains charismatic status as long as he or she is seen as charismatic. Or, as Robert Tucker has pointed out, "To be a charismatic leader is essentially to be *perceived* as such.[19] A charismatic must periodically demonstrate his or her exceptional gifts in order to maintain power.

The person-centered authority of the charismatic leader is a threat to societies governed according to either tradition or the force of law. In monarchies and other traditional systems, customs dictate the choice of leaders. (There is only one royal family in England, for example.) In legal-rational societies like the United States, well defined legal procedures govern the selection of leaders. If a legal-rational leader (Richard Nixon, for instance) violates the laws, then the right to rule is revoked. Charismatic leaders often replace traditional and legal-rational systems with structures based on their personal power. Because charismatic power rests on the qualities of the leader, charismatic authority frequently erodes after the charismatic dies. The social system then reverts back to a traditional or legal-rational form of leadership.[20]

A number of important details are missing from Weber's theory of charismatic leadership. The theory never describes the origin or exact nature of the charismatic leader's extraordinary powers or clarifies how charismatic authority can rest both on the traits of the leader *and* on the perceptions of followers. Weber left much to be discovered and defined. As a result, investigators from a number of other disciplines have added their insights to the discussion of charisma. Psychoanalysts, in particular, have been interested in the unique psychological characteristics of charismatic leaders and followers.

The Psychoanalytic Approach

The leading advocate of a psychoanalytic approach to leadership is Abraham Zaleznik of Harvard University. In 1981 Zaleznik was awarded the chair in leadership at Harvard, the first faculty position devoted entirely to the study of leadership at any major business school in the United States. Using the theories of Sigmund Freud, Zaleznik argues that leaders differ significantly from managers (a distinction we also make in Chapter 1). His description of leader characteristics has much in common with Weber's description of charismatic authority. According to Zaleznik, leaders introduce change, take risks and arouse emotions. These same elements can be found in Weber's definition of charismatic leadership. Zaleznik also identifies some of the communication behaviors of leaders. Leaders focus on what events mean for followers rather than on how to get things done. Unlike managers who send vague "signals" that promote compromise, leaders send clear messages that may anger others.[21]

Other psychoanalysts use Freudian concepts to describe the motivation of those who follow charismatic leaders. Many of these theorists believe that followers cope with feelings of inadequacy by making charismatic leaders into ideals or love objects. Ralph Hummel, for instance, uses Freud's projection theory to explain why the Israelites rallied behind the biblical prophets. In projection theory, individuals who suffer loss project their love on an outside object or person. Hummel contends that when the ancient nation of Israel came under attack from foreign enemies, citizens turned to a group they had once scorned—the prophets. The Israelites coped with the loss of their traditional way of life by making the prophets the recipients of their love.[22]

Political Charisma

A number of political scientists, sociologists and others apply Weber's definition of charisma to political figures. However, they don't always

put the charismatic label on the same people. To see how difficult it
is to determine who should be classified as charismatic, generate your
own list of charismatic leaders. Then form a small group with other
members of the class and create a composite list (see Application Exercise
5). A number of individuals that you label as charismatic may not be
accepted by other members of the group.

One extensive list of charismatic figures from this century was
developed by Arthur Schweitzer.[23] He calls the 20th century "The Age
of Charisma" since so many charismatic leaders have emerged during
the past several decades. Schweitzer believes there are different types
of charismatic political leaders. **Charismatic giants** take control of
governments in world powers. Franklin Roosevelt, Benito Mussolini,
Indira Gandhi and Adolph Hitler fall into this category. **Charismatic
luminaries** are leaders who have political authority in small countries
(i.e. Gamal Nasser in Egypt or Colonel Quadaffi in Libya). **Charismatic
failures** (such as Senator Joseph McCarthy) try for political control but
fail. **Charismatic aspirants** are still striving for leadership positions.

Political scientist Ruth Ann Willner's list of charismatic figures is
much shorter than Schweitzer's. She names only six people—Ayatollah
Khomeini, Mahatma Gandhi, Adolph Hitler, Franklin Roosevelt, Fidel
Castro, and Sukarno of Indonesia—as charismatic leaders.[24] Willner
defines charisma on the basis of the leader-follower relationship.
Charismatic followers: 1) attribute divine or semi-divine qualities to their
leaders; 2) believe that their leaders have supernatural abilities to do
magic, to prophesy or to escape from injury; 3) offer absolute devotion
and obedience; 4) are extremely loyal. Letters written to Franklin
Roosevelt reveal the deep devotion followers have for their charismatic
leaders. One highly committed follower, an Iowa congressman, told
Roosevelt: "I will do anything you ask. You are my leader." A citizen
wrote to say: "I have never had the urge to write to any President before,
but with you it is different. . . . To me you're a god in disguise."[25]

We can learn a great deal about how charismatics increase their power
by studying the lives of charismatic political figures. One key to their
success is the use of cultural myths. Charismatic leaders identify
themselves with past heroes and widespread beliefs. For example, many
Iranians thought that the Ayatollah Khomeini was the last descendant
of the prophet Mohammed. According to Moslem belief, this holy man
would return to help his people in their time of need.[26] Another key
to the emergence of charismatic leaders lies in their effective use of public
address. Charismatics are dynamic public speakers. Often the public
speeches delivered by charismatic leaders evoke powerful emotions in
followers. To see how one charismatic leader moved his audience

through the use of stirring language, read Martin Luther King's "I Have a Dream" speech reprinted in Figure 8.3.

Robert Tucker uses the idea of concentric circles to describe the development of charismatic movements.[27] In Tucker's model, a movement starts when a small circle of core followers surrounds the leader. Next, a larger circle emerges as the charismatic following grows and organizes. In the next largest circle, the charismatic group takes political power and the whole citizenry is effected. In the last and largest circle, the charismatic movement may become international in scope. The rise of Lenin demonstrates how these circles of influence emerge. Lenin first became an acknowledged revolutionary leader in a small colony of Bolsheviks in Geneva, Switzerland. Then the Bolsheviks became the dominant force in the Communist Party which seized control of the Russian government and nation in 1917. Soon a world Communist movement was formed.

Charismatic Behavior

Unlike political scientists who limit their discussion of charisma to famous social leaders, behavioral scientists argue that organizational leaders, like Thomas J. Watson, Sr. of IBM and George F. Johnson of Endicott-Johnson Shoes, can also be described as charismatic. Behavioralists try to quantify the differences between charismatic and noncharismatic leaders. By describing charisma as a set of behaviors, they hope to clarify what charisma is and predict the effects of charismatic leadership.[28]

Based on a behavioral model of charisma, Robert House and Bernard Bass developed a set of propositions or conclusions about charismatic leaders.[29] These propositions fall into three major categories:

- *Leader Behaviors.* Charismatic leaders have strong power needs, display high self-confidence, demonstrate competence, serve as role models, communicate high expectations, engage in effective argumentation, and create transcendent goals.

- *Leader-Follower Relations.* Charismatics serve as targets for follower hopes, frustrations and fears. They also create a sense of excitement and adventure. While charismatics lead groups toward new visions, they build their appeals to followers on widely shared beliefs, values and goals.

Figure 8.3   Case Study

"I Have a Dream" by Dr. Martin Luther King Jr.

On August 28, 1963 more than two hundred thousand people marched through Washington D.C. to protest racial inequality. The protesters hoped to focus attention on the need for civil rights legislation. The march extended nearly a mile from the Washington Monument to the Lincoln Memorial where the assembled protesters were addressed by a number of prominent entertainers and social activists. Among the speakers was Dr. Martin Luther King Jr. The following text of his speech is known as the "I Have a Dream" speech.

I am happy to join with you today in what will go down in history as the greatest demonstration for freedom in the history of our nation.

Five score years ago, a great American, in whose symbolic shadow we stand today, signed the Emancipation Proclamation. This momentous decree came as a great beacon light of hope to millions of Negro slaves who had been seared in the flames of withering injustice. It came as a joyous daybreak to end the long night of their captivity.

But one hundred years later, the Negro still is not free; one hundred years later, the life of the Negro is still sadly crippled by the manacles of segregation and the chains of discrimination; one hundred years later, the Negro lives on a lonely island of poverty in the midst of a vast ocean of material prosperity; one hundred years later, the Negro is still languished in the corners of American society and finds himself in exile in his own land.

So we've come here today to dramatize a shameful condition. In a sense we've come to our nation's capital to cash a check. When the architects of our republic wrote the magnificent words of the Constitution and the Declaration of Independence, they were signing a promissory note to which every American was to fall heir. This note was the promise that all men, yes, black men as well as white men, would be guaranteed the unalienable rights of life, liberty, and the pursuit of happiness.

It is obvious today that America has defaulted on this promissory note in so far as her citizens of color are concerned. Instead of honoring this sacred obligation, America has given the Negro people a bad check, a check which has come back marked "insufficient funds." But we refuse to believe that the bank of justice is bankrupt. We refuse to believe that there are insufficient funds in the great vaults of opportunity of this nation. And so we have come to cash this check, a check that will give us upon demand the riches of freedom and the security of justice.

We have also come to this hallowed spot to remind America of the fierce urgency of now. This is no time to engage in the luxury of cooling off or to take the tranquilizing drug of gradualism. Now is the time to make real the promises of democracy; now is the time to rise from the dark and desolate valley of segregation to the sunlit path of racial justice; now is the time to lift our nation from the quicksands of racial injustice to the solid rock of brotherhood; now is the time to make justice a reality for all of God's children. It would be fatal for the nation to overlook the urgency of the moment. This sweltering summer of the Negro's legitimate discontent will not pass until there is an invigorating autumn of freedom and equality.

Nineteen-sixty-three is not an end, but a beginning. And those who hope that the Negro needed to blow off steam and will now be content, will have a rude awakening if the nation returns to business as usual. There will be neither rest nor tranquility in America until the Negro is granted his citizenship rights. The whirlwinds of revolt will continue to shake the foundations of our nation until the bright day of justice emerges.

But there is something that I must say to my people, who stand on the warm threshold which leads into the palace of justice. In the process of gaining our rightful place, we must not be guilty of wrongful deeds. Let us not seek to satisfy our thirst for freedom by drinking from the cup of bitterness and hatred. We must forever conduct our struggle on the high plane of dignity and discipline. We must not allow our creative protests to degenerate into physical violence. Again and again we must rise to the majestic heights of meeting physical force with soul force. The marvelous new militancy, which has engulfed the Negro community, must not lead us to a distrust of all white people. For many of our white brothers, as evidenced by their presence here today, have come to realize that their destiny is tied up with our destiny. And they have come to realize that their freedom is inextricably bound to our freedom. We cannot walk alone. And as we walk, we must make the pledge that we shall always march ahead. We cannot turn back.

There are those who are asking the devotees of civil rights, "When will you be satisfied?" We can never be satisfied as long as the Negro is the victim of the unspeakable horrors of police brutality; we can never be satisfied as long as our bodies, heavy with the fatigue of travel, cannot gain lodging in the motels of the highways and the hotels of the cities; we cannot be satisfied as long as the Negro's basic mobility is from a smaller ghetto to a larger one; we can never be satisfied as long as our children are stripped of their selfhood and robbed of their dignity by signs stating "For Whites Only"; we cannot be satisfied as long as the Negro in Mississippi cannot vote and a Negro in New York believes he has nothing for which to vote. No! No, we are not satisfied, and we will not be satisfied until "justice rolls down like waters and righteousness like a mighty stream."

I am not unmindful that some of you have come here out of great trials and tribulations. Some of you have come fresh from narrow jail cells. Some of you have come from areas where your quest for freedom left you battered by the storms of persecution and staggered by the winds of police brutality. You have been the veterans of creative suffering. Continue to work with the faith that unearned suffering is redemptive. Go back to Mississippi. Go back to Alabama. Go back to South Carolina. Go back to Georgia. Go back to

Louisiana. Go back to the slums and ghettos of our Northern cities, knowing that somehow this situation can and will be changed. Let us not wallow in the valley of despair.

I say to you today, my friends, so even though we face the difficulties of today and tomorrow, I still have a dream. It is a dream deeply rooted in the American dream. I have a dream that one day this nation will rise up and live out the true meaning of its creed, "We hold these truths to be self evident, that all men are created equal." I have a dream that one day on the red hills of Georgia, sons of former slaves and sons of former slave-owners will be able to sit down together at the table of brotherhood. I have a dream that one day, even the state of Mississippi, a state sweltering with the heat of injustice, sweltering with the heat of oppression, will be transformed into an oasis of freedom and justice. I have a dream that my four children will one day live in a nation where they will not be judged by the color of their skin, but by the content of their character.

I HAVE A DREAM TODAY!

I have a dream that one day down in Alabama—with its vicious racists, with its governor having his lips dripping with the words of interposition and nullification—one day right there in Alabama, little black boys and black girls will be able to join hands with little white boys and white girls as sisters and brothers.

I HAVE A DREAM TODAY!

I have a dream that one day every valley shall be exalted, and every hill and mountain shall be made low. The rough places will be plain and the crooked places will be made straight, "and the glory of the Lord shall be revealed, and all flesh shall see it together."

This is our hope. This is the faith that I go back to the South with. With this faith we will be able to hew out of the mountain of despair a stone of hope. With this faith we will be able to transform the jangling discords of our nation into a beautiful symphony of brotherhood. With this faith we will be able to work together, to pray together, to struggle together, to go to jail together, to stand up for freedom together, knowing that we will be free one day. And this will be the day. This will be the day when all of God's children will be able to sing with new meaning, "My country, 'tis of thee, sweet land of liberty, of thee I sing. Land where my father died, land of the pilgrim's pride, from every mountainside, let freedom ring." And if America is to be a great nation, this must become true.

So let freedom ring from the prodigious hilltops of New Hampshire; let freedom ring from the mighty mountains of New York; let freedom ring from the heightening Alleghenies of Pennsylvania; let freedom ring from the snow-capped rockies of Colorado; let freedom ring from the curvaceous slopes of California. But not only that. Let freedom ring from Stone Mountain of Georgia; let freedom ring from Lookout Mountain of Tennessee; let freedom ring from every hill and mole hill of Mississippi. "From every mountainside, let freedom ring."

And when this happens, and when we allow freedom to ring, when we let it ring from every village and every hamlet, from every state and every city, we will be able to speed up that day when all of God's children, black men and white men, Jews and Gentiles, Protestants and Catholics, will be able to join hands and sing in the words of the old Negro spiritual: "Free at last. Free at last.Thank God Almighty, we are free at last."

Discussion Questions

1. Dr. King's speech had a tremendous impact on the civil rights movement in the United States. Why do you think this speech was so important?
2. Was Dr. King a charismatic leader? Why or why not?
3. Dr. King's speech incorporates images from the Bible and American political history. How do these images influence the effectiveness of the speech?
4. What types of vivid language does Dr. King use in this speech?
5. Some commentators consider this to be the finest speech delivered during the 20th century. Do you agree? Why or why not?

Source: "I Have a Dream." A speech by Dr. Martin Luther King, Jr. Copyright 1963. Reprinted by permission of the King Library and Archives

• *Elements of the Charismatic Situation.* Charismatic leaders are most likely to appear when groups are under stress. For a corporation, stress might involve bankruptcy or the loss of a major market. Chrysler's financial problems, for example, set the stage for Lee Iacocca's emergence as a charismatic figure. Societies experience tension when they move from an agricultural to an industrial economic base, fight a war, or face a depression. Ironically, the charismatic's success in rallying support in response to an emergency may also explain the strong resistance she or he faces. Charismatic leaders generate intense feelings of love or hate. Charismatic movie czar Louis B. Mayer convinced members of the financial community to back his movies at a time when the future of the film industry was in doubt. Yet, many considered him to be a vain tyrant. In fact, Samuel Goldwyn claimed that the reason so many people came to Mayer's funeral was to make sure he was really dead![30]

Bass identifies charisma as the most important element in transformational leadership. He found that transformational leaders rate highly on such items as "Makes everyone around him/her enthusiastic about assignments," and "Gives me a sense of overall purpose."[31] As we noted in Chapter 3, transformational leaders lift the performance of the group to higher levels. However, while all transformational leaders are charismatic, not all charismatic leaders are transformational. Transformational leadership results in higher moral standards. Charismatic leaders, on the other hand, can change society for good or for evil.[32] The difference between charismatic and transformational leadership can be seen in the life of Adolph Hitler. While Hitler was charismatic, he was not transformational since he appealed to lower human emotions by promoting hate and violence.

Charisma From a Communication Perspective

None of the perspectives on charisma that we have discussed so far view the topic from a communication vantage point. Nonetheless, all of these approaches acknowledge the prominent role that communication plays in charismatic leadership. Sociologist Weber emphasized that charisma is perceived by followers who look to the leader to illustrate his or her charismatic standing through communication. Psychoanalyst Abraham Zaleznik notes that leaders send clear messages and focus on the meaning that events have for followers. Both political scientists and behaviorists recognize the importance of 1) the charismatic leader's command of rhetoric and persuasion, 2) the charismatic's creation of a self-confident, competent image, and 3) the link between symbolic myths and goals and charismatic emergence. We think that communication is more than an important element of charismatic leadership, however. We believe that **charisma is the product of communication**.

In Chapter 1 we established that effective leaders must demonstrate communication skills associated with monitoring the environment and building relationships, thinking and reasoning (envisioning), and influencing others. Charismatic leaders excel in all three functions of communication:

Charismatics as Relationship Builders. Charismatic leaders are skilled at linking with others. Their relationships with followers are characterized by strong feelings. As we've seen, such terms as excitement, adventure, loyalty and devotion are frequently used to describe charismatic leader-follower relations. In addition, charismatics convince followers that as leaders they have a significant impact on the course of events—that they are "at the center of things."[33]

Charismatics as Visionaries. Charismatic leaders can also be defined in terms of their ability to create symbolic visions. Above all, charismatics emphasize the transcendent. According to one scholar, "They provide in themselves and in their visions an opportunity for the follower to imagine himself and his society transformed into something entirely new."[34]

Although the visions of charismatic leaders are new images of the group's future, they are built upon the foundation of previous myths and values. The power of the charismatic grows as larger and larger numbers of people accept his/her symbolic focus. Stressful events like unemployment, war, fear for the future and racial strife discredit current definitions of reality. This creates a more receptive audience for the charismatic leader's new vision. For example, the Civil Rights movement of the 1960s made many white Americans aware of the extent of racial injustice. Martin Luther King's nonviolent message gained wide acceptance because people of all racial groups could accept King's vision of a world united by love.[35]

Charismatics as Influence Agents. Charismatics are masters at influence and inspiration. In some instances, their influence is so great that followers never question their decisions or directives. Charismatic leaders project an image of confidence, competence, and trustworthiness. They utilize the power of positive expectations to generate high productivity and make effective use of language and persuasion to achieve their goals. Such leaders rely heavily on referent power (their influence as role models) to encourage others to sacrifice on behalf of the group.

If the perception of charisma is the result of communication behaviors, then we all have the potential to act as charismatic leaders. We can generate charismatic effects as small group, organizational, and public leaders. Though we may never influence millions like a Mahatma Gandhi or Martin Luther King, we can have a strong impact on the lives of others through shaping the symbolic focus of the group, generating perceptions of confidence and competence, communicating high expectations, and inspiring others.

Summary

In this chapter we examined the nature of public leadership. Public leaders influence the attitudes and behaviors of large audiences at all levels of society. These leaders use public address and persuasive campaigns to shape public opinion. A persuasive campaign consists of a series of messages aimed at changing the beliefs and behaviors of others. Successful campaigns pretest their messages and identify market segments, expose a large portion of the audience to campaign messages, use media which are most accessible to target groups, rely on the media to raise awareness, utilize interpersonal communication to bring about behavior change, employ high credibility sources, direct messages at individual needs, and emphasize positive rewards rather than prevention. There are six steps or stages to any type of persuasive campaign: 1) situation analysis, 2) objectives, 3) strategies, 4) budget, 5) implementation, and 6) evaluation.

We ended the chapter with a discussion of those public leaders—called "charismatic"—who exert extraordinary influence over followers. Scholars in many disciplines have been interested in charismatic leadership. Major perspectives on charisma include: 1) sociological, 2) psychoanalytical, 3) political, 4) behavioral, and 5) communication-based. While the first four perspectives make communication a prominent part of charismatic leadership, only the communication-based approach sees charisma as the product of symbolic activity. Charismatic leaders excel in every function of human communication. They form strong emotional bonds with followers, emphasize transcendent visions, generate perceptions of confidence, communicate high expectations, and inspire others.

Application Exercises

1. Consider the impact of public leaders on history. Do you agree with Carlyle's perspective that history is shaped by powerful leaders or Spencer's claim that history develops according to patterns that cannot be altered by a single individual? Think of some examples which support your position.

2. Clip out all the articles related to public speaking from one newspaper. Classify the news stories as local, regional, national or international. What conclusions can you draw about the relationship between public address and public leadership based on your sample?

3. Use the techniques discussed in Appendix A to prepare a speech. Concentrate on pre-speech preparation, organization, language, rehearsal and delivery. After the speech, evaluate your performance and record ways that you can make your future presentations more effective. As an alternative assignment, evaluate a speech delivered by someone else.

4. Analyze a recent persuasive campaign based on the characteristics of successful campaigns presented in the chapter. Based on these elements, why did the campaign succeed or fail? Write up your findings.

5. Make a list of ten charismatic leaders. Then form a small group and generate a composite list. To make the group's list, a leader must be accepted as charismatic by all the members of the group. Keep a record of those individuals who fail to receive unanimous support. Present your findings to the rest of the class. As part of your report, describe the criteria that the group used to compile its list. In addition, name those individuals who were rejected by the group. Explain why these leaders failed to make the master list.

6. Do an in-depth study of a public charismatic leader. Describe how this person's use of communication resulted in his/her emergence as a charismatic figure. As you gather research, don't overlook popular films and plays which focus on the lives of Douglas McArthur, Mahatma Gandhi, General Patton, Eva Peron, Martin Luther King and others. Used as a supplement to biographies, these dramatizations can help charismatic figures "come alive." Write up your findings.

Endnotes

1 Carlyle, T. (1907). *On heroes, hero-worship, and the heroic in history*. Boston: Houghton Mifflin. (Original work written 1840)

2 Spencer, H. (1884). *The study of sociology*. New York: D. A. Appleton. (First published 1873)

3 Tucker, R. C. (1965). The dictator and totalitarianism. *World Politics, 17*, 565-573.

4 Gardner, J. (1990). *On leadership*. New York: The Free Press, p. xiii.

5 Andersen, K., & Witteman, P., A spunky tycoon turned superstar. (1985, April 1). *Time*, pp. 30-39; Lucas, S. E. (1986). *The art of public speaking* (2nd ed.). New York: Random House, p. 9.

6 News items were taken from the April 14, 1990 edition of *The Oregonian*, Portland, Oregon.

7 Simons, H. W. (1986). *Persuasion: Understanding, practice, and analysis* (2nd ed.). New York: Random House, p. 227.

8 Woodward, G. C., & Denton, R. E., Jr. (1988). *Persuasion and influence in American life*. Prospect Heights, IL: Waveland, Ch. 10.

9 Star, S. A., & Hughes, H. (1950). Report on an educational campaign: The Cincinnati plan for the United Nations. *American Journal of Sociology, 55*, 389-400.

10 Miller, A., & Hager, M. (1989, September 11). The elderly duke it out. *Newsweek*, pp. 42-43.; Clift, E., & Hager, M. (1989, October 16). A victory for the haves? *Newsweek*, p. 38.

[11] Rogers, E. M., & Storey, J. D. (1987). Communication campaigns. In C. R. Berger & S. H. Chaffee (Eds.), *Handbook of Communication Science* (pp. 817-846). Newbury Park, CA: Sage. Some of the examples used in this section of the chapter also come from this article.

[12] Heath, R. L. (1988). The rhetoric of issue advertising: A rationale, a case study, a critical perspective—and more. *Central States Speech Journal, 39,* 99-109.

[13] The UN campaign also failed because messages weren't directed at the individual needs of audience members. Many Cincinnatians couldn't understand how the UN related to their daily lives. As a result, only those who were already interested in the United Nations paid much attention to campaign messages.

[14] Rogers & Storey, p. 837.

[15] Rogers, E. M. (1983). *Diffusion of innovations* (3rd ed.). New York: The Free Press, Ch. 8.

[16] Woodward & Denton, Ch. 10.

[17] Bass, B. (1985). *Leadership and performance beyond expectations.* New York: The Free Press, Ch. 3. Some contemporary Christian groups also consider their leaders to be gifted by God. The term "charismatic" can also refer to a particular style of religious worship.

[18] Weber, M. (1947). *The theory of social and economic organization.* (A. M. Henderson & T. Parsons, Trans.), Glencoe, IL: The Free Press, pp. 358-359.

[19] Tucker, R. C. (1968). The theory of charismatic leadership. *Daedalus, 97,* p. 737.

[20] Freund, J. (1968). *The sociology of Max Weber.* New York: Vintage Books, Ch. 4.

[21] Zaleznik, A. (1977, May-June). Managers and leaders: Are they different? *Harvard Business Review, 55,* 67-78.; See also: Kiechel, W. (1983, May 30). What makes a corporate leader? *Fortune,* pp. 135-140.

[22] Hummel, R. P. (1975). Psychology of charismatic followers. *Psychological Reports, 37,* 759-770. For other examples of the psychoanalytic perspective on charisma, see:

Post, J. M. (1986). Narcissism and the charismatic leader- follower relationship. *Political Psychology, 7,* 675-688.

Winer, J. A., Jobe, T., & Ferrono, C. (1984-85). Toward a psychoanalytic theory of the charismatic relationship. *Annual of Psychoanalysis, 12-13,* 155-175.

Woodward, B., & McGrath, M. (1988). Charisma in group therapy with recovering substance abusers. *International Journal of Group Psychotherapy, 38,* 223-236.

Schiffer, I. (1973). *Charisma: A psychoanalytic look at mass society.* Toronto: University of Toronto Press.

[23] Schweitzer, A. (1984). *The age of charisma.* Chicago: Nelson-Hall.

[24] Willner, R. A. (1984). *The spellbinders: Charismatic political leadership.* New Haven: Yale University Press. Although Willner identifies only six pure or true charismatic leaders, she acknowledges that other leaders — like Mussolini and John F. Kennedy — possessed charismatic qualities.

[25] Willner, pp. 20, 29.

[26] Willner, pp. 86-88.

[27] Tucker, The theory of charismatic leadership.

[28] Conger, J. A., & Kanungo, R. N. (1987). Toward a behavioral theory of charismatic leadership in organizational settings. *Academy of Management Review, 12,* 637-647.

[29] House, R. J. (1977). A 1976 theory of charismatic leadership. In J. G. Hunt & L. L. Larson (Eds.), *Leadership: The cutting edge* (pp. 189-207). Carbondale: Southern Illinois University Press.; Bass, Ch. 3.

[30] Bass. p. 61.

[31] Bass, Ch. 11.

[32] Tucker, The theory of charismatic leadership, p. 735.

[33] Geertz, C. (1977). Centers, kings, and charisma: Reflections on the symbolics of power. In J. Ben-David & T. Nichols (Eds.), *Culture and its creation: Essays in honor of Edward Shils* (pp. 150-171). Chicago: University of Chicago Press, p. 151.

[34] Dow, T. (1969). The theory of charisma. *Sociological Quarterly 10*, p. 316.

[35] Huggins, N. (1987). Martin Luther King, Jr: Charisma and leadership. *Journal of American History, 74,* 477-481.

9

Developing Effective Leadership Communication

Every year thousands of adult learners over the age of twenty-five return to college classrooms to complete their degrees and to upgrade their job skills. These nontraditional students (you may be among them) believe in lifelong learning. We do, too. Developing leadership communication skills is a continuous process. The moment we think we've "arrived" as leaders, our progress stops. For this reason, we will use this final chapter to talk about ways through which you can increase your ability to think creatively and ethically as a leader. We'll conclude by suggesting three components to include in a plan for personal leadership development.

Creative Leadership

Creativity is an integral part of leadership. Since leaders are change agents, they need to plan creatively for change. Visions, for instance, are creative acts since they are new pictures of reality. Creativity also comes into play when leaders respond to change. The New Deal, the Head Start program, civil rights laws, the space program and the interstate highway system were all developed by American leaders in response to changing economic, political and social conditions. Stanford creativity expert James Adams sums up the relationship between creativity and change this way:

> Creativity and change are two sides of the same coin. They are often linked, in that creativity is needed to respond successfully to change and creativity, in turn, results in change. Creativity and change both imply new directions. They are both associated with uncertainty and risk.[1]

The Creative Process

To clarify the relationship between creativity and leadership, we first need to understand how the creative process works. Most experts suggest that creativity involves making new combinations or associations with existing elements. For example, S. J. Parnes of the Creative Education Foundation of New York describes creating as "the fresh and relevant association of thoughts, facts, ideas, etc. in a new configuration." He calls this action the "Aha" experience.[2]

Creativity requires looking at problems from a number of different perspectives, thinking in broad categories, and generating a variety of solutions. In other words, creative thinking is lateral thinking. This type of problem solving is associated with the right side of the brain while analytical reasoning is centered in the left hemisphere. Studies done on epileptic patients, stroke victims and others (described in Figure 9.1) demonstrate that the left and right hemispheres of the brain have different, albeit overlapping, functions. A summary of these functions is given below.

Left Brain	Right Brain
Treats information serially, one piece at a time	Treats information as a whole
Logic, analytic thinking, calculation	Visualization, intuitive ability
Reading, speaking, reasoning, arithmetic	Spatial ability, touch, musical ability, motor abilities
Center of language ability, writing and speech	Some language functions

By examining the functions of the left and right hemispheres, we get a better understanding of why creative ideas apparently appear out of nowhere. What seems like sudden inspiration to the logical left hemisphere may really be the result of long periods of analysis by the intuitive, visual, right side of the brain. As important as the right hemisphere is to creativity, it would be inaccurate to say that creative thinking is solely a right brain activity. Though the right brain may suggest a solution, this idea can only be carried to completion through the reasoning and verbal abilities of the left hemisphere. For example, to develop his theory of relativity, Einstein first visualized himself as a passenger holding a mirror as he rode on a ray of light. He determined that his image would never reach the mirror because both he and the glass would move at the speed of light. In contrast, a stationary observer could catch Einstein's reflection in a mirror as the scientist passed by. Einstein started work on his theory of relativity as a result of this visualization. To complete the task, he worked for a decade using the left brain functions of calculation and reasoning.[3]

One widely used description of creative problem solving was developed by George Graham Wallas. Based on research done with problem solvers, Wallas claimed that there are four steps to the creative process.[4]

1. *Preparation.* Creativity often begins with a conscious attempt to define and solve a problem. The preparation stage involves days, months and even years of reading, gathering information, and repeated experiments. Composers, for example, may spend over ten years in study

Figure 9.1   Research Highlight

Brain Asymmetry

The idea that each side of the human brain might perform different functions was first advanced in 1836 by a French physician named Marc Dax.[1] Dax had treated many patients who suffered brain damage caused by blows to the head. Curiously enough, those who had been struck on the left side of the brain often experienced a permanent loss of speech while those hit on the right side exhibited no such disruption. Dax's observations went largely unnoticed until a young French surgeon named Paul Broca began to research brain physiology in the late 1800s. Broca noted that the frontal area of the left side (or hemisphere) of the brain seemed to be most closely associated with speech.[2] This portion of the left hemisphere is known today as "Broca's area."

Beginning in the 1950s a group of researchers at the California Institute of Technology began piecing together the complex connections between the left and right brain. The research, led by Nobel Prize winner Roger Sperry, shed new light on the function of the left and right hemispheres of the brain. Sperry and his colleagues discovered that the connecting cable between the two hemispheres, known as the corpus callosum, acts primarily as a transmitter shuttling information back and forth between the left and right brain.[3]

The two hemispheres operate asymmetrically, each with its own unique form of processing. When the corpus callosum is completely severed, each hemisphere operates independently. The separation of the left and right hemispheres, known as split-brain surgery, has been used as a treatment for severe forms of epilepsy.

Michael Gazzaniga tested the information processing skills of split-brain patients. By developing an elaborate transmission system, Gazzaniga was able to flash two images on a screen simultaneously. One image was sent to the left brain while the other image was transmitted to the right brain. In one such study, a picture of a spoon was transmitted to the right hemisphere of a split-brain patient while a picture of a knife was sent to the patient's left hemisphere. When asked by the researcher to identify the image, patients gave different responses. The image transmitted to the verbal left brain led patients to say they had seen a "knife." At the same time, the image of the spoon flashed to the visual right brain caused patients to pick up a spoon from a group of objects that included both a spoon and a knife. When asked by the experimenter to identify the object in their hand, patients would become confused and identify the spoon as a "knife."[4]

The results of studies such as Gazzaniga's suggest that both the left and right brain have their own unique functions. Certain activities may require greater use of one hemisphere or another. Robert Ornstein suggests that lawyers and artists use different hemispheres of the brain while working.[5] Regardless, the evidence strongly suggests that each of us possesses two uniquely different brains, each with its own way of processing information and interpreting reality.

[1] Springer, S. P., & Deutsch, G. (1985). *Left brain, right brain*. New York: W. H. Freeman.

[2] Critchley, M. (1970). *Aphasiology and other aspects of language*. London: Edward Arnold.

[3] See, for example:

Myers, R. E., & Sperry, R. W. (1958). Interhemispheric communication through the corpus callosum: Mnemonic carry-over between the hemispheres. *Archives of Neurology and Psychiatry, 80*, 298-303.

Sperry, R. W. (1968). Hemisphere disconnection and unity in conscious awareness. *American Psychologist, 23*, 723-733.

[4] Gazzaniga, M. (1972). The split brain in man. In R. Held & W. Richards, (Eds.), *Perception: Mechanisms and models* (pp. 29-34). San Francisco: W. H. Freeman.

[5] Ornstein, R. (1978). The split and whole brain. *Human Nature, 1*, 76-83.

before their first important compositions are finished. The more extensive the preparation, the more likely the creative solution. As two time Nobel Prize winner Linus Pauling once pointed out: "The best way to get a good idea is to get lots of ideas." In addition, valuable new insights often come from unrelated fields of study. Take the case of Steven Jobs who co-developed the Apple Computer. Before starting Apple, Jobs designed video games at Atari. He attributes his success in developing the game Breakout to what he learned about movement and perception in a college dance class.[5]

2. *Incubation.* During the incubation period, the conscious mind shifts to other interests and the right brain has an opportunity to make the new associations which lead to creative problem solving. To see how the incubation process works, build in an incubation period as you write your next major paper. Work as hard as you can for a few hours and then turn your attention to other matters. When you return to write, you may find that ideas come more easily.

3. *Illumination.* As we noted earlier, ideas frequently appear as sudden inspirations during the creative process. These flashes of insight come during the illumination stage, often when a person is alone and more sensitive to intuitive messages. Carol Orsag Madigan and Ann Elwood

compiled the stories of many such inspirational moments in a book called
Brainstorms and Thunderbolts.[6] Here are a few examples of famous
flashes of illumination:

- The ancient Greek scientist Archimedes discovered the principle
  that "a body immersed in liquid loses as much in weight as the
  weight of the fluid it displaces" while in the bathtub. Afterwards
  he celebrated his discovery by running naked through the streets,
  shouting "Eureka!" ("I have found it.")

- The formula for the structure of benzene came to German chemist
  Friedrich August Kekule (1847) in a dream. Dreams were also a
  source of story plots for Robert Louis Stevenson. Mary Shelley, on
  the other hand, got her inspiration for the novel *Frankenstein*
  during a sleepless night.

- William Booth, the founder of the Salvation Army, came home after
  a walk through the slums of London to announce to his wife,
  "Darling, I have found my destiny."

- Mary Baker Eddy used her recovery from a fall on the ice to launch
  a new faith—Christian Science.

4. *Verification.* In this last stage, the creator develops the ideas which
have come through preparation, incubation and illumination.
Verification can include writing poetry and novels, testing mathematical
theorems, or checking with suppliers and running cost data.

To summarize what we've said so far, creativity consists of making
new associations, a process that relies heavily on the right hemisphere
of the brain which controls visualization, spatial relationships and
intuition. The creative process involves preparation, a period of incubation, illumination and verification. Unfortunately, few of us take
advantage of our creative potential either as followers or leaders. In the
next section we'll take a look at a number of the barriers which keep
us from developing our creative abilities.

Creative Roadblocks

The belief that only a few people are blessed with creative ability is
one common misconception about creativity. According to this view,
some outstanding individuals like Einstein, Beethoven and Steven Jobs
have large amounts of creative talent while most people have little or
none. Research suggests, however, that everyone can think creatively—
not just a few creative superstars. There is little correlation between

creative ability and such factors as intelligence, gender or age. Studies of creative people reveal that they do not fit a single profile. Creative individuals are both aggressive and passive, introverted and extroverted, emotionally unstable and emotionally healthy. Studies of creative people show that they share only three characteristics: 1) they are hardworking and persevering; 2) they are nonconformist in their thinking; 3) they are more flexible thinkers who are able to shift their frames of reference.[7]

If we all have creative potential, then we need to identify those factors which keep us from being creative problem solvers. James Adams identifies four types of creative blocks in his book *Conceptual Blockbusting*.[8]

1. *Perceptual Blocks.* According to Adams, "Perceptual blocks are obstacles that prevent the problem-solver from clearly perceiving either the problem itself or the information needed to solve the problem." Such blocks can include seeing what you expect to see (stereotyping), difficulty in isolating the problem, putting too many constraints on the problem, being unable to see the problem from many different viewpoints, being too close to the problem (saturation), and failure to use all the senses to understand the problem.

2. *Emotional Blocks.* Our fears and emotions can also keep us from using our creative potential. We may fear risk, failure or uncertainty; we might be unenthusiastic and too quick to judge new ideas; or we might confuse fantasy with reality.

3. *Cultural and Environmental Blocks.* Not all blocks to creativity come from within. Society often imposes stringent guidelines which inhibit the creative process. Cultural taboos eliminate certain solutions, and societal norms frequently emphasize reason to the exclusion of other methods of problem solving. Reliance on tradition ("We never did it that way before") also inhibits creative thinking. Ours is a rational society. When was the last time you took a course in creativity, for example, or talked about intuition in class? The results of a study of Oregon teachers demonstrates how little time is devoted to creative activities in the classroom. These teachers spent 67% of their time teaching cognitive learning skills like reading, writing and math while another 15% of their school day was devoted to administrative tasks. Most of their instructional methods were analytical, centering on lecture, discussion, recitation and drill/practice.[9]

4. *Intellectual and Expressive Blocks.* Intellectual blocks come from using the wrong strategies to solve problems, from being inflexible, or from not having enough (or correct) information. Expressive blocks keep us from communicating ideas effectively. Using words, for instance, is not always the best way to share ideas with others. To demonstrate the

limitations of language, Adams suggests that you have someone place an unfamiliar object in a bag so that you can feel the item but not see it. Describe the object while others try to draw a picture based on your description. You will find this task to be extremely difficult if you rely on common verbal symbols ("the top is circular with a piece cut out, and the longest side comes down from this cut off area"). You will be more successful if you describe the object in coordinates or geometric terms.

Becoming a Creative Leader

Based on what we know about the creative process and blocks to creativity, there are a number of strategies you can use to increase your effectiveness as a creative problem solver. These strategies include:

Put more effort into preparation. Many would-be creators overlook the fact that *preparation precedes illumination*. For each exciting moment of inspiration, there are many hours of preparation. As the old saying notes, "Inspiration is 99% perspiration." To increase the chances that you will generate the new associations that are at the heart of creative problem solving, make your preparation as broad as possible. Read journals and magazines that you have never read before, talk to experts who work outside your normal field of study and so on.

Withhold judgment. Premature evaluation squelches creativity. Not only does criticism make people defensive, but few of us can generate suggestions and critique them at the same time. Evaluation should take place only *after* ideas have been generated.[10] Suspension of critical judgment is the major component of the creative brainstorming procedure developed by advertising executive Alex Osborn. In brainstorming, participants list as many ideas as possible. Group members can add to earlier suggestions but they cannot criticize ideas.[11]

Build in periods of incubation and isolation. This may be the hardest strategy to use for two reasons: 1) you may not want to halt your conscious effort to solve a problem, and 2) finding the time to let ideas incubate or to get away may be difficult when others are demanding immediate solutions. Nonetheless, the right side of your brain needs time to generate new ideas. These ideas may come more easily if you are able to concentrate in a quiet setting. Members of your group or organization also need periods of incubation and isolation. As a creative leader, give followers the time they need to come up with solutions and protect them from unnecessary intrusions.

Reward yourself and others. The satisfaction of discovering a creative solution to a problem illustrates how creativity can be its own reward. Finishing a difficult paper or project can boost self-esteem and spur further creative efforts. Outside or extrinsic rewards also encourage creative output. The results of a four-year study of engineering and art students at Carnegie Mellon University exemplify how extrinsic rewards boost creativity. The engineering students (who were rewarded for coming up with "right" answers) developed strong analytical skills but scored low on creativity tests. The art students, on the other hand, scored low in analysis and high in creativity because creative activities, not structured solutions, were rewarded in the university's art program.[12]

Many companies encourage creativity by giving cash awards to those who develop new products or make cost-saving suggestions. Psychological rewards like recognition and compliments also motivate creativity. Rewards should be given to those who make the effort to be creative even if they fail. A new product may not make it to market, but those who have labored long and hard on the project still deserve credit. They'll be more willing to try again if their efforts are recognized.

All too often, creativity is not rewarded. Consider the case of Ignaz Semmelweis. Semmelweis worked in a hospital in Vienna before scientists discovered the relationship between germs and disease. He suspected that the fever which killed many infants in the hospital was spread by doctors who didn't wash their hands before deliveries. Semmelweis insisted that the physicians wash their hands before performing any medical procedures. Although the rate of deaths dropped dramatically as a result of hand washing, the other doctors drove Semmelweis out of the hospital. They could not accept the fact that their dirty hands caused patients to die. Since creativity is not always rewarded, you must learn to persist in the face of adversity. As Winston Churchill admonished: "Never give up. Never give up. Never give up."

Practice lateral thinking. Those who teach creativity courses and workshops claim that creativity training pays off. After training, participants not only score higher on such measures of creativity as quantity of ideas and originality, but they also report that they feel more expressive and competent.[13] If you can't take a course or seminar in creative thinking, start a self-directed program instead. Creativity exercises can be found in a number of books including *Creative Growth Games* and *Training Your Creative Mind*.[14] These exercises range from identifying numbers or items in a sequence, to writing cartoon captions, to matching inventions with their counterparts in nature. For example, creativity consultant Roger von Oech suggests that you think of humorous or slightly crazy uses for the major products and services of

your organization. He also advocates the use of "What if" questions.
By asking what if the situation were different, you broaden your
perspective on the problem.[15]

Although the left and right sides of your brain process information
differently, the metaphor is one tool that you can use to bridge the gap
between the two hemispheres. Metaphors are simply comparisons of two
elements we normally think of as different. Educators Donald and Judith
Sanders describe how the metaphor ties together both the
analytical/verbal and intuitive portions of the brain:

> It [the metaphor] is, perhaps, the fastest and most effective route we
> have to link the right brain with the left. With the metaphor, the
> sequential, factual, verbal knowledge of the left brain becomes "real"
> to the right brain, which assumes a pattern, an image of what the
> "big picture" means. As such, the metaphor provides a bridge
> between the two separate thought processes of the brain, a bridge
> that allows imagery to be verbalized and creates images for specific
> facts. This bridge connects the literal and the figurative, the factual
> and the imaginative, the proven and the intuitive.[16]

Effective leaders have employed metaphors throughout recorded
history. Plato used the image of the cave to demonstrate how societies
fear new ideas. Franklin Roosevelt compared the Nazis to carriers of
contagious diseases and suggested that other nations place them under
quarantine. More recently, George Bush described the generous acts of
individual Americans as a "thousand points of light."

The Importance of Ethics

As we have suggested throughout this book, effective leadership is
a product of the creation and delivery of inspiring and compelling
messages. Humans, unlike other species, are capable of shaping reality
through the manipulation of symbols. We do not passively react, but
rather *act* to change the world around us.

This ability to reformulate our view of the world has received renewed
attention from medical practitioners. An increasing number of physicians
believe that human communication plays an important role in physical
well-being. One of the most vocal advocates of this perspective is Bernie
Siegel, a Yale University cancer specialist. Siegel teaches his patients
how to be aware of their own healing potential as a means for avoiding
and overcoming illness.[17]

You may have experienced some of this healing power in your own life. If you have ever been ill at a time when you had something very important to do (take a final examination or go to a job interview, for example) you might have used some of Siegel's strategies. You might have told yourself something like, "I don't have time to be sick today." This message, perhaps coupled with some chicken soup and Vitamin C, might have been enough to fight off your illness. Human communication is that powerful!

Because human communication is capable of triggering such dramatic change, the question of ethics, in the words of Gerald Miller, is "inextricably bound up with every instance of human communication."[18] Ethics refer to standards of moral conduct. Standards vary from culture to culture, but the dilemma of establishing the measure of right and wrong remains constant.

The investigation of ethics is critical when focusing on leadership. A leader communicates a plan for action to his or her followers. The ethical implications of a leader's plans must be considered since the exercise of unethical leadership can have devastating results. Consider, for example, the negative impact of historical leaders such as Adolph Hitler, Pol Pot of Cambodia, and Nicolae Ceausescu of Romania and you begin to see how important the relationship between leadership and ethics is.

Responsible leaders maintain the highest possible standards of ethics. Whether a leader is guiding a problem-solving group, a small business, a multimillion dollar organization, or a national government, he or she exerts significant influence. Leaders must consider the impact they have on their followers as well as others external to the group, organization, or society.

Ethical Dilemmas of Leadership

Ethical questions are rarely simple to answer. Leaders are faced with a variety of moral and ethical dilemmas as they exercise influence over others. Here are just a few of the many complicated ethical questions leaders must consider.

The question of honesty. The adage states that honesty is the best policy. Yet, we have probably all told a lie (even if it was merely "little" or "white") at one time or another. Sissela Bok, in her book *Lying: Moral Choice in Public and Private Life*, defines lies as messages designed to make others believe what we ourselves do not believe.[19]

Often leaders challenge followers to achieve nearly impossible results. How else could we explain the incredible success stories of sports teams like the 1969 New York Mets or the development of products like Apple's Macintosh Computer? Eric Eisenberg calls this style of open-ended communication *strategic ambiguity*.[20] For example, should Gil Hodges, the manager of the 1969 New York Mets (a team picked to finish last by knowledgeable sources) have told his players he honestly felt there was no chance they could win a championship? In this situation, strategic ambiguity (''we have as good a chance to win as anyone else'') might have enhanced the team's performance. But where does a leader draw the line? Is it ethical for a leader to ask followers to perform in ways that are clearly beyond possibility?

Another ethical question of honesty deals with intentional deception on the part of a leader in discussing factors affecting those outside the immediate group. The leaders of the Soviet Union concealed the truth about the disaster at the Chernobyl nuclear power plant in 1986. Only after scientists throughout Europe reported potentially dangerous levels of radiation did the Soviets finally admit that one of the Chernobyl plant's reactors had exploded. Information about the disaster is still sketchy and many experts speculate that the true magnitude of the disaster may never be fully disclosed. Although few would consider the Soviet government's deception ethical, some argue that it is appropriate to keep secrets from the public when the information hidden is in the national interest.

The question of responsibility. Positions of leadership are associated with social and material power. Leaders may reap social benefits such as status, privilege, or respect as well as material benefits including salaries, bonuses and other items of value. Is it ethical for a leader to take advantage of his or her position to achieve personal power or prestige? Should a leader's concern always be for the good of the collective? Former Philippine leader Ferdinand Marcos placed personal interests above concerns for the welfare of followers. While many Filipinos lived in impoverished conditions, Marcos and his family enjoyed a lavish lifestyle supported, in part, by government funds. Similarly, in the late 1980s, a number of Wall Street financiers used illegal inside information to make billions of dollars from their investments. These actions clearly appear to be an abuse of the benefits of leadership.

How much responsibility does a leader bear in considering the extent to which his or her actions influence others? A number of tobacco companies have been criticized for targeting products to certain segments of the population. The prime targets for cigarette advertisers are minorities and women.[21] What responsibility, if any, do leaders such as those in the tobacco industry have?

The question of empowerment. A leader must decide how much power he or she wishes to exert over followers. Is it ethical to dominate followers and demand action or must power be distributed? Is it ethical for a leader to demand compliance when a follower has a moral objection to the leader's request? The United States government, for example, allows those with a moral objection to war to register as conscientious objectors. Those who register for military service in this category will not be assigned to combat units, but rather would serve during war in non-combat environments such as hospitals.

Is it ever appropriate for a leader to insist that a follower behave in a way which he or she finds unacceptable? What if an employee finds a particular task morally objectionable or physically dangerous? Can a leader ethically insist that a follower perform the task? Some medical practitioners, for instance, refuse to participate in the performance of certain medical procedures such as abortions and sterilizations. Should these practitioners be punished for their views?

Followers who choose not to perform certain tasks, of course, must live with the consequences of their conviction whether it leads to a demotion, a narrowing of responsibilities, or re-assignment to another unit. Under what conditions should a leader respect a follower's right to choose his or her own behavior?

The question of loyalty. Recent political scandals including Watergate and the Iran Contra Affair bring to mind the ethical question of loyalty. Does a leader have an ethical responsibility to defend followers when they are censured for carrying out the leader's policies?

Imagine that you work as a cashier in a small grocery store. The owner of the store tells you to sell items marked with two prices at the higher price. If you have no moral objection to this policy, you will probably be willing to act as the owner wishes. A customer comes into the store to purchase a sandwich for lunch. When the customer arrives at the checkout counter, you notice two prices marked on the sandwich. You charge the customer the higher price. The customer complains to you, but you explain that you are carrying out store policy. Angry over this confrontation, the customer decides to complain about you to a local consumer group. Is the owner of the grocery store morally obligated to defend you for carrying out his or her wishes? Must a leader defend followers when they are acting on his or her behalf?

The question of consistency. Consistency is an important ethical concern. Consistency refers to equal treatment of followers through the establishment of clear and uniform policies and procedures. Leaders often work with followers from diverse ethnic and social backgrounds. Laws have been established which protect followers from discrimination based on gender, ethnic or social background. Still, prejudice and inequality exist. Can you think of any situation under which unequal treatment is ethical?

Ambiguity in policies and procedures is another form of inconsistent leadership. Imagine a crew member on an assembly line night shift who has been verbally warned that she will be fired if late for work on three occasions. The organization has no formal policy regarding tardiness; however, the night shift supervisor has informed her that this is *his* policy. One night she is late arriving to work because her child has been ill. She is concerned, but not overly worried as this is the first time she has been late to work. When she arrives at work she discovers that her supervisor is absent and a supervisor from the day shift has taken his place. The day shift supervisor calls her into his office and fires her after explaining that he does not condone tardiness. Is this fair? What could be done to provide more consistent leadership in this situation?

At times leaders ask followers to perform tasks they themselves will not do. Should there be a "golden rule of leadership" mandating that leaders must be willing to do what they have asked followers to do? If arriving for work on time, for example, is important to a leader, is he or she compelled to be on time in order to behave ethically?

We have asked a number of questions about the behavior of leaders. Although these questions are difficult to answer, we offer the following guidelines as the basis for a code of leadership ethics.

1. Ethical leaders do not transmit intentionally deceptive or harmful messages to followers.

2. Ethical leaders place concern for others above concern for personal gain.

3. Ethical leaders respect the opinions and attitudes of followers and allow followers the freedom to consider the consequences of their actions.

4. Ethical leaders defend followers when they are censured for carrying out policies supported by the leader.

5. Ethical leaders are consistent in their treatment of followers regardless of gender, ethnic or social background.

6. Ethical leaders establish clear and uniform policies and procedures which are implemented consistently throughout the group, organization or society.

7. Ethical leaders follow the "golden rule of leadership" by demonstrating a willingness to meet the expectations required of followers.

The guidelines we offer may seem somewhat simplistic or impractical in certain situations. In some cases, they may be. But we believe that adopting these guidelines enhances your chances of engaging in ethical and responsible leadership, thereby increasing your overall level of leadership effectiveness. (Take a look at the case study in Figure 9.2 to see what happens when leaders ignore ethical concerns.)

Establishing an Ethical Climate

Once a leader has considered ethical issues on the personal level, he or she can focus attention on one of the primary ethical responsibilities of leadership—the establishment of an "ethical climate." Richard Johannesen, an expert on ethical responsibility in human communication, has synthesized results of research on corporate ethics. He identifies five behaviors through which you as a leader can promote the development of an ethical climate.[22]

1. *Demonstrate a personal commitment to ethical behavior.* A leader's high standards of ethics often set the tone for followers. Although ethical behavior on the part of a leader does not guarantee ethical followership, unscrupulous leader behavior rarely encourages a clear commitment to ethics among followers.

2. *Develop a formal code of ethics.* Encourage the establishment of a set of ethical expectations. These expectations can be agreed upon orally or, preferably, put in writing. Realize that a formal code of ethics is not cast in stone and will continue to evolve over time.

3. *Commit resources to ethical concerns.* A leader communicates a belief in the importance of ethics by committing resources to ethical concerns. Resources devoted to ethics may be human (time devoted to the discussion of ethics in a problem-solving group, the establishment of an ethics committee in an organization) or material (hiring an ethics officer to oversee implementation of a formal code of ethics, sending followers to an ethics workshop).

Figure 9.2   Case Study

The Cost of Care at Mercy General Hospital

Mercy General* is a private hospital serving a large metropolitan community. The majority of nurses working at Mercy General are Registered Nurses (RNs); a handful are lower paid Licensed Practical Nurses (LPNs). RNs are traditionally responsible for the most complex patient care as well as staff leadership. LPNs, who receive less training, perform limited patient care under the supervision of RNs. Professional guidelines mandate that LPNs are not to perform certain duties. Among the responsibilities assigned only to RNs are the administration of intravenous medication, the interpretation of physicians' orders, and various forms of complicated patient assessment.

In a cost cutting move, the administration at Mercy General ordered LPNs to perform one form of patient assessment previously assigned only to RNs. This move enabled the hospital to staff wards with more LPNs, resulting in salary savings of several thousand dollars per day. To appease the professional association monitoring the LPNs, the administration instructed RNs to sign patient charts indicating they, not the LPNs, had completed the necessary assessments. A number of nurses complained that they would be jeopardizing their careers—not to mention the well-being of their patients—if LPNs performed tasks that clearly fell outside the scope of their training. The hospital administration ignored the concerns of the nurses and informed those who were unwilling to comply with the new policy that they would be scheduled to work in lower paying non-nursing jobs.

Complaints about the new policy led to an investigation by an external agency. A number of nurses were cited for performing inappropriate patient care. Although the nurses were only carrying out administration policy, the hospital suspended several nurses to avoid censure from the professional association.

Discussion Questions

1. Was the administration at Mercy General justified in asking RNs to sign patient assessments performed by LPNs? Why or why not?
2. Under what circumstances is it ethical for leaders to ask followers to perform objectionable tasks?
3. Under what circumstances should leaders solicit the viewpoints of followers before initiating changes in policy?
4. What action would you recommend the administration at Mercy General take to deal with the citations given to the nurses who provided inappropriate care?
5. How could the administration at Mercy General have implemented a more ethical change in policy?

6. Which of the ethical guidelines discussed earlier were breached by the administration at Mercy General?

* The hospital and situation depicted in this case are fictional.

4. *Schedule a periodic "ethics audit."* Develop a procedure for a formal and periodic assessment of overall ethical performance. Evaluate compliance with ethical guidelines among all members of the group or organization.

5. *Encourage a cultural concern for ethics.* As suggested in Chapter 7, one of a leader's primary functions is the creation and management of culture. A leader can promote high ethical standards by incorporating a concern for ethics into group or organizational culture. As Johannesen explains, "Ethical concerns must be regarded as on a par with economic and pragmatic concerns in decision-making. Procedures must be established so that ethical issues automatically are confronted as part of a decision."[23]

Three Components of Leadership Development

We began this chapter by noting that leadership development is a lifelong process. If becoming an effective leader is your goal, then the following components should be part of your plan for personal leadership development:

Component 1: Leadership Learning

There is no shortage of opportunities to learn about leadership. As a matter of fact, it would be hard to avoid hearing about leaders since we track their successes and failures in the newspaper, read about them in history books, and follow them at school and on the job. We can learn a great deal from the experiences of other leaders. We will want to adopt some of their strategies and behaviors; others we will want to avoid. Unfortunately, we often learn very little from the examples of other leaders because we merely observe them without understanding the reasons behind their successes and failures. One way to become a more perceptive student of leadership is to keep current with leadership research. The explosion of leadership knowledge in recent years demonstrates why it is so important to view leadership learning as an ongoing process. The second edition of *Stogdill's Handbook of Leadership* cited forty-seven hundred books and articles in 1981. This massive volume was soon outdated. Nine years later the updated, third edition of the *Handbook* appeared with seventy-five hundred citations.[24]

Component 2: Leadership Experience

Any opportunity to master your communication skills, whether it be at home, at work or at school, is preparation for leadership. The most useful experiences, though, are those that put you in the leader role. Since leadership experience is so vital, seek out chances to act as a leader. Volunteer to coordinate a campus or community activity, be a crew manager, teach a skill to a group, or offer to serve in any capacity to further your leadership skills. What you learn from your successes and perhaps more importantly your failures is preparation for future leadership assignments. Warren Bennis notes that leaders engage in ''innovative learning.'' While others often feel trapped by their experiences, leaders build on the past to anticipate and to shape future events. According to Bennis, innovative learning involves reflection:

> Experiences aren't truly yours until you think about them, analyze them, examine them, question them, reflect on them, and finally understand them. The point, once again, is to use your experiences rather than being used by them, to be the designer, not the design, so that experiences empower rather than imprison.[25]

One way to gain leadership experience without having to pay for your mistakes is through training. In addition to participating in traditional educational and corporate training programs, you may have the opportunity to be a part of a leadership simulation. In a simulation exercise, trainees become managers of a fictitious company and cope with budgets, meetings, memos and interruptions. Perhaps the best known leadership simulation is Looking Glass Inc. which was developed by researchers at the Center for Creative Leadership.[26] Looking Glass is a mythical glass manufacturing company with four thousand employees and $200 million in annual sales. Managers from such corporations as Monsanto, Dow Jones and Union Pacific take charge of Looking Glass for a day or more in order to learn about their own management and leadership styles and the demands of corporate life.

Component 3: Find a Mentor

Finding someone who will serve as your mentor can greatly increase your chances of emerging as a leader in an organizational context. The term "mentor" originated from the character Mentor who was the friend of the ancient Greek king Ulysses in Homer's *Odyssey*. He watched the king's son while Ulysses was away, acting as a personal and professional counselor and guide. Modern day mentors perform many of the functions of the original, including:[27]

1. *Providing sponsorship and visibility.* Mentors fight for their proteges by standing up for them in meetings, putting their names in for promotions and so on. Proteges gain power through their association with powerful mentors. Those who would normally refuse a request from a new manager, for instance, will frequently honor such a request if that manager is associated with a high level executive.

2. *Helping to learn the ropes.* Mentors help proteges learn the ins and outs of the organization, including how decisions are made, what the key values are, who holds power and so forth. Mentors have been totally immersed in the corporate culture (see Chapter 7) and can help acclimate the protege.

3. *Giving assignments and protection.* As we noted in our discussion of the Pygmalion Effect, the type of assignments that a new manager receives can determine whether that person becomes a low or high performer. Low expectations communicated through unchallenging or overly demanding assignments can generate a negative performance cycle. Effective mentors set challenging yet realistic goals and are less likely to dwell on poor performance. In addition, the mentor provides protection for the employee should she or he fail.

4. *Acting as a role model.* Mentors are role models who demonstrate leadership skills. During their apprenticeships, proteges learn how to manage conflict, build teams, gather information, and make ethical choices.

5. *Providing counseling.* Mentors often become trusted counselors who provide helpful advice on such topics as career choices and problem solving.

6. *Serving as a friend.* In healthy mentor-protege partnerships, the parties become friends who provide support and encouragement to each other. Even when the original relationship ends because

of a promotion, job transfer or some other factor, the friendship remains. Friendship is one reward for serving as a mentor. Mentors also profit from the help that proteges provide with job related tasks, and they get a feeling of satisfaction from seeing their proteges develop. In some organizations like the Jewell company and the Security Pacific Bank, mentors receive company-wide recognition for their efforts.

Based on what mentors can do for their proteges, it's not surprising that those who have organizational sponsors are generally more successful. A researcher surveyed all the executives who appeared in the "Who's News" column of the *Wall Street Journal* during one year. Two-thirds of those who responded reported having one or more mentors during their careers. Most were mentored when they were in their twenties and thirties and they stated that their sponsors had either an extraordinary or substantial influence on their careers.[28] Mentor relationships are also important to faculty success. College instructors who receive mentoring support have higher rank and salaries and are more likely to be tenured.[29] Yet, mentor-protege relationships can fail if 1) mentors demand too much from their proteges, 2) mentors lose their organizational power, or 3) proteges become too dependent on their sponsors.[30]

The development of mentor-protege relationships is especially critical to women since nearly all women who make it to the top of established organizations do so with the help of sponsors.[31] As we noted in our discussion of the gender leadership gap, however, there are few women available to be mentors. In addition, many men are reluctant to act as mentors for females. Fortunately, peers can function much as mentors do, supplying information, feedback and friendship. Effective peer relationships can serve as an alternative for both women and men who cannot find sponsors. Kathy Kram and Lynn Isabella identify three types of peer relationships.[32] *Information peers* are casual acquaintances whose chief function is information sharing. *Collegial peers* help with career strategies and provide job related feedback as well as friendship. *Special peers* act like best friends, giving confirmation, emotional support and personal feedback. Kram and Isabella suggest that developing a network which includes all three types of peers can help fill the gap when mentors can't be found.

Taking the Next Step

In the course of these nine chapters, we've defined leadership from a communication perspective, described leadership theories, identified key leadership communication skills and looked at leaders in the small group, organizational and public contexts. Along the way we've touched upon everything from power and credibility to team building and creativity. While our job as authors is ending, your task is just beginning. If you want to continue to develop your leadership communication, the next step is up to you. We hope we have provided a solid foundation from which your quest for leadership will be successfully launched.

Summary

In this chapter, we focused on the lifelong process of developing leadership communication skills. We talked first about creativity which is an integral part of leadership. Leaders need to think creatively in order to plan for change and to respond to change. Creative problem solving is the process of combining existing elements in new ways and involves lateral thinking — the type of thinking most closely associated with the right hemisphere of the brain. Creating incorporates preparation, incubation, illumination and verification. Blocks to creativity can be: 1) perceptual, 2) emotional, 3) cultural and environmental, 4) intellectual and expressive. These blocks can be overcome by putting more effort into preparation, avoiding premature judgment of ideas, building in periods of incubation and isolation, rewarding ourselves and others, and practicing associative thinking.

Next we looked at the importance of ethical leadership. Effective leaders develop standards to deal with ethical questions related to honesty, responsibility, empowerment, loyalty and consistency. Leaders establish an ethical climate for followers when they 1) demonstrate a personal commitment to ethical behavior, 2) develop a formal code of ethics, 3) commit resources to ethical concerns, 4) schedule a periodic ethics audit, and 5) encourage a cultural concern for ethics.

We concluded the chapter by proposing that learning about leadership, gaining leadership experience and finding mentors should be part of your plan for your personal development as a leader. Mentors 1) act as sponsors, 2) give assignments and protection, 3) help proteges learn the ropes, 4) act as role models, 5) provide counseling when needed, and 6) serve as friends. When mentors are not available, peers can serve as a substitute by supplying information, feedback and friendship.

Application Exercises

1. The Brick Uses Test

   One well known test of creativity asks participants to list all the uses they can think of for an ordinary brick. See how well you can do alone and then generate a master list in a group. Use the same procedure with other familiar objects of your choice—used tires or cereal boxes, for example. If you have the time, talk about criteria that you might use to evaluate answers. When is an idea conventional but not creative or creative but not useful?

2. Think of a time when you came up with a creative solution to a major problem. Analyze your problem solving effort based on the four stages of the creativive process identified by Wallas and others: preparation, incubation, illumination, verification. Did you experience each stage? Which was the most difficult for you? How can you increase your flow of creative ideas in the future? Report your findings.

3. Develop your own metaphor for leadership. Share your metaphor with a small group or with the rest of the class.

4. Review the list of Ethical Guidelines for Leaders. Do you think it is possible for a leader to follow all of these guidelines? Are there any circumstances in which a leader is justified in behaving unethically?

5. Research a leader you consider to be either highly ethical or unethical. What impact did this leader have on others? Share your findings with the class.

6. Pair off with someone else and discuss mentor relationships. Have you served as a mentor or protege? How would you evaluate this experience? If you haven't been in this type of relationship, identify someone who could serve in this capacity and consider how you might ask them to be your mentor. Describe the peer relationships that have been most helpful to you at work or in school.

Endnotes

[1] Adams, J. L. (1986). *The care and feeding of ideas*. Reading, MA: Addison-Wesley, p. 3.

[2] Sanders, D. A., & Sanders, J. A. (1984). *Teaching creativity through metaphor*. New York: Longman, p. 24.; Parnes, S. J. (1975). "Aha!." In I. A. Taylor & J. W. Getzels (Eds.), *Perspectives on creativity* (pp. 224-248). Chicago: Aldine.

[3] A number of examples for this chapter are taken from Hunt, M. (1982). *The universe within: A new science explores the human mind.* New York: Simon and Schuster, Chs. 8, 9.

[4] Wallas, G. (1926). *The art of thought.* New York: Harcourt.

[5] von Oech, R. (1986). *A kick in the seat of the pants.* New York: Harper & Row, pp. 30, 32.

[6] Orsag Madigan, C., & Elwood, A. (1983). *Brainstorms and thunderbolts.* New York: Macmillan.

[7] Hunt, Ch. 9.

[8] Adams, J. L. (1986). *Conceptual blockbusting* (3rd ed.). Reading, MA: Addison-Wesley.

[9] Sanders & Sanders, p. 19.

[10] Roger von Oech suggests that one of the roles of a creator is to act as a judge who passes judgment on the value of ideas. However, von Oech argues that this role should not be played until late in the creative process, after information has been gathered and put into the form of creative proposals.

[11] Osborn, A. (1957). *Applied imagination.* New York: Charles Scribner's Sons.

[12] Adams, *The care and feeding of ideas,* pp. 138-140.

[13] Davis, G. A., & Bull, K. S. (1978). Strengthening affective components of creativity in a college course. *Journal of Educational Psychology, 70,* 833-836.; Parnes, "Aha."

[14] Raudsepp, E., & Hough, G. P. (1977). *Creative growth games.* New York: Harvest/Jove.; VanGundy, A. B. (1982). *Training your creative mind.* Englewood Cliffs, NJ: Prentice-Hall.

[15] von Oech, R. (1983). *A whack on the side of the head.* New York: Warner Books.

[16] Sanders & Sanders, pp. 18-19.

[17] See:

Siegel, B. S. (1989). *Peace, love & healing.* New York: Harper & Row.

Siegel, B. S. (1986). *Love, medicine & miracles.* New York: Harper & Row.

[18] Miller, G. R. (1969). Contributions of communication research to the study of speech. In A. H. Monroe & D. Ehninger, *Principles and types of speech communication* [6th brief ed.] (pp. 334-357). Glenview, Ill: Scott, Foresman, p. 355.

[19] Bok, S. (1979). *Lying: Moral Choice in Public and Private Life.* New York: Vintage Books.

[20] Eisenberg, E. M. (1984). Ambiguity as strategy in organizational communication. *Communication Monographs, 51,* 227-242.

[21] For more information on the targeting of tobacco advertisements, see:

Ernster, V. L. (1985, July). Mixed messages for women: A social history of cigarette smoking and advertising. *New York State Journal of Medicine,* pp. 335-340.

Warner, K. E. (1986). *Selling smoke: Cigarette advertising and public health.* Washington D.C: American Public Health Association.

[22] Johannesen, R. L. (1990). *Ethics in human communication* (3rd ed.). Prospect Heights, IL: Waveland, pp. 154-155.

[23] Johannesen, p. 155.

[24] Bass, B. (Ed.) (1981). *Stogdill's handook of leadership* (2nd ed.). New York: The Free Press.; Bass, B. (1990). *Bass and Stogdill's handbook of leadership* (3rd ed.). New York: The Free Press.

[25] Bennis, W. (1989). *On becoming a leader.* Reading, MA: Addison-Wesley, p. 98. For more information on innovative learning, see: Botkin, J. W., Elmandjra, M., & Malitza, M. (1979). *No limits to learning.* New York: Pergamon Books.

[26] Petre, P. (1984, October 29). Games that teach you to manage. *Newsweek,* pp. 65-72.

[27] See, for example:

Hunt, D. M., & Michael, C. (1983). Mentorship: A career training and development tool. *Academy of Management Review, 8,* 475-485.

Kanter, R. M. (1977). *Men and women of the corporation.* New York: Basic Books.

Kram, K. E., & Isabella, L.A. (1985). Mentoring alternatives: The role of peer relationships in career development. *Academy of Management Review, 28,* 110-132.

Woodlands Group. (1980, November). Management development roles: Coach, sponsor, and mentor. *Personnel Journal, 59,* 918-921.

[28] Roche, G. R. (1979). Much ado about mentors. *Harvard Business Review, 57,* 14-28.

[29] Kogler Hill, S. E., Bahniuk, M. H., & Dobos, J. (1989). The impact of mentoring and collegial support on faculty success: An analysis of support behavior, information adequacy, and communication apprehension. *Communication Education, 38,* 15-33.

[30] For a more complete discussion of the potential problems of the mentor-protege relationship and how to solve them, see:

Phillips-Jones, L. (1982). *Mentors and proteges.* New York: Arbor House, Ch. VIII.

[31] For a discussion of mentors and female career success, see:

Hennig, M., & Jardim, A. (1977). *The managerial woman.* New York: Anchor Press/Doubleday.

Morrison, A. M., White, R. P, & Van Velsor, E. (1987). *Breaking the glass ceiling: Can women reach the top of America's largest corporations?* Reading, MA: Addison-Wesley.

Kanter. *Men and women of the corporation.*

[32] Kram & Isabella.

Appendix A

Developing Effective Public Speeches

Overview

Element 1: Pre-speech Planning

Element 2: Organization

Element 3: Language

Element 4: Rehearsal

Element 5: Delivery

Public leadership is a product of effective public communication. Although many public campaigns rely on pamphlets, position papers and other written materials, the majority of interaction between public leaders and their followers takes place via public address. Whether you aspire to be President of the United States, a social activist, or the leader of a fraternity or sorority, you must be able to speak effectively in public to influence large numbers of followers.

The following material is designed to assist you in developing effective public speeches. Regardless of where you speak, whether in the classroom, political rally or business meeting, you will discover that the delivery of an effective public speech enhances audience perceptions of your personal power and leadership potential.

The effectiveness of a public speech is dependent on five primary elements: pre-speech planning, organization, language, rehearsal and delivery.

Element 1: Pre-speech Planning

Planning is essential in the development of successful public messages. The following factors should be considered before delivering a public presentation.

Mode of delivery. The principal modes of delivery are *impromptu*, *extemporaneous*, and *manuscript*. Impromptu speeches are delivered "off the cuff" with little advance preparation. Situations which might require an impromptu presentation include responding to an unexpected disaster or crisis, accepting an award, or participating in a meeting. When speaking in the impromptu mode, try to maintain a clear focus or theme. Always avoid long, rambling impromptu messages.

Speaking from a prepared outline or set of notes is known as extemporaneous speech. This is the most common mode of public address. Extemporaneous speech gives you an opportunity to develop a clear presentational purpose or goal and adequate reasoning and support. The extemporaneous speech also offers you freedom in the construction of the message. Since your notes consist of an outline or a few key phrases, you have greater flexibility.

Working from a manuscript—a written transcript of the speech— allows for the greatest control of subject matter. Many political leaders use the manuscript mode of delivery. Manuscripts are most effective when the content of the message must be very precise. However, the manuscript mode does not allow a speaker to be spontaneous. When using a manuscript, it is advisable to use a teleprompter or similar mechanical device so that eye contact with the audience is not disrupted.

Audience analysis. It is essential that you have an understanding of the attitudes and expertise of your listeners. Although audience size may vary from a small group to a worldwide audience, an understanding of the needs, aspirations, experiences and intellectual abilities of those in the audience helps to create a more effective message. For example, a political candidate addressing a group of union employees will be more effective if he or she is aware of the issues that have the greatest impact on union members. A well prepared speaker will seek information about the audience from a variety of sources. The speaker might research the previous positions of audience members, observe current actions, or question, interview or survey selected audience members as a means of uncovering information.

Element 2: Organization

The logic and structure of the ideas presented within a public speech are critical. Successful presentations are organized around a central theme with supporting points. Three factors are most important in organizing a public speech.

Developing a thesis. The purpose or objective of a speech is known as the thesis. In general terms, the thesis identifies your goals (to inform, persuade, entertain, etc.). More specifically, the thesis outlines exactly what you hope to achieve in your presentation. A thesis statement is prepared in the initial stages of speech organization and usually consists of one declarative sentence. The thesis statement itself should be as specific as possible in identifying the feelings, knowledge or understanding you wish to convey to your audience. For example, "My speech is on John F. Kennedy" is ineffective. This thesis provides no explanation regarding the specific purpose of the speech. A better thesis would be, "John F. Kennedy was one of the most effective public communicators of the twentieth century." This thesis statement provides a detailed description of the argument you wish to make. Be certain that you have a clear idea of what you want to accomplish in your presentation before moving on.

Arranging ideas. Once the thesis has been developed, arrange the main points you have selected to support your thesis. The number of main points should be kept to a minimum, and each main point should be supported with statistics, examples, illustrations, anecdotes, or other forms of evidence. Main points can be arranged in chronological order (from the earliest to the most recent event), spatial order (by some physical or geographical relationship), in order of size or impact (from largest to smallest or vice-versa), or, when no other logical pattern seems appropriate, in what is known as a topical arrangement pattern. Topical arrangement involves creating an organizational pattern that fits the ideas presented. For example, a persuasive speech describing the benefits of a particular university would be difficult to organize chronologically, spatially or in relation to size. Developing a series of arguments which can be strung together in a topical pattern would be more effective.

Topics could include tuition and housing costs, location, and the quality of the faculty.

Linking ideas. Statements that link ideas together are known as transitions. Be careful to include transitions in your presentation so that audience members can follow along with your message. Phrases such as "now that we have discussed the affordable housing at State University, let's focus on the desirability of the surrounding area" help to shift an audience's attention from one main point to the next.

Element 3: Language

The effective use of language is the key to producing memorable and moving public speeches. We remember Martin Luther King's "I Have a Dream" speech reprinted in Chapter 8 primarily because of the way King used words to create dramatic images. Successful speakers use language that is clear, vivid and appropriate.

Clarity. The best rule of thumb in a presentation is to use specific, understandable language. Technical and complicated words should be used sparingly, particularly when dealing with mass audiences. Further, avoid the use of jargon and euphemisms. Political leaders often create pleasant descriptions of unpleasant events. During the Reagan administration, for instance, MX missiles were known as "peacekeepers" and taxes were referred to as "revenue enhancements."[1] This type of "doublespeak" only serves to confuse and distract audience members. The more you complicate your message by using technical or convoluted language, the more likely it is that your message will be misunderstood.

Vividness. Clear language does not have to be dull. Public speeches should be descriptive and distinctive. The use of affect and imagery serve to enliven public address. Affective language sparks emotion while imagery creates visual connections for the audience. Franklin Roosevelt's Declaration of War following the Pearl Harbor attack of 1941 began as follows:

> Yesterday, December 7, 1941 — a date which will live in infamy —
> the United States was suddenly and deliberately attacked by naval
> and air forces of the Empire of Japan.

Roosevelt's words expressed the shock of a nation. To this day, many people look at the calendar on December 7th and think back to that infamous day in 1941. The image persists.

The mark of effective public speakers is their ability to create stirring representations for audiences. While a picture may paint a thousand words, it is equally true that a gifted speaker can fashion a word into a thousand pictures.

Appropriateness. Avoid using language which might offend members of the audience. The use of profane or obscene language is almost always inappropriate. In addition, promoting racial or sexual stereotypes can damage a speaker's image. Al Campanis, the former general manager of the Los Angeles Dodgers, was forced to resign after he announced on national television that blacks lacked the "necessities" required to manage professional baseball teams. Campanis claimed that his remark was not indicative of racial prejudice, but public outcry over the "inappropriateness" of his comment led to his dismissal. Although this incident did not occur during a public speech, it did occur in a public context. This incident demonstrates how most audiences react to racial or sexual stereotyping.

Some forms of humor lower a speaker's credibility. One type of humor which can be particularly detrimental is disparaging humor. Disparagement involves using yourself or another as the object or brunt of a humorous comment or joke. This form of humor is commonly referred to as a "put down."

Disparagement focusing on personal shortcomings (such as height, weight, complexion, or social skills) has been found to be detrimental to a speaker's image. Informative speakers who belittled themselves were rated as less competent, less expert and less likeable while speakers who belittled others were rated as having lower character.[2] Other research suggests that a speaker's use of milder forms of disparaging humor aimed at one's occupation or profession are not as harmful.[3] All in all, the evidence suggests that public speakers should generally avoid using disparaging humor whether aimed at the self or others.

Element 4: Rehearsal

Practicing gives you the opportunity to simulate a public presentation. This experience helps you refine content and increase your confidence level. Just as a dress rehearsal can serve to make a marriage ceremony or theater production less confusing and stressful, a speech rehearsal can help polish a public presentation.

The most important thing to remember when rehearsing a speech is that you must practice *out loud*. As we noted in Chapter 6, we are able to think more rapidly than we speak. As a result, internal thought and external speech operate differently. Thought is characterized by condensed grammar and syntax which makes the structure of internal thought incomplete. Our thoughts are composed of fleeting images and words. External speech, on the other hand, is grammatically and syntactically complete. Speech consists of fully constructed messages which follow a distinctive organizational pattern. Since presentations are delivered in external speech, the external form of communication must be used during rehearsal. Rehearsing only in internal thought (just thinking about what you will say without saying it out loud) may contribute to the same feelings of anxiety that are associated with inadequate speech preparation.[4]

Element 5: Delivery

Delivery refers to the physical aspects of speechmaking. A speaker's delivery should not be awkward or distracting. The delivery of a message is most effective when it appears natural. Several factors directly affect the delivery of public messages.

Physical appearance. Public speakers should be appropriately groomed and clothed before appearing in front of an audience. Expectations regarding hygiene and dress vary from one situation to another. For example, it is generally acceptable to deliver a classroom presentation dressed in jeans and a t-shirt, but this casual attire would not be acceptable for a speech to a group of civic leaders. In general, it is best to tailor your appearance to the situation, region or culture in which you will be speaking. Your audience analysis should help you decide what will be acceptable.

Gesturing. Gestures occur naturally in conversation and do not need to be planned for in public address. When did you last worry about gesturing while conversing casually with your best friend? Unfortunately, many speakers are uncomfortable about body language during their presentations. Instead of allowing the natural tendency to gesture to operate, they *plan* where to insert gestures in the speech. As a result, their movements are awkward and distracting. Pay attention to your natural pattern of gestures. When rehearsing, include these natural gestures in your presentation. Allow the same natural gestures to occur when you make your appearance in front of an audience.

Movement. Movement can be used to heighten interest in a speech. Movement that minimizes physical distance between the speaker and audience also serves to reduce psychological distance. Getting physically closer to the audience often creates an emotional and spiritual connection with listeners. This might explain why so many speeches by religious and political leaders end with the speaker shaking hands with audience members.

Eye contact. In western culture, looking others in the eyes is a sign of respect and honesty. Effective public speakers maintain eye contact with audience members. Staring at your notes or letting your eyes dart around leads to the perception that you are not trustworthy. Use your notes sparingly. Avoid eye dart by focusing for a few seconds on individuals seated in different sections of the audience.

Voice Quality. Avoid monotonous or strident tones. An expressive voice conveys emotion and interest without being harsh. Most unpleasant vocal patterns can be improved with training and practice. George Bush worked during the 1988 Presidential campaign to reduce the nasality of his voice and to make the quality of his voice more pleasing to listeners.

Incorporating these suggestions for pre-speech planning, organization, the use of language, rehearsal, and delivery can help to make your presentations more effective. Remember, as with any skill, hard work and practice are the keys to success.

Endnotes

[1] For more examples of this kind of deceptive communication, see:

Lutz, W. (1989). *Doublespeak*. New York: Harper & Row.

This highly readable and entertaining book describes how government, business, advertisers, and others use language to distort reality. Among the more comical examples: an 18 page recipe for fruitcake for Army chefs which includes instructions describing how the cake should "conform to the inside contour of the can or can liner," with "no point on the top of the lid greater than 3/4-inch from the side of the can where the cake did not touch the lid during baking"; and the U.S. government's description of the 1983 early morning paratroop invasion of Grenada as a "pre-dawn vertical insertion."

[2] See:

Hackman, M. Z. (1988). Audience reactions to the use of direct and personal disparaging humor in informative public address. *Communication Research Reports*, 5, 126-130.

Hackman, M. Z. (1988). Reactions to the use of self-disparaging humor by informative public speakers. *Southern Speech Communication Journal*, 53, 175-183.

[3] Chang, M. & Gruner, C. R. (1981). Audience reaction to self-disparaging humor. *Southern Speech Communication Journal*, 46, 419-426.

[4] For a more complete discussion of the importance of internal thought and external speech in public address, see:

Hackman, M. Z. (1989). The inner game of public speaking: Applying intrapersonal communication processes in the public speaking course. *Carolinas Speech Communication Annual*, 5, 41-47.

Bibliography

Adams, J. L. (1986). *Conceptual blockbusting* (3rd ed.). Reading, MA: Addison-Wesley.

Adams, J. L. (1986). *The care and feeding of ideas*. Reading, MA: Addison-Wesley.

Adams, J., Rice, R., & Instone, D. (1984). Follower attitudes toward women and judgments concerning performance by female and male leaders. *Academy of Management Journal, 27*, 636-643.

Adler, M. J. (1967). *The difference of man and the difference it makes*. New York: Holt, Rinehart and Winston.

Akin, G., & Hopelain, D. (1986). Finding the culture of productivity. *Organizational Dynamics, 14*, 19-32.

Andersen, K. & Witteman, P. (1985, April 1). A spunky tycoon turned superstar. *Time*, pp. 30-39.

Andrews, P. (1984). Performance, self-esteem and perceptions of leadership emergence: A comparative study of men and women. *Western Journal of Speech Communication, 48*, 1-13.

Applbaum, R. C., & Anatol, W. E. (1972). The factor structure of credibility as a function of the speaking situation. *Speech Monographs, 39*, 216-222.

Ashour, A. S. (1973). The contingency model of leadership effectiveness: An evaluation. *Organizational Behavior and Human Performance, 9*, 339-355.

Atkinson, J. W. (1957). Motivational determinants of risk-taking behavior. *Psychological Review, 64*, 359-372.

Aufderheide, P. (July, 1986). Paul Harvey, good day!. *The Progressive*, pp. 20-25.

Auger, B. Y. (1972). *How to run better business meetings*. New York: AMACOM.

Axelrod, R. (1984). *The evolution of cooperation*. New York: Basic Books.

Baird, J. E. (1977). Some nonverbal elements of leadership emergence. *Southern Speech Communication Journal, 42*, 352-361.

Baird, J., & Wieting, G. K. (1979, September). Nonverbal communication can be a motivational tool. *Personnel Journal*, 607-610 + .

Baldwin, D. A. (1971). The costs of power. *Journal of Conflict Resolution, 15,* 145-155.

Bales, R. F. (1970). *Personality and interpersonal behavior.* New York: Holt, Rinehart & Winston.

Bales, R. F., & Cohen, S. P. (1979). *Symlog: A system for the multiple level observation of groups.* London: Collier.

Barnard, C. I. (1938). *The functions of the executive.* Cambridge, MA: Harvard University Press.

Barnlund, D. C. (1962). Consistency of emergent leadership in groups with changing tasks and members. *Speech Monographs, 29,* 45-52.

Barnlund, D. C. (1962). Toward a meaning-centered philosophy of communication. *Journal of Communication, 12,* 197-211.

Bass, B. M. (1960). *Leadership, psychology, and organizational behavior.* New York: Harper & Row.

Bass, B. M. (Ed.). (1981). *Stogdill's handbook of leadership.* New York: The Free Press.

Bass, B. M. (1985). *Leadership and performance beyond expectations.* New York: The Free Press.

Bass, B. M. (Ed.). (1990). *Bass and Stogdill's handbook of leadership.* New York: The Free Press.

Bazerman, M. H., & Neale, M. A. (1983). Heuristics in negotiation: Limitations to effective dispute resolution. In M. H. Bazerman & R. J. Lewecki (Eds.), *Negotiating in organizations* (pp. 51-67). Beverly Hills: Sage.

Beebe, S. A., & Masterson, J. T. (1986). *Communicating in small groups: Principles and practices* (2nd ed.). Glenview, IL: Scott Foresman.

Benne, K. D., & Sheats, P. (1948). Functional roles of group members. *Journal of Social Issues, 4,* 41-49.

Bennis, W. (1976). *The unconscious conspiracy: Why leaders can't lead.* New York: AMACOM.

Bennis, W. (1989). *On becoming a leader.* Reading, MA: Addison-Wesley.

Bennis, W., & Nanus, B. (1985). *Leaders: The strategies for taking charge.* New York: Harper & Row.

Berlew, D., & Hall, D. (1966). The socialization of managers: Effects of expectations on performance. *Administrative Science Quarterly, 2,* 208-223.

Blake, R. R., & Mouton, J. S. (1978). *The new managerial grid.* Houston: Gulf Publishing.

Blake, R. R., & Mouton, J. S. (1985). *The managerial grid III: The key to leadership excellence.* Houston: Gulf Publishing.

Blake, R. R., Mouton, J. S., Barnes, L. B., & Greiner, L. E. (1964). Breakthrough in organization development. *Harvard Business Review, 42,* 133-155.

Bok, S. (1979). *Lying: Moral choice in public and private life.* New York: Vintage Books.

Bormann, E. G. (1975). *Discussion and group methods* (2nd ed.). New York: Harper & Row.

Boster, F. J., & Stiff, J. B. (1984). Compliance-gaining message selection behavior. *Human Communication Research, 10,* 539-556.

Botkin, J. W., Elmandjra, M., & Malitza, M. (1979). *No limits to learning.* New York: Pergamon Books.

Bradac, J., & Mulac, A. (1984). A molecular view of powerful and powerless speech styles: Attributional consequences of specific language features and communicator intentions. *Communication Monographs, 51,* 307-319.

Brembeck, W. L., & Howell, W. S. (1976). *Persuasion: A means of social influence* (2nd ed.). Englewood Cliffs, NJ: Prentice Hall.

Brilhart, J. K. (1982). *Effective group discussion* (4th ed.). Dubuque, IA: Wm. C. Brown.

Burke, K. (1966). *Language as symbolic action.* Berkeley: University of California Press.

Burns, J. M. (1978). *Leadership.* New York: Harper & Row.

Burns, T., & Stalker, G. M. (1961). *The management of innovation.* Chicago: Quadrangle Books.

Cantrill, J. G., & Seibold, D. R. (1986). The perceptual contrast explanation of sequential request strategy effectiveness. *Human Communication Research, 13,* 253- 267.

Carlyle, T. (1907). *On heroes, hero-worship, and the heroic in history.* Boston: Houghton Mifflin. (Original work written in 1840)

Chang, M., & Gruner, C. R. (1981). Audience reaction to self-disparaging humor. *Southern Speech Communication Journal, 46,* 419-426.

Cialdini, R., Vincent, J., Lewis, S., Catalan, J., Wheeler, D., & Darby, B. (1975). Reciprocal concessions procedure for inducing compliance: The door-in-the-face technique. *Journal of Personality and Social Psychology, 31,* 206-215.

Clift, E., & Hager, M. (1989, October 16). A victory for the haves? *Newsweek,* p. 38.

Cody, M. J., & McLaughlin, M. L. (1980). Perceptions of compliance-gaining situations: A dimensional analysis. *Communication Monographs, 47,* 132-148.

Cody, M. J., McLaughlin, M. L., & Schneider, M. J. (1981). The impact of relational consequences and intimacy on the selection of interpersonal persuasion tactics: A reanalysis. *Communication Quarterly, 29,* 91-106.

Conger, J. A., & Kanungo, R. N. (1987). Toward a behavioral theory of charismatic leadership in organizational settings. *Academy of Management Review, 12,* 637-647.

Cragan, J. F., & Wright, D. W. (1980). *Communication in small group discussion: A case study approach.* St. Paul: West Publishing.

Crawford, K. S., Thomas, E. D., & Fink, J. J. (1980). Pygmalion at sea: Improving the work effectiveness of low performers. *Journal of Applied Behavioral Science, 16,* 482-505.

Daly, J. A., McCroskey, J. C., & Richmond, V. P. (1980). Relationship between vocal activity and perception of communication in small group interaction. *Western Journal of Speech Communication, 41*, 175-187.

Dance, F. E.X. (1982). A speech theory of human communication. In F. E.X. Dance (Ed.), *Human communication theory* (pp. 120-146). New York: Harper & Row.

Dance, F. E.X., & Larson, C. (1976). *The functions of human communication: A theoretical approach*. New York: Holt, Rinehart & Winston.

Dandridge, T. C. (1983). Symbols' functions and use. In L. R. Pondy, P. J. Frost, G. Morgan, & T. C. Dandridge (Eds.), *Organizational symbolism* (pp. 69-79). Greenwich, CT: JAI Press.

Dandridge, T. C., Mitroff, I., & Joyce, W. (1980). Organizational symbolism: A topic to expand organizational analysis. *Academy of Management Review, 5*, 77-82.

Davis, G. A., & Bull, K. S. (1978). Strengthening affective components of creativity in a college course. *Journal of Educational Psychology, 70*, 833-836.

Deal, T. E., & Kennedy, A. A. (1982). *Corporate cultures: The rites and rituals of corporate life*. Reading, MA: Addison-Wesley.

Deaux, K., & Emswiller, T. (1974). Explanations of successful performance on sex-linked tasks: What is skill for the male is luck for the female. *Journal of Personality and Social Psychology, 29*, 80-85.

Deutsch, M. (1973). *The resolution of conflict*. New Haven: Yale University Press.

Dillard, J. P., & Burgoon, M. (1985). Situational influences on the selection of compliance-gaining messages: Two tests of the predictive utility of the Cody-McLaughlin typology. *Communication Monographs, 52*, 289-304.

Dillard, J., Hunter, J., & Burgoon, M. (1984). Sequential-request persuasive strategies: Meta-analysis of foot-in- the-door and door-in-the-face technique. *Human Communication Research, 10*, 461-488.

Dobbins, G., & Platz, S. (1986). Sex differences in leadership: How real are they? *Academy of Management Review, 11*, 118-127.

Donnell, S. M., & Hall, J. (1980). Men and women as managers: A significant case of no significant difference. *Organizational Dynamics, 8*, 60-77.

Dow, T. (1969). The theory of charisma. *Sociological Quarterly, 10*, 306-318.

Eden, D. (1984). Self-fulfilling prophecy as a management tool: Harnessing Pygmalion. *Academy of Management Review, 9*, 64-73.

Eden, D., & Ravid, G. (1982). Pygmalion vs. self-expectancy: Effects of instructor and self-expectancy on trainee performance. *Organizational Behavior and Human Performance, 30*, 351-364.

Eden, D., & Shani, A. B. (1982). Pygmalion goes to boot camp: Expectancy, leadership, and trainee performance. *Journal of Applied Psychology, 67*, 194-199.

Eisenberg, E. M. (1984). Ambiguity as strategy in organizational communication. *Communication Monographs, 51*, 227-242.

Ernster, V. L. (1985, July). Mixed messages for women: A social history of cigarette smoking and advertising. *New York State Journal of Medicine*, pp. 335-340.

Etzioni, A. (1964). *Modern organizations.* Englewood Cliffs, NJ: Prentice-Hall.

Falbo, T. (1977). Multidimensional scaling of power strategies. *Journal of Personality and Social Psychology, 35,* 537-547.

Fiedler, F. E. (1967). *A theory of leadership effectiveness.* New York: McGraw-Hill.

Fiedler, F. E. (1972). Personality, motivational systems, and the behavior of high and low LPC persons. *Human Relations, 25,* 391-412.

Fiedler, F. E. (1978). The contingency model and the dynamics of the leadership process. In L. Berkowitz (Ed.), *Advances in Experimental Social Psychology.* (pp. 60-112) New York: Academic Press.

Fiedler, F. E., (1986). The contribution of cognitive resources and leader behavior to organizational performance. *Journal of Applied Social Psychology, 16,* 532-548.

Fiedler, F. E., & Garcia, J. E. (1987). *New approaches to effective leadership: Cognitive resources and organizational performance.* New York: Wiley.

Fisher, B. A. (1970). Decision emergence: Phases in group decision making. *Speech Monographs, 37,* 53-66.

Fisher, B. A. (1980). *Small group decision making* (2nd ed.). New York: McGraw-Hill.

Fisher, R., & Ury, W. (1981). *Getting to yes.* New York: Penguin Books.

Foti, R. J., Fraser, S. L., & Lord, R. G. (1982). Effects of leadership labels and prototypes on perceptions of political leaders. *Journal of Applied Psychology, 67,* 326-333.

Foulke, E. (1971). The perception of time compressed speech. In D. L. Horton & J. J. Jenkins (Eds.), *The perception of language* (pp. 79-107). Columbus, OH: Charles E. Merrill.

French, J. R. P., & Raven, B. (1959). The bases of social power. In D. Cartwright, *Studies in Social Power,* (pp. 150-167). Ann Arbor: University of Michigan, Institute for Social Research.

Freund, J. (1968). *The sociology of Max Weber.* New York: Vintage Books.

Freedman, J. L., & Fraser, S. L. (1966). Compliance without pressure: The foot-in-the-door technique. *Journal of Personality and Social Psychology, 4,* 195-202.

Gardner, J. (1990). *On leadership.* New York: The Free Press.

Geertz, C. (1977). Centers, kings, and charisma: Reflections on the symbolics of power. In J. Ben-David & T. Nichols (Eds.), *Culture and its creation: Essays in honor of Edward Shils* (pp. 150-171). Chicago: University of Chicago Press.

Geier, J. G. (1967). A trait approach to the study of leadership. *Journal of Communication, 17,* 316-323.

Giles, H., & Powesland, P. F. (1975). *Speech style and social evaluation.* London: Academic Press.

Ginter, G., & Lindskold, S. (1975). Rate of participation and expertise as factors influencing leader choice. *Journal of Personality and Social Psychology, 32,* 1085-1089.

Glazer, M. P., & Glazer, P. M. (1989). *The Whistleblowers,* New York: Basic Books.

Goffman, E. (1959). *The presentation of self in everyday life.* Garden City, NY: Doubleday.

Goldberg, A., Cavanaugh, M., & Larson, C. (1984). The meaning of power. *Journal of Applied Communication Research, 11,* 89-108.

Good, T., & Brophy, J. (1980). *Educational psychology: A realistic approach.* New York: Holt, Rinehart and Winston.

Goss, B., & O'Hair, D. (1988). *Communicating in interpersonal relationships.* New York: Macmillan.

Hackman, M. Z. (1988). Audience reactions to the use of direct and personal disparaging humor in informative public address. *Communication Research Reports, 5,* 126-130.

Hackman, M. Z. (1988). Reactions to the use of self-disparaging humor by informative public speakers. *Southern Speech Communication Journal, 53,* 175-183.

Hackman, M. Z. (1989). The inner game of public speaking: Applying intra-personal communication processes in the public speaking course. *Carolinas Speech Communication Annual, 5,* 41-47.

Haiman, F. S. (1949). An experimental study of the effects of ethos in public speaking. *Speech Monographs, 16,* 190-202.

Hart, R. P., & Burks, D. M. (1972). Rhetorical sensitivity and social interaction. *Speech Monographs, 39,* 75-91.

Hart, R. P., Carlson, R. E., & Eadie, W. F. (1980). Attitudes toward communication and the assessment of rhetorical sensitivity. *Communication Monographs, 47,* 3-22.

Hawes, L. C. (1974). Social collectivities as communication: Perspectives on organizational behavior. *Quarterly Journal of Speech, 60,* 497-502.

Heath, R. L. (1988). The rhetoric of issue advertising: A rationale, a case study, a critical perspective—and more. *Central States Speech Journal, 39,* 99-109.

Hennig, M., & Jardim, A. (1977). *The managerial woman.* New York: Anchor Press/Doubleday.

Hersey, P. (1984). *The situational leader.* Escondido, CA: Center for Leadership Studies.

Hersey, P., & Blanchard, K. H. (1988). *Management of organizational behavior: Utilizing human resources* (5th ed.). Englewood Cliffs, NJ: Prentice-Hall.

Hill, N. (1976, August). Self-esteem: The key to effective leadership. *Administrative Management,* pp. 24-25, 51.

Hirokawa, R., & Pace, R. (1983). A descriptive investigation of the possible communication-based reasons for effective and ineffective group decision making. *Communication Monographs, 50,* 363-379.

Hollander, E. (1978). *Leadership dynamics: A practical guide to effective relationships.* New York: The Free Press.

House, R. J. (1971). A path-goal theory of leader effectiveness. *Administrative Science Quarterly, 16,* 321-338.

House, R. J. (1977). A 1976 theory of charismatic leadership. In J. G. Hunt & L. L. Larson (Eds.), *Leadership: The cutting edge* (pp. 189-207). Carbondale: Southern Illinois University Press.

House, R. J., & Mitchell, T. R. (1974). Path-goal theory of leadership. *Journal of Contemporary Business, 3,* 81-97.

Hovland, C., Janis, I., & Kelley, H. H. (1953). *Communication and persuasion.* New Haven: Yale University Press.

Hovland, C. I., & Weiss, W. (1951). The influence of source credibility on communication effectiveness. *Public Opinion Quarterly, 15,* 635-650.

Huggins, N. (1987). Martin Luther King, Jr: Charisma and leadership. *Journal of American History, 74,* 477-481.

Hummel, R. P. (1975). Psychology of charismatic followers. *Psychological Reports, 37,* 759-770.

Hunt, D. M., & Michael, C. (1983). Mentorship: A career training and development tool. *Academy of Management Review, 8,* 475-485.

Hunt, M. (1982). *The universe within: A new science explores the human mind.* New York: Simon and Schuster.

Hunter, J. E., & Boster, F. J. (1987). A model of compliance-gaining message selection. *Communication Monographs, 54,* 63-84.

Instone, D., Major, B., & Bunker, B. B. (1983). Gender, self-confidence, and social influence strategies: An organizational simulation. *Journal of Personality and Social Psychology, 44,* 322-333.

Jacobs, T. O. (1970). *Leadership and exchange in formal organizations.* Alexandria, VA: Human Resources Research Organization.

Johannesen, R. L. (1990). *Ethics in human communication* (3rd ed.). Prospect Heights, IL: Waveland.

Johnson, C., & Vinson, L. (1987). "Damned if you do, damned if you don't?": Status, powerful speech and evaluations of female witnesses. *Women's Studies in Communication, 10,* 37-44.

Johnson, C., Vinson, L., Hackman, M., & Hardin, T. (1989). The effects of an instructor's use of hesitation forms on student ratings of quality, recommendations to hire, and lecture listening. *Journal of the International Listening Association, 3,* 32-43.

Kahn, R. L. (1956). The prediction of productivity. *Journal of Social Issues, 12,* 41-49.

Kanter R. M. (1977). *Men and women of the corporation.* New York: Basic Books.

Kanter, R. M. (1977). Some effects of proportions on group life: Skewed sex ratios and responses to token women. *American Journal of Sociology, 82,* 965-990.

Kanter, R. M. (1983). *The change masters: Innovation for productivity in the American corporation.* New York: Simon and Schuster.

Katz, D., Maccoby, N., Gurin, G., & Floor, L. (1951). *Productivity, supervision, and morale among railroad workers.* Ann Arbor: University of Michigan, Institute for Social Research.

Katz, D., Maccoby, N., & Morse, N. (1950). *Productivity, supervision and morale in an office situation.* Ann Arbor: University of Michigan, Institute for Social Research.

Kearney, P., Plax, T. G., Sorensen, G., & Smith, V. R. (1988). Experienced and prospective teachers' selections of compliance-gaining messages for "common" student misbehaviors. *Communication Education, 37*, 150-164.

Kelman, H. C., & Hovland, C. I. (1953). "Reinstatement" of the communicator in delayed measurement of opinion change. *Journal of Abnormal and Social Psychology, 48*, 327-335.

Kenny, D. A., & Zaccaro, S. J. (1983). An estimate of variance due to traits in leadership. *Journal of Applied Psychology, 68*, 678-685.

Kerr, S., & Harlan, A. (1973). Predicting the effects of leadership training and experience from the contingency model: Some remaining problems. *Journal of Applied Psychology, 57*, 114-117.

Kiechel, W. (1983, May 30). What makes a corporate leader? *Fortune*, pp. 135-140.

Knittel, R. E. (1974). Essential and nonessential ritual in programs of planned change. *Human Organization, 33*, 394-396.

Knutson, T. J., & Holdridge, W. E. (1975). Orientation behavior, leadership and consensus: A possible functional relationship. *Speech Monographs, 42*, 107-114.

Kogler Hill, S. E. (1982). The multistage process of interpersonal empathy. In S. E. Kogler Hill (Ed.), *Improving interpersonal competence: A laboratory approach* (pp. 83-89). Dubuque, IA: Kendall/Hunt.

Kogler Hill, S. E., Bahniuk, M. H., & Dobos, J. (1989). The impact of mentoring and collegial support on faculty success: An analysis of support behavior, information adequacy, and communication apprehension. *Communication Education, 38*, 15-33.

Korba, R. J. (1986). *The rate of inner speech*. Unpublished doctoral dissertation, University of Denver.

Kouzes, J. M., & Posner, B. Z. (1987). *The leadership challenge: How to get extraordinary things done in organizations*. San Francisco: Jossey-Bass.

Kram, K. E., & Isabella, L. A. (1985). Mentoring alternatives: The role of peer relationships in career development. *Academy of Management Review, 28*, 110-132.

Krech, D., & Crutchfield, R. S. (1948). *Theory and problems of social psychology*. New York: McGraw-Hill.

Landauer, T. J. (1962). Rate of implicit speech. *Perceptual and Motor Skills, 15*, 646.

Larson, C. E., & LaFasto, F. M. J. (1989). *Teamwork: What must go right/What can go wrong*. Newbury Park, CA: Sage.

Lawrence, P. R., & Lorsch, J. W. (1967). *Organization and environment*. Cambridge: Harvard University Press.

Leathers, D. G. (1986). *Successful nonverbal communication: Principles and applications*. New York: Macmillan.

Lewin, K., Lippitt, R., & White, R. K. (1939). Patterns of aggressive behavior in experimentally created "social climates." *Journal of Social Psychology, 10*, 271-299.

Littlejohn, S. (1989). *Theories of Human Communication* (3rd ed.). Belmont, CA: Wadsworth.

Livingston, J. S. (1969). Pygmalion in management. *Harvard Business Review, 47*, 81-89.

Lord, R. G., De Vader, C. L., & Alliger, G. M. (1986). A meta-analysis of the relation between personality traits and leadership perceptions: An application of validity generalization procedures. *Journal of Applied Psychology, 71*, 402-410.

Lucas, S. E. (1986). *The art of public speaking* (2nd ed.). New York: Random House.

Lutz, W. (1989). *Doublespeak*. New York: Harper & Row.

Magaree, E. I. (1969). Influence of sex roles on the manifestation of leadership. *Journal of Applied Psychology, 53*, 377-382.

Mann, R. D. (1959). A review of the relationships between personality and performance in small groups. *Psychological Bulletin, 56*, 241-270.

Martin, J., & Powers, M. E. (1983). Truth or corporate propaganda: The value of a good story. In L. R. Pondy, P. J. Frost, G. Morgan, & T. C. Dandridge (Eds.), *Organizational symbolism* (pp. 93-107). Greenwich, CT: JAI Press.

Martin, J., & Siehl, C. (1983). Organizational culture and counterculture: An uneasy symbiosis. *Organizational Dynamics, 12*, 52-64.

Marwell, G., & Schmitt, D. (1967). Dimensions of compliance gaining behavior: An empirical analysis. *Sociometry, 30*, 350-364.

Maslow, A. H. (1970). *Motivation and personality*. New York: Harper & Row.

Massengill, D., & DiMarco, N. (1979). Sex-role stereotypes and requisite management characteristics: A current replication. *Sex Roles, 5*, 561-570.

McCroskey, J. C., & Young, T. J. (1981). Ethos and credibility: The construct and its measurement after three decades. *Central States Speech Journal, 32*, 24-34.

McGlone, E. L., & Anderson, L. J. (1973). The dimensions of teacher credibility. *Communication Education, 22*, 196-200.

McGregor, D. (1960). *The human side of enterprise*. New York: McGraw-Hill.

McMahan, E. M. (1976). Nonverbal communication as a function of attribution in impression formation. *Communication Monographs, 43*, 287-294.

Miller, A., & Hager, M. (1989, September 11). The elderly duke it out. *Newsweek*, pp. 42-43.

Miller, G. R. (1969). Contributions of communication research to the study of speech. In A. H. Monroe, & D. Ehninger, *Principles and Types of Speech Communication*, [6th brief ed.] (pp. 334-357). Glenview, IL: Scott, Foresman.

Miller, G., Boster, F., Roloff, M., & Seibold, D. (1977). Compliance-gaining message strategies: A typology and some findings concerning effects of situational differences. *Communication Monographs, 44*, 37-51.

Morris, C. G., & Hackman, J. R. (1969). Behavioral correlates of perceived leadership. *Journal of Personality and Social Psychology, 13*, 350-361.

Morrison, A. M., White, R. P., & Van Velsor, E. (1987). *Breaking the glass ceiling: Can women reach the top of America's largest corporations?* Reading, MA: Addison-Wesley.

Mortensen, C. D. (1966). Should the discussion group have an assigned leader? *The Speech Teacher, 15*, 34-41.

Neale, M. A., & Bazerman, M. H. (1983). The role of perspective taking ability in negotiating under different forms of arbitration. *Industrial and Labor Relations, 36*, 378-388.

Nichols, R. G. (1961). Do we know how to listen? Practical helps in a modern age. *The Speech Teacher, 10*, 120-124.

O'Barr, W. (1984). Asking the right questions about language and power. In C. Kramarae, M. Schulz, & W. O'Barr (Eds.), *Language and power* (pp. 260-280). Beverly Hills, CA: Sage.

O'Day, R. (1974). Intimidation rituals: Reactions and reforms. *Journal of Applied Behavioral Science, 10*, 373-386.

O'Keefe, D. J. (1987). The persuasive effects of delaying identification of high and low-credibility communicators: A meta-analytic review. *Central States Speech Journal, 38*, 63-72.

Orsag Madigan, C., & Elwood, A. (1983). *Brainstorms and thunderbolts.* New York: Macmillan.

Osborn, A. (1957). *Applied imagination.* New York: Charles Scribner's Sons.

Osborn, R. N., & Vickers, W. M. (1976). Sex stereotypes: An artifact in leader behavior and subordinate satisfaction analysis? *Academy of Management Journal, 19*, 439-449.

Pacanowsky, M. E., & O'Donnell-Trujillo, N. (1983). Organizational communication as cultural performance. *Communication Monographs, 50*, 126-147.

Parnes, S. J. (1975). "Aha!" In I. A. Taylor & J. W. Getzels (Eds.), *Perspectives on creativity* (pp. 224-248). Chicago: Aldine.

Patton, B. P., Giffin, K., & Patton, E. N. (1989). *Decision-making group interaction* (3rd ed). New York: Harper & Row.

Peters, T. (1987). *Thriving on chaos.* New York: Borzoi/Alfred A. Knopf.

Peters, T., & Austin, N. (1985). *A passion for excellence: The leadership difference.* New York: Warner Books.

Peters, T. J., & Waterman, R. H., Jr. (1982). *In search of excellence.* New York: Harper & Row.

Petre, P. (1984, October 29). Games that teach you to manage. *Newsweek*, pp. 65-72.

Pettigrew, A. M. (1979). On studying organizational cultures. *Administrative Science Quarterly, 24*, 570-582.

Phillips-Jones, L. (1982). *Mentors and proteges.* New York: Arbor House.

Poole, M. S. (1983). Decision development in small groups II: A study of multiple sequences in decision making. *Communication Monographs, 50*, 206-232.

Poole, M. S. (1983). Decision development in small groups III: A multiple sequence model of group decision development. *Communication Monographs, 50*, 321-341.

Post, J. M. (1986). Narcissism and the charismatic leader-follower relationship. *Political Psychology, 7*, 675-688.

Powell, G. N. (1989). *Women and men in management.* Beverly Hills, CA: Sage.

Powell, G. N., & Butterfield, A. D. (1982). Sex, attributions, and leadership: A brief review. *Psychological Reports, 51,* 1171-1174.

Pruitt, D. G. (1981). *Negotiation behavior.* New York: Academic Press.

Putman, L. L., & Jones, T. S. (1982). The role of communication in bargaining. *Human Communication Research, 8,* 262-280.

Raudsepp, E., & Hough, G. P. (1977). *Creative growth games.* New York: Harvest/Jove.

Regula, C. R., & Julian, J. W. (1973). The impact of quality and frequency of task contributions on perceived ability. *Journal of Social Psychology, 89,* 115-122.

Riecken, H. (1975). The effect of talkativeness on ability to influence group solutions of problems. In P. V. Crosbie (Ed.), *Interaction in small groups* (pp. 238-249). New York: Macmillan.

Roche, G. R. (1979). Much ado about mentors. *Harvard Business Review, 57,* 14-28.

Rogers, E. M. (1983). *Diffusion of innovations* (3rd ed.). New York: The Free Press.

Rogers, E. M., & Storey, J. D. (1987). Communication campaigns. In C. R. Berger & S. H. Chaffee (Eds.), *Handbook of communication science* (pp. 817-846). Newbury Park, CA: Sage.

Roloff, M. E., & Barnicott, E. F. (1978). The situational use of pro-and antisocial compliance-gaining strategies by high and low Machiavellians. In B. Ruben (Ed.), *Communication Yearbook 2* (pp. 193-208). New Brunswick, NJ: Transaction Books.

Rosenthal, R., & Fode, K. L. (1963). The effect of experimenter bias on the performance of the albino rat. *Behavioral Science, 8,* 183-189.

Rosenthal, R., & Jacobson, L. (1968). *Pygmalion in the classroom.* New York: Holt, Rinehart and Winston.

Rubin, J. Z., & Brown, B. R. (1975). *The social psychology of bargaining and negotiation.* New York: Academic Press.

Sabin, R. (1989, November 20). Women's growing role in the workplace. *San Francisco Chronicle,* p. C1 + .

Sanders, D. A., & Sanders, J. A. (1984). *Teaching creativity through metaphor.* New York: Longman.

Sandler, L. (1986, February). Self-fulfilling prophecy: Better management by magic. *Training,* pp. 60-64.

Sattler, W. M. (1947). Conceptions of ethos in ancient rhetoric. *Speech Monographs, 14,* 55-65.

Scheidel, T. M., & Crowell, L. (1964). Idea development in small discussion groups. *Quarterly Journal of Speech, 50,* 140-145.

Schein, E. H. (1983). The role of the founder in creating organizational culture. *Organizational Dynamics, 12,* 13-28.

Schein, E. H. (1985). *Organizational culture and leadership.* San Francisco: Jossey Bass.

Schiffer, I. (1973). *Charisma: A psychoanalytic look at mass society.* Toronto: University of Toronto Press.

Schriesheim, C. A., & Kerr, S. (1977). Theories and measures of leadership: A critical appraisal. In J. G. Hunt and L. L. Larson (Eds.), *Leadership: The Cutting Edge* (pp. 9-45). Carbondale: Southern Illinois University Press.

Schultz, B. (1979). Predicting emergent leaders: An exploratory study of the salience of communicative functions. *Small Group Behavior, 9,* 109-114.

Schultz, B. (1980). Communicative correlates of perceived leaders. *Small Group Behavior, 11,* 175-191.

Schwartz, H., & Davis, S. (1981). Matching corporate culture and business strategy. *Organizational Dynamics, 10,* 30-48.

Schweitzer, A. (1984). *The age of charisma.* Chicago: Nelson-Hall.

Sebeok, T. A., & Rosenthal, R. (Eds.). (1981). *The Clever Hans Phenomenon: Communication with horses, whales, apes, and people.* (Annals of the New York Academy of Sciences, Vol. 364). New York: New York Academy of Sciences.

Sebeok, T. A., & Umiker-Sebeok, J. (1979). *Speaking of apes: A critical anthology of two-way communication with man.* New York: Plenum.

Shockley-Zalabak, P., Staley, C. C., & Morley, D. D. (1988). The female professional: Perceived communication proficiencies as predictors of organizational advancement. *Human Relations, 41,* 553-567.

Siegel, B. S. (1986). *Love, medicine & miracles.* New York: Harper & Row.

Siegel, B. S. (1989). *Peace, love & healing.* New York: Harper & Row.

Sillars, A. L. (1980). The stranger and the spouse as target persons for compliance-gaining strategies: A subjective utility model. *Human Communication Research, 6,* 265-279.

Simons, H. W. (1986). *Persuasion: Understanding, practice, and analysis* (2nd ed.). New York: Random House.

Smith, P. B., & Peterson, M. F. (1988). *Leadership, organizations and culture.* London: Sage.

Sorenson, R., & Pickett, T. (1986). A test of two teaching strategies designed to improve interview effectiveness: Rating behavior and videotaped feedback. *Communication Education, 35,* 13-22.

Spencer, H. (1884). *The study of sociology.* New York: D. A. Appleton. (First published 1873)

Staley, C. C., & Shockley-Zalabak, P. (1986). Communication proficiency and future training needs of the female professional: Self-assessment vs. supervisors' evaluations. *Human Relations, 39,* 891-902.

Stang, D. J. (1973). Effect of interaction rate on ratings of leadership and liking. *Journal of Personality and Social Psychology, 27,* 405-408.

Star, S. A., & Hughes, H. (1950). Report on an educational campaign: The Cincinnati plan for the United Nations. *American Journal of Sociology, 55,* 389-400.

Stech, E. L. (1983). *Leadership communication.* Chicago: Nelson-Hall.

Stewart, L., & Gudykunst, W. B. (1982). Differential factors influencing the hierarchical level and number of promotions of males and females within an organization. *Academy of Management Journal, 25,* 586-597.

Stogdill, R. M. (1948). Personal factors associated with leadership: A survey of the literature. *Journal of Psychology, 25,* 35-71.

Stogdill, R. M. (1950). Leadership, membership and organization. *Psychological Bulletin, 47,* 1-14.

Stogdill, R. M. (1965). *Managers, employees, organizations.* Columbus: Ohio State University, Bureau of Business Research.

Stogdill, R. M. (1974). *Handbook of leadership.* New York: The Free Press.

Stogdill, R. M., & Coons, A. E. (1957). *Leader behavior: Its description and measurement.* Columbus: Ohio State University, Bureau of Business Research.

Strong, S. R., & Dixon, D. N. (1971). Expertness, attractiveness, and influence in counseling. *Journal of Counseling Psychology, 18,* 562-570.

Strong, S. R., & Schmidt, L. D. (1970). Expertness and influence in counseling. *Journal of Counseling Psychology 17,* 81-87.

Tannenbaum, R., & Schmidt, W. H. (1958). How to choose a leadership pattern. *Harvard Business Review, 36,* 95-101.

Terrace, H. S., Pettito, L. A., Sanders, R. J., & Bever, T. G. (1979). Can an ape create a sentence? *Science, 206,* 891-902.

Thayer, L. (1988). Leadership/communication: A critical review and a modest proposal. In G. M. Goldhaber & G. A. Barnett (Eds.), *Handbook of organizational communication* (pp. 231-263). Norwood, NJ: Ablex Publishing.

Thibault, J. W., & Kelly, H. H. (1978). *Interpersonal relations: A theory of interdependence.* New York: John Wiley.

Tompkins, P. K. (1982). *Communication as action: An introduction to rhetoric and communication.* Belmont, CA: Wadsworth.

Trice, H. M., & Beyer, J. M. (1984). Studying organizational cultures through rites and ceremonials. *Academy of Management Review, 9,* 653-669.

Trice, H. M., & Beyer, J. M. (1985). Using six organizational rites to change culture. In R. H. Kilmann, M. J. Saxton, & R. Serpa (Eds.), *Gaining control of the corporate culture* (pp. 370-399). San Francisco: Jossey-Bass.

Tucker, R. C. (1965). The dictator and totalitarianism. *World Politics, 17,* 565-573.

Tucker, R. C. (1968). The theory of charismatic leadership. *Daedalus, 97,* 731-756.

VanGundy, A. B. (1982). *Training your creative mind.* Englewood Cliffs, NJ: Prentice-Hall.

Vinson, L. (1988, November). *An emotion-based model of compliance-gaining message selection.* Paper presented at the Speech Communication Association convention, New Orleans, Lousiana.

von Oech, R. (1983). *A whack on the side of the head.* New York: Warner Books.

von Oech, R. (1986). *A kick in the seat of the pants.* New York: Harper & Row.

Walker, S. (1983). *Animal thought.* London: Routledge & Kegan Paul.

Wallas, G. (1926). *The art of thought.* New York: Harcourt.

Ward, C. D., & McGinnies, E. (1974). Persuasive effects of early and late mention of credible and non-credible sources. *Journal of Psychology, 86,* 17-23.

Warner, K. E. (1986). *Selling smoke: Cigarette advertising and public health.* Washington DC: American Public Health Association.

Warren, I. D. (1969). The effects of credibility in sources of testimony and audience attitudes toward speaker and topic. *Speech Monographs, 36,* 456-458.

Weber, M. (1947). *The theory of social and economic organization* (A. M. Henderson & T. Parsons, Trans.), Glencoe, IL: The Free Press.

White, L. A. (1949). *The science of culture.* New York: Farrar, Strauss and Cudahy.

White, R., & Lippitt, R. (1968). Leader behavior and member reaction in three "social climates." In D. Cartwright & A. Zander (Eds.), *Group Dynamics* (pp. 318-335). New York: Harper & Row.

Wilkins, A. L. (1984). The creation of company cultures: The role of stories and human resource systems. *Human Resource Management, 23,* 41-60.

Willner, R. A. (1984). *The spellbinders: Charismatic political leadership.* New Haven: Yale University Press.

Wilson, G. L., & Hanna, M. S. (1986). *Groups in context: Leadership and participation in small groups.* New York: Random House.

Winer, J. A., Jobe, T., & Ferrono, C. (1984-85). Toward a psychoanalytic theory of the charismatic relationship. *Annual of Psychoanalysis, 12-13,* 155-175.

Woodlands Group. (1980, November). Management development roles: Coach, sponsor, and mentor. *Personnel Journal, 59,* 918-921.

Woodward, B. & McGrath, M. (1988). Charisma in group therapy with recovering substance abusers. *International Journal of Group Psychotherapy, 38,* 223-236.

Woodward, G. C., & Denton, R. E., Jr. (1988). *Persuasion and influence in American life.* Prospect Heights, IL: Waveland.

Woodword, J. (1965). *Industrial organization: Theory and practice.* Oxford: Oxford University Press.

Young, J. (1984, March). Innovation and the education process. *T.H.E. Journal,* pp. 72-74.

Yukl, G. (1981). *Leadership in organizations.* Englewood Cliffs, NJ: Prentice-Hall.

Zaleznik, A. (1977, May-June). Managers and leaders: Are they different? *Harvard Business Review, 55,* pp. 67-78.

Index